Photoshop 5.5/Imageready 2.0 | H·O·T

lynda.com/books

By Lynda Weinman

Design: Ali Karp

Photoshop 5.5 /Imageready 2.0 | H·O·T Hands-On Training

Lynda Weinman

lynda.com/books | Peachpit Press

1249 Eighth Street • Berkeley, CA • 94710

800.283.9444 510.524.2178 • 510.524.2221 (fx)

http://www.lynda.com/books

http://www.peachpit.com

lynda.com/books are published in association with Peachpit Press.

Peachpit Press is a division of Addison Wesley Longman.

Copyright © 2000 by lynda.com

ISBN 0-201-35452-7

0 9 8 7 6 5 4 3 2 1
Printed and bound in the
United States of America

H•O•T | **Credits**

Book Design: Ali Karp (alink@earthlink.net)
Alink Newmedia

Peachpit Editor: Cary Norsworthy

Peachpit Production Coordinator: Cary Norsworthy

lynda.com Developmental Editor: Kathryn Van Sant

lynda.com Editors: Jane Van Tassel
Marla Fergeson

Beta Testers: Lisa Brenneis,
Lana Swanson
Jane Van Tassel

Tech Editors: Joe Maller
Doug Meisner

Cover Illustration: Bruce Heavin (bruce@stink.com)

Photographs: Carol Topalian

Indexer: Steve Rath

CD-ROM Coordinator: Victor Gavenda

H•O•T | **Colophon**

The preliminary art direction for Photoshop 5.5 / Imageready 2.0 H•O•T was sketched on paper. The layout was heavily influenced by online communication—merging a traditional book format with a modern Web aesthetic.

The text in Photoshop 5.5/Imageready 2.0 H•O•T was set in Akzidenz Grotesk from Adobe and Triplex from Emigre. The cover illustration was created in Adobe Photoshop 5.5 and Adobe Illustrator 8.0.

This book was created using QuarkXPress 4.0, Adobe Photoshop 5.5, ImageReady 2.0, Microsoft Word, and Snapz Pro on a MacOS G3. It was printed on 70lb Influence Soft Gloss — disk-to-plate on a web press at Graphic Arts Center/Shepard Poorman, Indianapolis, IN.

Photoshop 5.5/Imageready 2.0 H•O•T_____**Table of Contents**

7. Background Images _____ 180

I3.   Automation   396

I.

Introduction

| H•O•T |

| Hands-On Training |

Photoshop 5.5 / ImageReady 2.0

For the Web

A Note from Lynda

I was motivated to create a hands-on training book series because it's my experience that people buy computer books to educate themselves. Most books and manuals are reference based, and while there is nothing wrong with reference books in general, it seemed to me that a book with hands-on tutorials would be of great value. I know that I am the type of learner who learns by doing. I enjoy a reference manual or book after I know my way around a program, but those types of materials don't help me get up to speed as quickly as I like. I guess I wrote this series of books with my own learning style in mind. I know I am not alone in my impatience to get productive in a tool as soon as humanly possible.

In this book, you will find carefully developed lessons and exercises that have been tested in my digital arts training center to help you learn Photoshop 5.5 and ImageReady 2.0. If you are new to Photoshop or even if you've owned Photoshop for years, this book will teach you many new things that you didn't know. That's mostly because there are so many new features in Photoshop 5.5 and Image-Ready 2.0 that even experienced Photoshop users will be on new ground.

This book is targeted toward beginning – to intermediate – level Web developers who are looking for a great tool to create graphics and Web content. The premise of the hands-on exercise approach is to get you up to speed quickly in Photoshop 5.5 and ImageReady 2.0, while actively working through the book's lessons. It's one thing to read about a product, and an entirely different one to try the product and get measurable results.

Many exercise-based books take a paint-by-numbers approach to teaching by offering instructions that tell you what to do but not why or when the instruction will apply to your work later. While this approach sometimes works, it's often difficult to figure out how to apply those lessons to a real-world situation, or understand why or when you would use the technique again. What sets this book apart is that the lessons contain lots of background information for each given subject, which are designed to help you understand the process as well as the particular exercise.

At times, pictures are worth a lot more than words. When necessary, I have also included short QuickTime movies to show any process that's difficult to explain in writing. These files are located on the **H•O•T CD-ROM** inside a folder called **movies**. I approach teaching from many different angles because I know that some people are visual learners, while others like to read, and still others like to get out there and try things. This book combines a lot of teaching approaches so you can learn Photoshop 5.5 and ImageReady 2.0 as thoroughly as you want to.

I didn't set out to cover every single aspect of Photoshop and ImageReady – the manual and many other reference books are great for that! What I saw missing from the bookshelves was a process-oriented book that taught readers core principles, techniques, and tips in a hands-on training format. I've been making graphics for the Web since 1995, and it used to be a lot tougher than it is today. This version of Photoshop and Image-Ready in particular is oriented toward making Web graphics faster to download and easier to make. Additionally, ImageReady even writes JavaScript code and HTML, something which traditional imaging programs have never broached.

It's my hope that this book will raise your skills in Web design and digital imaging. If it does, then I have accomplished the job I set out to do!

• I welcome your comments
  psirhot@lynda.com

• Please visit my Web site as well
  http://www.lynda.com

• The URL for support for this book
  http://www.lynda.com/books/psirhot

Lynda Weinman

How This Book Works

This book has several components, including step-by-step exercises, commentary, notes, tips, warnings, and movies. Step-by-step exercises are numbered, and file names and command keys are bolded so they pop out more easily. You might notice that certain words are capitalized, such as **Style**, **Layer Effect**, **Preferences**, etc. I chose to capitalize these terms to call more attention to them and to mimic how they appear in Photoshop and Image-Ready. When you see italicized text, it signifies a picture caption and when the italicized text is green, it signifies commentary.

• Whenever you're being instructed to go to a menu or multiple menu items, it's stated like this: **File > Open…**

• Code is in a monospace font: `<HTML></HTML>`

• URLs are in a bold font: **http://www.lynda.com**

• Macintosh and Windows interface screen captures: Most of the screen captures in the book were taken on a Macintosh. Windows shots were taken only when the interface differed from the Macintosh. I made this decision because I do most of my design work and writing on my Mac. I also own and use a Windows system, so I noted important differences when they occurred.

Exercise Files and the H•O•T CD-ROM

All of your course files are located inside a folder called **exercise_files** on the **H•O•T CD-ROM**. These files are divided into chapter folders. Please copy the chapter folders to your hard drive because you will be required to alter them, which is not possible if they stay on the CD. **Warning:** Unfortunately, when files originate from a CD-ROM, the Windows operating system defaults to making them write-protected, meaning that you cannot alter them. If you use Windows, you will need to remove this setting, so please read the following note for instructions.

Warning | **Platform Concerns**

Windows: Missing Windows File Extensions
By default, Windows 95/98 users will not be able to see file extension names, such as .gif, .jpg, or .html. Don't worry, you can change this setting!

Windows 95 Users
1. Double-click on the **My Computer** icon on your desktop. (**Note:** If you or someone else has changed the name, it will not say **My Computer**).

2. Select **View > Options**. This will open the **Options** dialog box.

3. Click on the **View** tab at the top. This will open the **View** options screen so you can change the view settings of Windows 95.

4. Make sure there is no checkmark in the **Hide MS-DOS file extensions for file types** that are registered options. This will ensure that the file extensions are visible, which will help you better understand the exercises in the book.

Windows 98 Users
1. Double-click on the **My Computer** icon on your desktop. (**Note:** If you or someone else has changed the name, it will not say **My Computer**).

2. Select **View > Folder Options** to open the **Folder Options** dialog box.

3. Click on the **View** tab at the top. This will allow you to access the different view settings for your computer.

4. Uncheck the checkbox inside the **Hide file extensions for known file types** option. This will make all of the file extensions visible.

Software Files on the CD-ROM

The **H•O•T CD-ROM** includes a Mac and Windows version of Netscape 4.7 as well as QuickTime 4.0. All software is located inside the CD's software folder (imagine that!).

Troubleshooting FAQ

If you find yourself getting stuck in an exercise, be sure to read the Trouble-shooting FAQ in the back of the book. If you don't find your answer there, send an email to **psirfaq@lynda.com** and I'll post an update on the compan-ion Web site for the book, **http://www.lynda.com/books/psirhot/** as quickly as I can. Obviously, I can't offer personal technical support for everyone who reads the book, so be sure to refer to this FAQ before you request extra help.

Note: This FAQ is intended to support the exercises in this book. If you have other questions about Photoshop or ImageReady, as a registered owner of the program you can call Adobe's technical support line (800)49-ADOBE or visit their excellent Web site at **http://www.adobe.com**.

Skill Level

This book assumes that you possess a basic knowledge of Photoshop. If you have never used Photoshop before, you should go through the tutorial in the manual before you begin this book. Web design and digital imaging are chal-lenging, somewhat technical, somewhat creative mediums. You must have good general computer skills to work with Web applications, as they require that you save and open numerous files and often work in multiple programs at the same time.

RAM, RAM, and More RAM

It's ideal to keep Photoshop, ImageReady, and a Web browser open at the same time. To do this, I recommend that you have at least 128 MB of RAM. This book assumes that you can open all these programs simultaneously. If you cannot, you will need to quit whichever program you're in whenever you are requested to enter another. This is possible to do but will grow tiring, I assure you. Photoshop and ImageReady are professional tools and require professional-level systems to run optimally.

System Requirements

This book requires that you use either the MacOS operating system (on a Macintosh running System 7.6 or later) or Windows 95, Windows 98, or Windows NT. That's another reason I suggest that you have at least 128 MB of RAM. More RAM is better, especially on Macintosh computers, which do not offer dynamic RAM allocation like Windows.

About lynda.com

lynda.com is dedicated to helping Web designers and developers understand tools and design principles. lynda.com offers training books, CDs, videos, hands-on workshops, training seminars, and on-site training. The Web site contains online tips, discussion boards, training products, and a design job board. Be sure to visit our site at **http://www.lynda.com** to learn more!

Check out Lynda's other books at: **http:www.lynda.com/books**.

Check out Lynda's training videos and DVDs at: **http:www.lynda.com/videos**.

lynda.com/books

About Me

I've been practicing computer design and animation since 1984, when I bought one of the first Macintosh computers. I worked as an animator and motion graphics director in the special-effects industry for seven years before having a daughter in 1989. At that time, I was asked to teach my first workshop in multimedia animation, and eventually became a full-time faculty member at Art Center College of Design in Pasadena, California. I've worked as a beta tester for imaging and animation software packages since 1984, and have worked as a consultant for Adobe, Macromedia, and Microsoft. I've conducted workshops at Disney, Microsoft, Adobe, and Macromedia, and have been a keynote speaker and/or moderator at numerous design, broadcast-design, animation, Web-design, and computer-graphics conferences. With my husband Bruce Heavin (who is responsible for the beautiful covers of all my books!), I co-founded lynda.com, inc., which specializes in Web-design training via hands-on classes, seminars, training videos, books, Web tips, and CD-ROMs. The list could go on and on, but I basically love teaching and sharing knowledge, and that's what I spend most of my waking hours doing. I hope you'll visit **http://www.lynda.com**, to learn more.

lynda.com offers a hands-on training in Ojai, California. The lab includes the latest Web-design software, plus state-of-the-art networked Mac and Windows computers utilizing a T1 Internet connection. *Lynda* is shown above, teaching color theory to a group of Web-design professionals.

Book designer Ali in Eastern Europe checks for *lynda.com* titles at a local Budapest Bookstore!

Lynda and her husband/partner *Bruce Heavin*.

Lynda and her beautiful 10-year-old daughter, *Jamie*. This wonderful photo was taken by Jamie's dad, Mark Kirkland

Acknowledgements

I could not have written this book without the help of many key people.

Special thanks to... _____

My **husband** and partner in crime, **Bruce Heavin**, who inspires me like no other.

My **book designer**, **Ali Karp**, who always runs the final mile with me. This marks our 11th book together. Wow, Ali!

My **daughter**, **Jamie**, who is growing into the kind of woman I always hoped she would become – smart, witty, funny, kind, and unpredictable. It's a joy to be your mom.

My **agent**, **David Rogelberg**, who helped make my dream of a **lynda.com/book** imprint come true.

My **developmental editor**, **Kathryn Van Sant**, whose humor and warmth is infectious to all on our team who have the good fortune to work with her.

My **editor**, **Jane Van Tassel**, who joined our team for this book.

My **Peachpit Press editor** and dear pal, **Cary Norsworthy**, whose hard work and keen intelligence brought extra greatness to this project. I thank you for who you are and all you give.

My **technical editor**, **Joe Maller**, whose passion for detail and deeper knowledge is unsurpassed.

My **production artist**, **Heidi Goodspeed**, who Quarked again until the cows came home and beta tested, and tested, and re-tested again. Thanks for your great attitude and devotion to this project.

My **copyeditor**, **Marla Ferguson** the preposition queen and mother of Eva-to-be.

My **entire beta testing team**, with special appreciation to **Lisa (Bee) Brenneis**, the FinalCut queen and sister Beck fan.

One awesome **photographer**, **Carol Topalian** for giving us toy dinosaur dioramas, Ojai flowers, and other interesting photographic images for the book.

The **Adobe folks** who made these amazing products – extra smooches to **Doug Meisner** and the entire team in Minneapolis. A tip of the hat and fond farewell to **Doug Olson** to whom all ImageReady users owe a great deal of thanks for his vision and foresight.

Extra-big appreciation to the **ever-funkadelic lynda.com staff**. You make having a business much more fun than working out of my garage ;-).

2.

Interface

| Interface Overview | Photoshop / ImageReady Toolbars |
| Jump To | Moving Palettes and Tabs | Shortcuts |

Photoshop 5.5 / ImageReady 2.0

For the Web

One thing that Adobe has always been known for is its consistency in interfaces. An Adobe application feels like just that – once you learn one Adobe product, it's a lot easier to learn another.

In this chapter, I'm not planning to go in depth into each palette and tool. In my opinion, that's best left to each exercise so you can learn about the features in context with what you're learning. This chapter will outline some of the key interface concepts in both Photoshop 5.5 and ImageReady 2.0, and point out some of the significant similarities and differences.

Interface Overview

Photoshop and ImageReady both began their lives as separate applications. While they are still separate, now they ship together for the first time and are designed to work together. The good news is that, from an interface standpoint, you're in for an easy learning curve. That's because Photoshop and ImageReady's toolbars, palettes, and menu items are organized in a very logical way, and support your workflow to a higher degree than just about any other software tool I can think of.

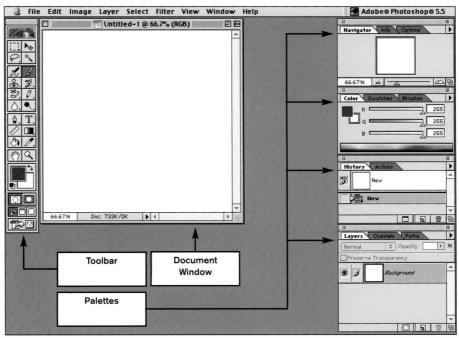

*When you first open Photoshop, it defaults to showing the toolbar and a few key palettes. The figure above also shows an open, untitled document, which you can create by choosing **File > New**. Notice the tabs inside the palettes? You can move these items around or, via the Window menu, show or hide them.*

The Photoshop 5.5 and ImageReady 2.0 Toolbars

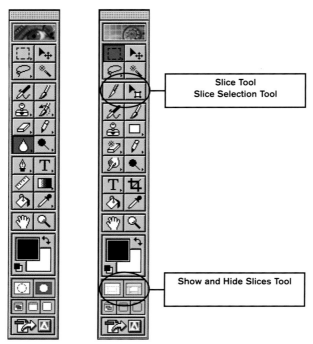

Slice Tool
Slice Selection Tool

Show and Hide Slices Tool

The toolbar is almost identical in Photoshop 5.5 and ImageReady 2.0. The key difference is that the ImageReady toolbar contains a series of slicing tools which help you cut apart graphics, buttons, and animated graphics to reassemble them into HTML tables for Web publishing. You'll learn more about this in Chapter 10, "Slicing."

Jump To Buttons

The big new thing in Photoshop 5.5 and ImageReady 2.0 is the addition of a **Jump To** button located at the bottom of both toolbars. It lets you switch between Photoshop and ImageReady with a convenient click of a button.

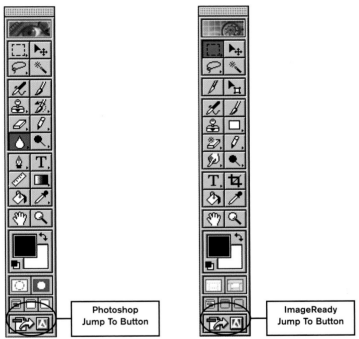

Photoshop
Jump To Button

ImageReady
Jump To Button

*You'll have plenty of opportunities to use the **Jump To** button throughout this book. When you have an open document and click this button, the same document reopens in the other application. If you don't have a document open, the **Jump To** button will not work.*

Note | Jump To Customization

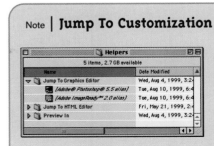

You can customize the **Jump To** button to go to a different graphics application by putting an alias inside the **Jump To Graphics Editor** directory, located inside the Adobe® Photoshop® 5.5 folder. However, I recommend that you don't customize this feature while reading this book because many of the exercises rely on jumping from ImageReady to Photoshop or vice-versa.

I. ————————**Using Flexible Palettes and Tabs**

What's distinctive about Photoshop and ImageReady is that you can reorganize items by docking or undocking a tab to form a new palette. This is a very convenient thing to do if you find that you are only working with a few palettes that are not grouped together, or if you don't want to crowd your workspace with palettes you don't use.

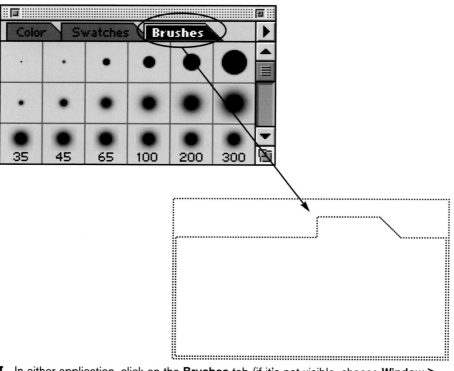

I. In either application, click on the **Brushes** tab (if it's not visible, choose **Window > Show Brushes**) and drag it off the palette.

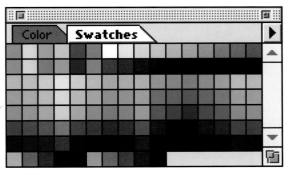

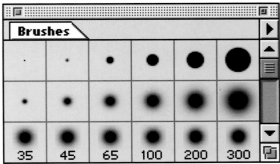

*By dragging the **Brushes** tab off the palette, it will form its own palette.*

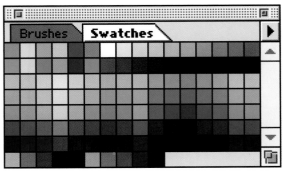

2. Click on the **Swatches** tab and drag it into the new **Brushes** palette you just made. You've just reorganized your palettes!

I do this often when I'm working in Photoshop or ImageReady because I find myself using just a few features and I don't want to clutter up my screen with all the default palettes.

2. ——————**Returning the Palettes to Default Settings**

The fact that you can rearrange palettes and tabs is wonderful until you wish you could set them back to the way Photoshop or ImageReady had them in the first place. I often create my own custom groupings of tabs and palettes to support a single project, and then return to the defaults when I'm finished. In the example below, I have used ImageReady, but this is the same procedure for both applications.

I. Choose **File > Preferences > General....**

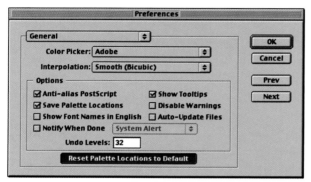

2. Click on the **Reset Palette Locations to Default** button.

This restores the default positions of all your palettes. Easy!

3. Click **OK** and all your palettes will appear in their default positions.

Obviously, there is a lot more to say about the Photoshop and ImageReady interfaces, but I think it will all be easier to absorb if these elements are introduced when you need them. Keep on reading, and by the end of the book you'll know the two interfaces intimately and be able to work them both comfortably!

Palette Shortcuts

There are several identical shortcuts for displaying or hiding the two applications' often-used palettes. Here's a handy chart for you to consult until you know these function-key shortcuts by heart.

	Palette Shortcuts	
F-key	**Photoshop 5.5**	**ImageReady 2.0**
F5	Brushes	Brushes
F6	Color	Color
F7	Layers	Layers
F8	Info	Info
F9	Actions	Actions
F10		Optimize
F11		Animation

If you memorize the F-keys for the palettes, you will probably never need to venture under the Window menu again in either application. You can also customize these shortcuts, which can be done through **Actions** in either Photoshop or ImageReady. You'll learn how to do this in Chapter 13, *"Automation."*

Shortcuts

I thought it would be a good idea to share with you some of the most useful shortcuts when doing Web work in Photoshop 5.5 and ImageReady 2.0. Here are two big ones.

• The Tab key shows/hides all palettes and the toolbar. To show or hide only the palettes, leaving the toolbar as is, press **Shift+Tab**.

• To select a tool quickly, press its shortcut key on your keyboard. To see a tool's shortcut key, point your mouse over the tool in the toolbox.

The two charts below give the keyboard letter shortcuts to the most commonly used tools when doing Web design.

Photoshop	
Tool	**Shortcut Key**
Eraser	E
Eyedropper	I
Hand	H
Move	V
Switch Colors	X
Type	T
Zoom	Z

ImageReady	
Tool	**Shortcut Key**
Slice	Y
Slice Selection	A
Hide/Show Slices	Q

How to Set a Tool's Default Settings in Photoshop

*Double-click the tool in the toolbar to access that tool's **Options** palette. Click the arrow on the palette's upper-right corner. Choose **Reset Tool** to reset one tool or **Reset All Tools**, to reset every tool.*

How to View Hidden Tools in Photoshop and ImageReady

In the toolbar of either application, the right-pointing arrow on certain tools means other kinds of tools are available. Click a tool and hold down your mouse until a pop-up menu of other choices appears, then click whichever tool you want to access.

Click the tool's arrow, hold down your mouse, and a pop-up menu will appear, displaying other tools. Click whichever tool you need.

3.
Color Management

| Color Management Assistant | Disabling Color Profiles |
| Adobe Gamma | Preference Settings for the Web |

chap_03

Photoshop 5.5 / ImageReady 2.0
H•O•T CD-ROM

This chapter focuses on how to maximize Photoshop's and ImageReady's color-management settings for Web graphics purposes. Photoshop 5.0 introduced color management in the form of profile settings, which many longtime Photoshop users found confusing. These same profile settings are also present in Photoshop 5.5. Since most of these features relate to print and not to the Web, I'm going to show you how to turn them off.

The Color Management Assistant

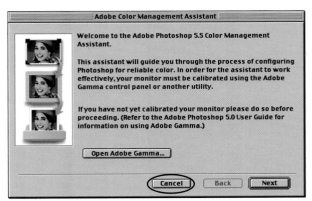

When you open Photoshop 5.5 for the first time, the **Color Management Assistant** will appear. If you plan to use Photoshop for print graphics, I recommend that you click on the **Next** button and go through the questions that are posed. Adobe basically walks you through the steps to build a color profile for your system, which will be stored and accounted for when you go to print your file. The trouble with this procedure is that it is counter productive to the creation of Web graphics.

If you are planning to use Photoshop for Web graphics, which is, of course, the orientation of this book, click the **Cancel** button. Exercise 1 in this chapter will show you how to properly set up your system for the Web and disable everything that the **Color Management Assistant** will set.

If you plan to use Photoshop for both print and Web graphics, you can always re-access the **Color Management Assistant** by choosing **Help > Color Management ....** Or you can create an **Action** script to automatically go back and forth between two settings — one that disables all the color-management features and another that enables them. Chapter 13, *"Automation,"* explains how to make Photoshop Actions.

Warning | **Why Disable Color Profiles?**

Until recently, computer color reliability has been an unexacting science. Digital artwork almost always looks different on the computer monitor than it does once it's printed. A number of computer software and hardware vendors, such as Adobe, Apple, Hewlett Packard, and Microsoft, got together to form some standards around computer color, and came up with the concept of color profiles. The premise was that computer files could carry information about where they were created and how they were supposed to look, and that printing devices could read the information and duplicate the intended settings. Sounds good so far, right?

The thing is, unless there's a receiving device that understands color profiles, they are of little use to anyone. Sadly, that is the case on today's Web, though at some point it will likely change for the better. Today, if you use color profiles in your Web graphics, not only will no other software or hardware recognize them, but the result is that your images will look different in Photoshop than they do anywhere else — even in other Adobe products!

While I think color profiles could ultimately be a great thing, I don't advocate using them just yet. I believe it will be more damaging to leave them turned on because you won't have an accurate idea of how your artwork looks in other applications, such as Explorer, Fireworks, Freehand, GoLive, Illustrator, ImageReady, Netscape, etc. Photoshop's display will be adjusted, actually changing the appearance of otherwise absolute RGB pixels into something completely different. Your document will look the same in every other program except Photoshop, effectively ruining Photoshop's ability to integrate with other applications.

[PS] **I.** ─────────**Changing Photoshop Color Settings for Web Design**

In order to disable color management in Photoshop, you'll need to adjust three settings: the **Profile Setup**, **RGB Setup**, and **Preview**.

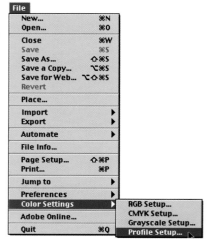

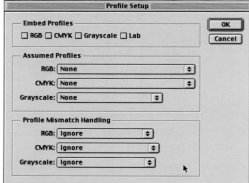

I. Choose **File > Color Settings > Profile Setup....**

2. Uncheck all the **Embed Profile** checkboxes. Change all **Assumed Profiles** pop-up menus to **None** and all **Profile Mismatch Handling** pop-up menus to **Ignore**. Click **OK**.

These color profiles are useful for print graphics, not Web graphics. Color profiles increase the file size of Web graphics and can't be read by other Web applications such as browsers and HTML editors (with the exception of Adobe's GoLive). The only Web publishers who would enable color profiles are those who have taken special measures to match colors perfectly, which requires the use of a proprietary Web Plug-In, and is outside the scope of this book. Most of us would not use this feature today because of that size impact and need for a proprietary browser Plug-In.

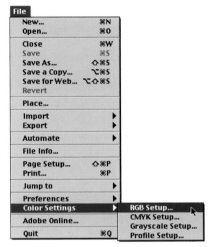

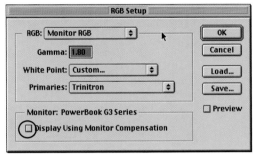

3. Choose **File > Color Settings > RGB Setup**....

4. Change the **RGB** pop-up menu to **Monitor RGB**. Uncheck **Display Using Monitor Compensation**. Click **OK**.

*Monitor RGB leaves the appearance of your monitor set to its defaults (just like in browsers, graphics applications other than Photoshop, and HTML editors. Once you uncheck **Display Using Monitor Compensation**, artwork on your screen will appear without any alteration, like it did in the days of Photoshop 4.0 and earlier, before color profiles were introduced.*

Now that you've finished these steps, all the color profile and preview options will be turned off, and your images will look exactly like they did in Photoshop 4.0 and in every other graphics and browser application you use.

Tip | **Additional Color Help**

Photoshop 5.5 ships with additional documentation about color management, which you can access by choosing **Help > Color Management....** I'm intentionally not bogging you down with all the technical details of this highly complex subject, so that the book stays focused on the Web instead of print. However, if this chapter piques your curiosity, be sure to give this **Help** system a read. Additional Color Management information is also available inside the **Adobe Photoshop 5.5 User Guide Supplement**.

Note | **Adobe Gamma on Macintoshes**

The "gamma" of your monitor sets a midpoint for gray, meaning that it affects not the white point or black point display but the grays or values in between white and black. Windows has a setting of 2.2 gamma, while Macintosh uses a setting of 1.8. This is why Web graphics look darker on Windows than they do on Macintoshes. Many Web developers who develop on Macs like to change their gamma settings to match that of Windows. If you make this change, it will affect all applications, not just Photoshop. I leave my gamma settings alone because I primarily design Web graphics for the lynda.com site, which has a large Mac audience. If you think that your site might have a larger Windows audience, this change might save you from potential revisions to lighten your graphics so they read better on Windows machines.

You can access **Adobe Gamma** by going to the **Apple** menu and choosing **Control Panels > Apple Gamma**. Check the **Control Panel** button, since this can be accessed at any time from within any application, not just Photoshop or ImageReady.

This opens the **Adobe Gamma** control panel, where you can choose **Desired: Windows Default 2.2**, which is the setting you want if you do a lot of Web authoring for a Windows audience.

---

2. ———————**Changing Your Photoshop Preferences for the Web**

There are numerous **Preference** settings in Photoshop, and many of them are related to workflow, while others will directly impact whether you are set up properly for the Web or print. The following setup emulates how I prefer to change my **Photoshop Preferences** for the Web. For a complete list of **Preferences** and their settings, refer to the Adobe Photoshop manual.

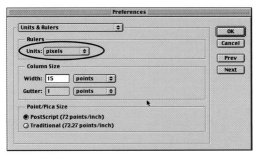

I. Select **File > Preferences > Units & Rulers....** Change the **Rulers Units** to **pixels** and click **OK**.

When you work on the Web you measure everything by pixels and points, not picas, as you would in print.

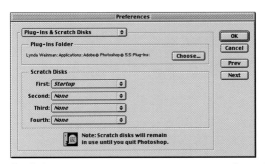

2. Select **File > Preferences > Plug-Ins & Scratch Disks....** This is the default setting for this Preference. If you have more than one hard drive, choose the one with the most space on it for your **First:** setting, and click **OK**. **Note:** This change will not take effect until you quit and reopen Photoshop.

*Scratch disk space helps Photoshop manage memory, so you want as much free space on your primary disk as you can get. I only have one hard drive on my laptop (which I am using to write this book) so my **First:** Scratch Disk is set to **Startup**.*

4.
Optimization

GIF, JPEG, and PNG	Bit Depth	Optimizing in Photoshop
Optimizing in ImageReady	Palette Descriptions
Matte Color on JPEG	Previewing and Writing HTML

chap_04

Photoshop 5.5 / ImageReady 2.0
H•O•T CD-ROM

Anyone who has ever used the Web has surely been frustrated by slow-loading Web pages. There's never been a design medium before where the file size of your artwork translates into the speed at which someone can view it. Making small Web graphics is both an art and a science. Fortunately, Photoshop 5.5 and ImageReady 2.0 are the ideal tools with which to master this craft.

Prepare for a long chapter since optimization is a fairly complex subject that both Photoshop and ImageReady handle with great detail. If terms like dither, Adaptive palettes, bit depth, JPEG, and GIF are unfamiliar to you, they won't be for long. Even if you're a pro at optimizing Web graphics, you will be impressed by Photoshop's and ImageReady's superb optimization capabilities.

Every image you work with is different and each has its own challenges. I've intentionally selected images that expose you to different optimization principles, so that you'll be able to apply a wide variety of tips and techniques that you learn here once you start optimizing images of your own.

What Affects Speed on the Web?

I wish that I could tell you that making your file sizes small in Photoshop or ImageReady guarantees fast Web site performance, because that would be so easy. Sadly, there are more factors involved than just your images' file size. Here are some of the other factors that slow down Web sites.

• Slow Web-server connection speed.

• Clogged arteries in the Information Highway (otherwise known as router problems "somewhere" in the system).

• Large service providers, such as AOL, Earthlink, or GeoCities, sometimes have so much traffic that your site's performance might slow down during heavy usage hours.

Solutions? Make sure that you run your Web site off of a fast connection or that you hire a hosting company that guarantees a fast connection. If you have a serious business site, get a dedicated hosting service instead of a large consumer-based Web service. If the Web is slow because of router problems, it affects everyone. Such is life. The best thing you can do is to control the things that you can (like file size) and accept that you can't control everything. The only predictable thing about the Web is that it won't always perform in a predictable manner. You can make your mark on speed by making images that are small in file size, which is what this chapter is going to get to as soon as some of this background information stuff is out of the way.

GIF or JPEG?

GIF stands for **Graphic I**nterchange **F**ormat and **JPEG** stands for **J**oint **Photographic E**xperts **G**roup. I've intentionally bolded the words "graphic" and "photographic" to point out what each file format is best for. It isn't that GIF is better than JPEG or JPEG better than GIF, but that these compression schemes are best suited for certain types of images.

• GIFs are best for flat or simple graphic images that contain a lot of solid areas of color, including but not limited to logos, illustrations, cartoons, line art, etc.

• JPEGs are best for continuous-tone images, including but not limited to photographs, landscapes, glows, gradients, drop shadows, etc.

Of course, some images don't fall into either category because they are hybrids of line art and continuous-tone artwork. In those cases, experiment with GIF and JPEG to see which works better.

GIF Transparency and Animation

Whether a graphic is a line art or continuous tone is not the sole deciding factor for whether to choose GIF or JPEG. The GIF format can do a couple of things that the JPEG format cannot – transparency and animation. This book has a chapter devoted to each, but I thought I'd provide a brief explanation of these terms in this chapter, too, since it may factor into your optimization strategy.

GIF Definitions	
GIF Transparency	What if you have a button design that's in a circle instead of a square or rectangle? You would need to use transparency to mask the shape so it would appear in a circle inside the Web browser. The GIF file format supports 1-bit masking, meaning that the image can be turned off in specified areas, making it possible to create irregularly shaped images. By only supporting 1-bit transparency, the GIF can only tell parts of the image to be visible or invisible, and subtle changes in opacity are not possible. For more information, check out Chapter 8, *"Transparent GIFs."*
GIF Animation	A single GIF document can contain multiple images and display them in a slide-show fashion. GIF files that contain multiple images are called "animated GIFs." For more information on how the GIF file format supports animation, check out Chapter 12, *"Animated GIFs."*

Lossy or Lossless?

In past books I've reported that the JPEG file format is **Lossy** and the GIF file format is **Lossless**. That's what I and everyone else thought until the release of Photoshop 5.5 and ImageReady 2.0. Those crafty Adobe engineers figured out a way to apply **Lossy** compression to the GIF file format. While this may mean nothing to you, to me it was quite exciting because no one had figured out a new way to make GIF files smaller until this breakthrough. So what does **Lossy** and **Lossless** mean, you must be thinking? **Lossy** means that the compression scheme reduces file size by discarding information, while **Lossless** means that it reduces file size without throwing away information.

Warning | **Don't Recompress a Compressed Image**

Because JPEG compression is **Lossy**, this format will cause your image to lose quality each time it is compressed. This is perfectly controllable as long as you start with a clean original. Compression artifacts can get out of control if you apply JPEG to an image that already had JPEG compression applied to it. Always start with an uncompressed file, and your JPEGs will look as good as it gets.

This same warning applies to the GIF format when **Lossy** compression is added. If you recompress an image that already contains **Lossy** compression, it will look much worse than if you began with an uncompressed original image.

How Can You Make Small JPEGS?

The JPEG file format best compresses images that are continuous tone. Here is a handy chart that shows what can be done to compress an image most effectively in this format.

JPEG Compression	
Start with an image that has tonal qualities, such as a photograph, blurry graphic, glow, drop shadow, etc.	The JPEG file format looks for areas of low contrast, subtle variation, and slight tonal shifts, and does its best job compressing this type of data. It can't compress areas of solid color well at all, and it doesn't work well for graphic-style artwork.
Add blur.	Unlike GIF, the JPEG format compresses blurry images well.
Add more JPEG compression.	The more JPEG compression you add, the smaller the file size becomes. Too much JPEG compression can cause unwanted compression artifacts to appear when you are using the optimization features of Photoshop or ImageReady. It's your job to find the balance between making the file small and making it look good.
Decrease the saturation.	If you decrease the color saturation of a JPEG, it will most often result in greater file savings.
Decrease the contrast.	Decreasing a JPEG's contrast usually reduces file size.

How Can You Make Small GIFs?

The principles of making a small GIF are almost opposite from those of making a small JPEG. The GIF file format works best on areas of solid color – and that's why it's best for line art, logos, illustrations, and cartoons.

GIF Compression	
Start with an image that has large areas of solid color.	The GIF file format looks for patterns in artwork, such as large runs of a single color that span in a horizontal, vertical, or diagonal direction. **Note:** The moment a color changes, the file size increases.
Reduce the number of colors.	Reducing the number of colors in a GIF image also reduces the file size. At some point during the color reduction process the image won't look right, and that's when you'll have to back up and add some colors. The objective is to find that exact threshold where the image looks good but contains the fewest number of colors.
Reduce the amount of dithering.	Dithering is a process in which the computer adds different colored pixels in close proximity to each other to simulate secondary colors or smooth gradations of color. A dithered image often looks noisy or has scattered pixels. Some images have to contain dithering to look good, but it's best to use the least amount of dithering necessary and you'll be able to see better file-size savings.
Add Lossy compression.	Lossy compression is new to Photoshop 5.5 and ImageReady 2.0. Adding a little to your GIF file will likely reduce your file size.

Note | **Recompressing GIF Images**

Compression artifacts are not an issue with GIF as they are with the JPEG format. You can recompress a GIF with no ill compression effects, though it's sometimes preferable to begin with a clean original .psd, .pict, or .bmp rather than to recompress an already compressed GIF. If, for example, you recompressed a GIF that had been set to six colors, you wouldn't be able to introduce any more colors even if you wanted to. You would have more latitude with your choices if instead you compressed a GIF from an original image source.

What About PNG?

Both Photoshop and ImageReady write the **PNG** file format, which stands for **P**ortable **N**etwork **G**raphics. Many people, myself included, believe that PNG is a superior file format to GIF and JPEG, but sadly it still isn't supported by the two major browsers, Explorer and Netscape. PNG is superior because it supports better transparency than GIF, plus it can achieve smaller file sizes than GIF for photographic and graphic-based images.

Another reason why PNG is attractive is that the GIF file format is patented by the company that developed it, Unysis. For this reason, technically you are supposed to pay a royalty to use the GIF compression scheme. The good news is that Adobe has a license for GIF which will cover anyone using Photoshop or ImageReady, so this patent shouldn't concern you. Still, many people are looking to PNG as an alternative to GIF so this patent issue would go away completely.

Until PNG is supported by the main Web browsers, however, the penalty of using it could result in broken images on your Web pages. That's just not acceptable, so I would say the risks of PNG outweigh the benefits right now. I hope this changes soon, and frankly I thought it would have already. The good news is that once PNG is supported by Web browsers, both Photoshop and ImageReady will be able to write the format perfectly.

What is Bit Depth?

Bit depth has to do with the number of colors in a graphics file. For your information, GIF is an 8-bit file format and JPEG is a 24-bit file format. I'm not suggesting that you memorize these numbers, but if you ever need to refer to a chart that lists bit depth, here you go.

Bit-Depth Chart	
32-bit	16.7 million colors plus an 8-bit masking channel
24-bit	65.5 million colors
16-bit	16.7 million colors
8-bit	256 colors
7-bit	128 colors
6-bit	64 colors
5-bit	32 colors
4-bit	16 colors
3-bit	8 colors
2-bit	4 colors
1-bit	2 colors

—————Saving For Web Using JPEG

This first exercise will walk you through saving a JPEG. It will introduce you to a new feature in Photoshop 5.5 called **Save For Web**. This saving feature gives you control over so many options that you will be able to make the smallest possible Web graphics once you master its nuances.

1. Open Photoshop 5.5 and choose **File > Open** to select **orangeflower.psd** from the **chap_ 04** folder you transferred to your hard drive from the **H•O•T CD-ROM**.

2. Choose **File > Save for Web....**

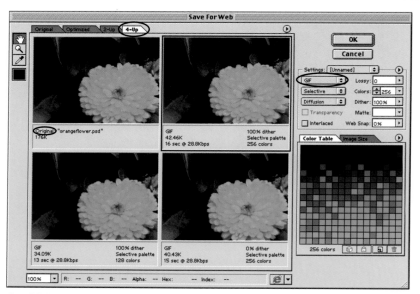

3. Click on the **4-Up** tab in the **Save For Web** dialog box, as this will let you compare different compression settings.

*Notice that the upper-left preview has the term "**Original**" in it? This allows you to compare compression choices to how the image looked in its original, uncompressed state. All of the other states in my example are set to **GIF**, which was chosen for me automatically. If you have already used the **Save For Web** feature before reading this book, your version of Photoshop might default to a different setting. That's because the **Save For Web** feature memorizes whichever compression settings were last set.*

4. Click on the upper-right preview (it is probably selected already) and change the pop-up menu that reads **GIF** to **JPEG** (if it needs to be changed).

Notice that the JPEG is smaller and better looking than any of the other previews that are GIFs? This is what I was talking about earlier when I wrote that continuous-tone images always compress better as JPEGs than as GIFs.

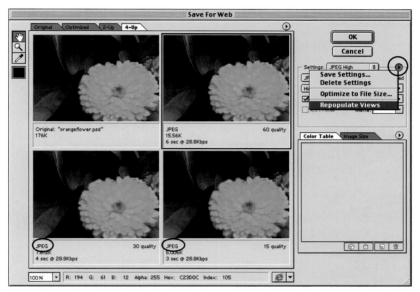

5. Click on the arrow circled above to access the pop-up menu and choose **Repopulate Views**.

Notice that this just turned the other two bottom previews to JPEG settings as well?

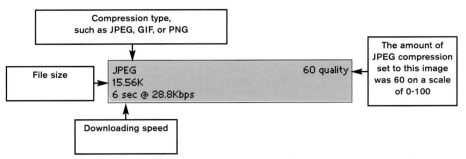

*Notice the readout below each preview? The first preview region you changed was set to **High Quality**, by default, which has a compression level of **60**. Photoshop is estimating how long this graphic will take to download over a slow connection. Note that this is a theoretical estimate of speed, and it might not be accurate due to other factors such as server speed and bottlenecks in the Internet.*

*Judging the quality and file-size savings of all these choices, it looks like the best quality would lie between a JPEG setting of **30** and **15**. Every image you optimize will have a different threshold of quality versus size, but isn't this readout handy for making your final decision?*

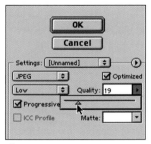

6. This time, use the slider by clicking on the arrow next to the **Quality** field and try some settings between **30** and **15**. **Note:** You must release the slider for the results of the new setting to take effect.

The slider is useful because it lets you easily experiment with different settings instead of requiring you to use the keyboard to type in different values.

7. Try adding a tiny amount of blur to the image. It will result in a slight file savings but you can't add too much or you will adversely affect the quality. When you're happy with the result, click **OK**.

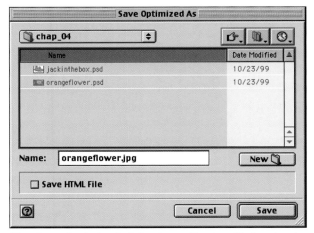

The **Save Optimized** dialog box will open. Notice that it puts a .jpg suffix on the file name for you? It also automatically generates a file name, which you can change. You could choose to check the box to **Save HTML File** as well, and Photoshop would generate an HTML file that places this image at the upper-left corner. You can upload this HTML file to the Web or open it in any HTML editor to further modify it.

At this point, I'm happy with the way the image looks once it weighs in at about 4.8K.

8. Click **Save** and keep this file open for the next exercise.

Notice when you click **Save** that the original, uncompressed **orangeflower.psd** file remains open in your program? That's because you haven't altered the original a bit. When you choose **Save for Web...**, it saves a copy on your hard drive and does not harm the original file.

Saving Options in Photoshop

In the last exercise, you learned how to use Photoshop's **Save For Web** feature. You might be familiar with a feature called **Save As….** In addition to plain old **Save**, there is a fourth way to save from Photoshop, **Save a Copy….** Here's a useful chart to show you when you would use each of the four Photoshop save options.

Which Type of Save Is Best?	
Save	To write over an existing file. If, for example, you have a .psd file open and you make a change that you want to keep, all you need to do is choose **File > Save** and the file will be overwritten. It's important to note that .psd is the only format that will save layers, filter effects, adjustment layers, etc. No other file format will save these things.
Save a Copy...	When you want to choose a file format other than the type of file you've opened. For example, if you have a .psd open but you want to save a version of it as a TIFF, EPS, PICT, BMP, or something else. This is also useful for when you want to keep an alternative version with a different name while not overwriting the original. It's a good way of keeping snapshots of different versions of a project. It leaves the original open and saves a copy to the hard drive. For example, if you were working on **orangeflower.psd** and saved a copy as **purpleflower .psd, orangeflower.psd** would remain open and unsaved.

Continued...	
Save As...	To save the same type of file you already have open as another name. In effect, this creates a copy of the file but it will only create a copy in the identical format that you have open. For example, if you have a file called **orangeflower.psd** and want to save a purple version of it as **purpleflower.psd**, you would choose **Save As...** In this example, **purpleflower.psd** would remain open, and **orangeflower.psd** would close.
Save for Web...	To optimize graphics and create a copy of your file in a Web format, such as GIF, JPEG, or PNG and leave your original open and unchanged.

Note | **Issues with Save**

If you are using the **Save** function to overwrite an image, Photoshop will honor whichever file format you are starting with, such as a GIF, JPEG, TIFF, EPS, etc. The only time it will not let you write over an existing format is when you add attributes that aren't supported by that format, such as layers, masks, adjustments, etc. It will then force you to write a .psd unless you choose **Save a Copy...**, and then you can change the file format.

2.————————Saving For Web Using GIF

The GIF file format is far more complex than the JPEG file format in terms of optimizing because there are so many more settings that affect file size. This exercise will expose you to some of the key settings to optimize a GIF, such as lowering the number of colors, adjusting the dither options, and choosing a palette.

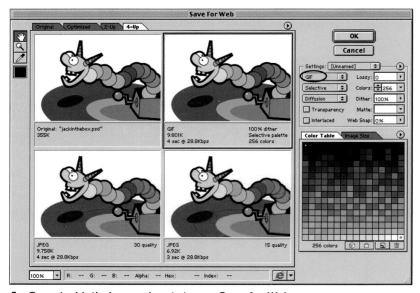

1. Open **jackinthebox.psd** and choose **Save for Web…**.

2. You still should be seeing the **4-Up** view, if not, click on the **4-Up** tab. Notice that all the views are in JPEG? The upper-right preview should read around 8K (it might be slightly smaller or larger depending on how the setting was set in the last exercise) and be set to **JPEG**. Click on the **JPEG** pop-up menu and select **GIF**. Change the **Colors** to **256** and make sure that all the other settings match those above.

Notice that the file size of this preview weighs in at half its previous size, to around 9.8K. Although the two previews on the bottom are smaller in file size than the upper-right quadrant set to GIF, notice that they don't look very good, especially the bottom-right image.

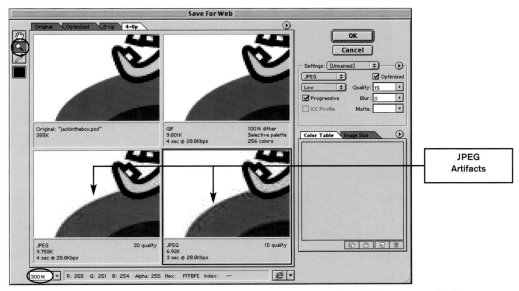

JPEG
Artifacts

3. Click on the **Zoom** tool of the **Save For Web** dialog box toolbar. Click once on the bottom-right image to select it and two more times to change the magnification to **300%**.

Notice how the two bottom JPEG images look distressed upon closer examination, and the top-right image set to GIF looks much more like the original on the upper left? As I mentioned before, flat-style graphics such as this image are better suited for the GIF format.

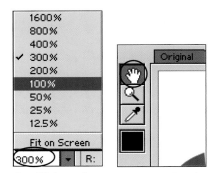

4. Click on the arrow next to the size readout on the bottom left of this window to return the view to **100%**. (You could alternately type **100%** into this field.) No one will ever see your Web images at anything other than 100% so don't fuss too much with an image at a high magnification. Next, select the hand icon on the **Save For Web** dialog box's toolbar.

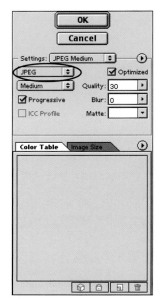 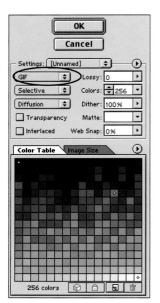

5. Click on the upper-right preview that is set to GIF. Notice that lots of things change on the far right of this window? Click to the bottom-left preview and keep your eye on the settings at the far right of the window. As you switch between a JPEG to GIF, notice the additional settings available for GIF.

*When the image is set to a **GIF**, the feedback of this window changes drastically. This is called a context-sensitive interface. When the **Save For Web** dialog box is set to **GIF**, it shows you all the compression options for GIF; when it's set to **JPEG**, it displays all the options for JPEG. Notice when this is set to the **GIF** format it contains a color palette while the **JPEG** does not? That's because the GIF file format's color is mapped to whichever palette appears in this window. A JPEG file supports up to millions of colors and doesn't need to map to a palette, while a GIF format only supports a maximum of 256 colors.*

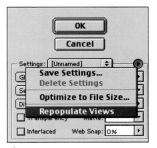

6. With the upper-right GIF preview selected again, hold your mouse down on the arrow next to **Settings** and choose **Repopulate Views** from the pop-up menu. This changes all the views to GIF.

You can always choose to **Repopulate Views** when you want to see variations on one compression setting, as you just did with the GIF format, to which it should now be set.

7. Leave this file open in the **Save For Web** dialog box for the next exercise.

*Note: If you press **Cancel**, the **Save For Web** dialog box will not remember all of these settings. For the purposes of this exercise, it is best if you leave the **Save For Web** dialog box open. If you cannot do so, expect to re-enter the settings.*

JPEG and GIF Photoshop Options

You are probably wondering what all the options mean inside the **GIF** and **JPEG** settings area of the **Save For Web** dialog box. The following descriptions might be helpful for quick reference until you try out the majority of these features in later chapters.

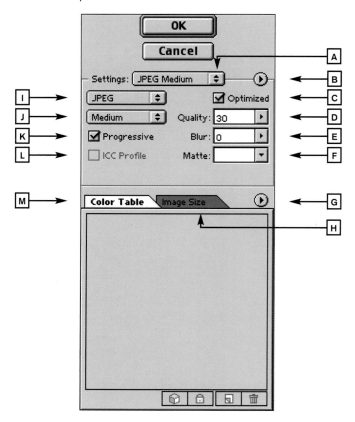

	JPEG Context-Sensitive Properties	
A	**Settings**	Settings contain preset compression values. You can use the ones that ship with Photoshop, or you can make your own by choosing **Save Setting** in the **Save Settings...** in the **Optimize** Menu (B).
B	**Optimize**	To see it, hold your mouse down on the arrow. This is where you are able to save and load settings for the **Settings Menu** (A).
C	**Optimized**	Highly recommended for making the smallest possible JPEG files.
D	**Quality**	Enter the quality value in this field. You can type it in or, hold your mouse down on the arrow — a slider will appear and you can drag it to a value.
E	**Blur**	Blurry images compress better as JPEGs than sharp images. This value field allows you to blur the image by typing or by holding your mouse down on the arrow to access a slider. I prefer using the slider because it's easier to make small incremental changes to the blur, which is usually what you'll want so the image doesn't appear too blurry.
F	**Matte**	If you begin with an image that is against a transparent background, you can change its matte color. Exercise 10 in this chapter shows you how to set the matte color for a JPEG.
G	**Color Palette**	This has no effect on JPEG settings.
H	**Image Size**	You can change the pixel dimensions of your image if you click on this tab and enter changes to the values.
I	**File Format**	This controls whether you're going to apply JPEG, GIF, or PNG compression to an image.
J	**Quality**	Preset quality values for the JPEG format. You can alternately enter values into the **Quality** setting (D).
K	**Progressive**	Progressive JPEGs are like Interlaced GIFs, in that they appear chunky and come into focus as they download. I don't recommend this format because it won't work on browsers below Netscape 3.0 or Explorer 3.0.
L	**ICC Profiles**	ICC (**I**nternational **C**olor **C**onsortium) Profiles work with some printing devices, but not with Web browsers (unless you use proprietary Plug-Ins). They add a lot of file size to a compressed image. I don't recommend them. However, there might come a day when browsers recognize this setting.
M	**Color Table**	The **Color Table** displays here.

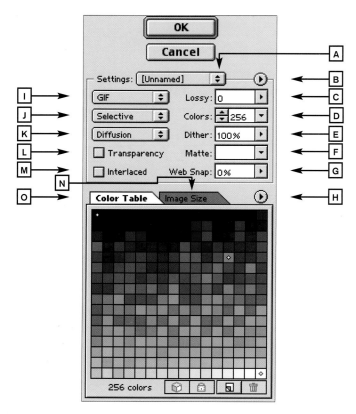

	GIF Context-Sensitive Properties	
A	**Settings Menu**	Settings contain preset compression values. You can use the ones that ship with Photoshop, or you can make your own by choosing **Save Settings…** in the **Optimize** Menu (**B**).
B	**Optimize Menu**	To see it, hold your mouse down on the arrow. This is where you can save and load settings for the **Settings** Menu (**A**).
C	**Lossy**	Changing the value in this field will add **Lossy** compression to your GIF images, this decreases the file size. It works much better on continuous-tone GIFs(such as photographs that you want to make transparent or animate).
D	**Color**	Reducing the number of colors in a GIF image results in file-size savings. The trick is to keep your image looking good with the fewest colors.

GIF Continued...

E	**Dither**	Adding dither to a GIF always increases file size but is sometimes necessary for the image to look its best.
F	**Matte Algorithm**	If you begin with an image that is set against a transparent background, you can change its matte color. You'll get a chance to do this in Chapter 8, *"Transparent GIFs."*
G	**Web Snap:**	If an image contains non-Web-safe colors, you can set a threshold so that any colors which are close will "snap" to become Web safe. You'll learn more about this in Chapter 5, *"Web Color."*
H	**Color Palette Menu**	This menu allows you to sort the colors in your palette, to load and save color palettes, and to create new colors in your palette.
I	**File Format**	This menu controls whether you're going to apply JPEG, GIF, or PNG compression to an image.
J	**Color Reduction Algorithms**	The Adobe engineers give you a lot of options as to which type of algorithm to use for best compressing your GIF images. You'll try them out in several upcoming exercises.
K	**Dithering Algorithms**	Bet you didn't know that your dithering could have algorithms! This is just a fancy way of saying that there are a few types of dithering options. You'll get to try these out in this chapter, too.
L	**Transparency**	Check this box when you want to make transparent GIF images. You might find that it won't work and that is most likely because your image doesn't contain any transparent areas. You'll learn all about how to make perfect transparent GIFs in Chapter 8, *"Transparent GIFs."*
M	**Interlaced**	Check this box if you want your GIFs to be interlaced, which means they will look chunky until they finish downloading. Interlaced GIFs work on all browsers, so you don't have to worry about backwards compatibility. I don't like to use them on text because I think it is frustrating to wait for an image to appear in focus when you have to read it. I prefer to use interlacing on graphics that contain no text, but the truth is I don't ever use interlaced GIFs because I don't like the way they look. To each his or her own preference.
N	**Image Size**	You can change the pixel dimensions of your image if you click on this tab and enter changes to the values.
O	**Color Table**	This area displays the colors that are being assigned to the GIF image. You'll get to explore this setting in great depth in Chapter 5, *"Web Color."*

3. ————Choosing the Right Palette

In the classes that I teach, I find that palette settings are among the most confusing things to my students. I thought it best to start with these mysterious settings, so you can cut to the chase and get through the confusing parts of optimizing GIFs.

1. Make sure that the upper-right preview is selected in the **Save For Web** dialog box containing **jackinthebox.psd** from the previous exercise.

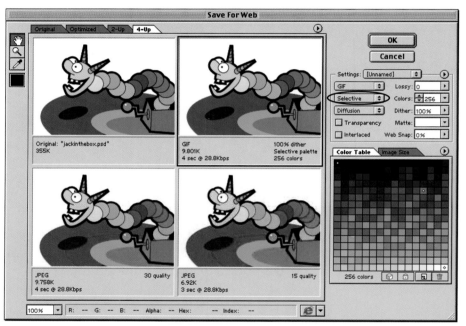

2. Change the palette setting from **Selective** to **Perceptual**, then **Adaptive**, and then **Web**, just to see the effect that these settings have on the file size and the image.

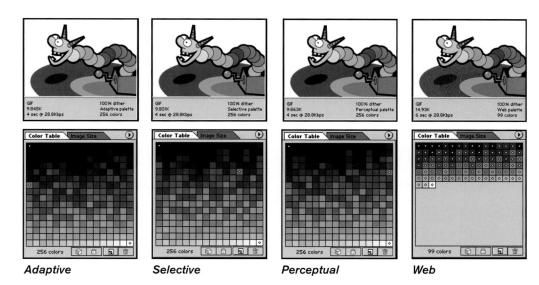

Adaptive   **Selective**   **Perceptual**   **Web**

*Notice how most of the **Color Table** feedback looks almost identical? While the **Web** setting resulted in a smaller file size, it didn't look very good. I almost always use **Adaptive**, **Perceptual**, or **Selective** instead of **Web**.*

3. Once you've looked at all of them, change the setting back to **Selective**. Make sure that the **Dither** method is set to **Diffusion**.

4. Leave the **Save For Web** dialog box as it is and move to the next exercise. If you have to quit Photoshop right now to start the next exercise later, be sure to save the .psd file. The next time you enter the **Save For Web** dialog box, the last settings will still be remembered.

The Meaning of Perceptual, Selective, Adaptive, and Web

If you are wondering what these four terms mean, here's a chart that shows how the Photoshop manual differentiates them.

Definitions	
Perceptual	Gives priority to colors for which the human eye has the greatest sensitivity.
Selective	Similar to perceptual but favors broad areas of color and the preservation of Web colors.
Adaptive	Samples colors from hues that appear most commonly in the image.
Web	Limits the **Color Table** to the 216 Web-safe colors which makes the most sense in relation to the image.

I always think of the **Perceptual**, **Selective**, and **Adaptive** palettes as variations of the same thing — algorithms that look to the colors in the image and build a different palette for each image on which they're applied. In contrast, the Web palette is made up of fixed colors that sometimes don't relate to the image being compressed.

You probably still have questions about these palettes and they will hopefully all be addressed in Chapter 5, *"Web Color."* For now, in the interest of time and the subject at hand, I'm going to skip past the deeper issues of the palette subject.

Reducing the Colors

In order to make a GIF image small in file size, it's necessary to reduce the number of colors until you arrive at the fewest that are necessary to ensure that the image looks good. The battle between looking good and having a small file is always present when you're optimizing Web graphics.

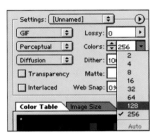

I. While still in the Web setting from the previous exercise, change the number of colors to **128** by accessing the pop-up menu next to the **Colors:** setting. You'll see the file size get smaller right away. Compare this image to the original, and it still looks great. Try smaller values until the image stops looking good.

*I'm satisfied with this image at **64** colors, which results in a file size of about 7.5K. Notice when you take this image down to **32** that some of the colors start looking dotted with other colors? Those dots are called dithering and in this example they don't look good. I still think this image can be coaxed to go smaller, though.*

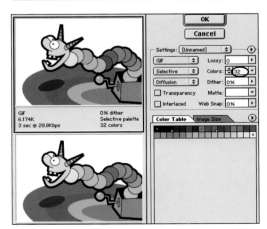

2. Take the **Colors** setting to **32** and turn the **Dither** slider to **0%**.

Wow, the image is now 6.2K. Dithering adds to file size with GIFs just like colors do.

I did notice that something unwanted happened, however. The purple circle in the neck turned blue and lost its purple hue. When you're reducing colors, you have the power to control this.

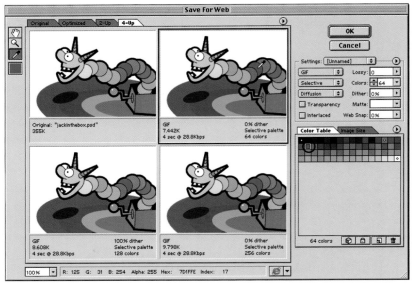

3. Change the value back to **64** colors and you'll get the purple back. Using the **Eyedropper** tool in the left side of the **Save For Web** dialog box, click on the **purple** color.

Notice how the purple highlights inside the Color Table?

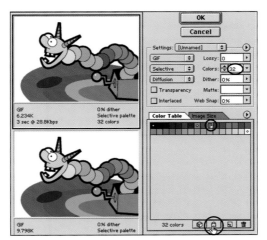

4. Click on the **lock** button at the bottom of the **Color Table** and reduce the colors to **32** again. Notice the little white square that appears at the bottom right of the color selection? This is a "lock" symbol that indicates the color is locked. Now, no matter how few colors you tell Photoshop to use, the purple that you locked will be one of them.

This time the purple didn't shift, but the blue did. Repeat the same procedure.

5. Go back to **64** colors again, select the blue you want to preserve, and lock it before returning the value to **32**.

You may have to do this several times, as the colors shift slightly. Instead of letting Photoshop decide mathematically which colors to discard, you can lock the ones you want to keep. Pretty powerful stuff, eh?

6. Stay in the **Save For Web** dialog box for the next exercise. If for some reason you have to quit or cancel, Photoshop will not remember the settings and you may have to re-enter them.

Previewing Gamma and Browser Dither

This particular image looks great, and it's down from approximately 9K to 6K. Not bad considering it still looks good. However, there are a few unseen gremlins in it. Before a tool like Photoshop 5.5 was developed, you wouldn't have discovered what the gremlins were until you published this image to the Web and someone with a different system saw it. This exercise teaches you how to take a look at the preview features for **Gamma** and **Browser Dither**, and it may save you a trip to browser hell.

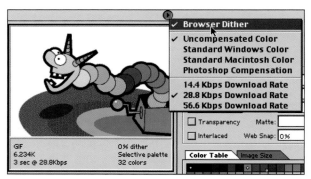

1. With **jackinthebox.psd** still open from the previous exercise, click on the arrow above the upper-right preview and select **Browser Dither** from the pop-up menu.

Notice that the image has some dithering that you didn't know about? This is how the image will be visible to an audience that has their systems set to 8-bit color, or 256 colors. No one knows how sizable this audience is, but there are quite a number of systems out there that can't see 16-bit or 24-bit color. If you want to make this image look good to them, too, shift the offending colors that are dithering to colors that won't dither.

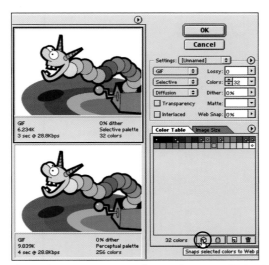

2. Use the **Eyedropper** (in the **Save For Web** dialog box's toolbar) to select a color that contains dithering. It will highlight in the **Color Table**. Click on the **cube** icon. Once this is clicked, a diamond shape will appear on the selected color in the **Color Table**, and the cube will no longer be accessible. The diamond symbol indicates that the color is within the Web-safe color spectrum. **Tip:** A color swatch in the **Color Table** must be selected before the cube icon will be active.

*This will change the colors from non-safe to Web-safe and the dithering will disappear before your eyes. You don't need to do this to every color, just the offending ones. The **Browser Dither** preview is really helpful in locating problematic colors. **Hint:** Some colors might appear dithered even after you've shifted them. In this event you might have to click on some colors and shift them twice. This is because the dots in the image sometimes translate to two different Web colors rather than one. In order to shift another color, be sure to first select it with the **Save For Web** dialog box's **Eyedropper** tool and then click on the **cube** icon.*

3. Be sure to turn off the **Browser Dither** preview once you've fixed the image. Just access the pop-up menu again.

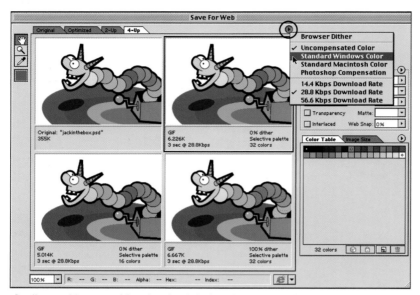

4. I'm working on a Mac, but it might be nice to see what this image looks like on a Windows machine. If you're on a Windows machine, you can see what the image looks like on a Mac. No matter where you are, you can access the same pop-up menu and choose the opposite platform to preview. You can return the preview to display whatever platform you are working on by accessing this menu again and selecting that choice.

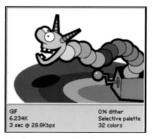

Color on a Macintosh is usually lighter.

Color on a Windows machine is usually darker.

There is not anything you can do about the gamma differences between Mac and Windows, which is what causes the difference in brightness between the two platforms. It is nice to be able to preview this problem when you're working, so you can adjust an image to be brighter or darker if it looks intolerable on the other platform.

5. Keep the image inside the **Save For Web** dialog box. You're almost finished with it!

[PS]

6. ———— Changing the Dimensions of a Graphic

There is only one more thing that can make this image smaller — changing its dimensions. This isn't always an option, since you might have sized it to the perfect dimensions before you started optimizing. The cool thing is that you can change the dimensions if you want to and you don't even have to leave the **Save For We**b dialog box. Another advantage is that it leaves the original untouched and only resizes the Web version of the graphic.

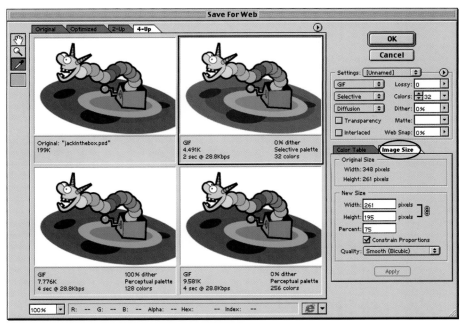

1. With **jackinthebox.psd** still open from the previous exercise, click on the **Image Size** tab to the right of the **Color Table** tab.

2. Enter **Percent: 75%**, click the **Apply** button, and watch the image get smaller in all four preview windows.

You just couldn't do all this at once before Photoshop 5.5. Those of us who have been slugging it through optimizing and sizing images for the past few years have great big smiles on our faces right now. The best news of all is that this image is now under 5K. Not bad for a few minutes' work. Well, it probably took you longer than that, but it won't in the future when you know how to do all this stuff without reading these steps.

3. Leave this file open in the **Save For Web** dialog box for the next exercise.

7.————————**Previewing in a Browser**

[PS]

Photoshop is now capable of previewing in a browser, right from the **Save For Web** dialog box.

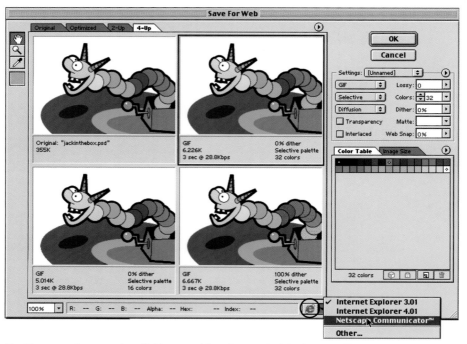

1. Choose a browser by clicking on either the symbol for Internet Explorer at the bottom of the **Save For Web** dialog box or the arrow to its right to access a pop-up menu for other browser choices. I chose Netscape Communicator instead of the default Internet Explorer by using this technique.

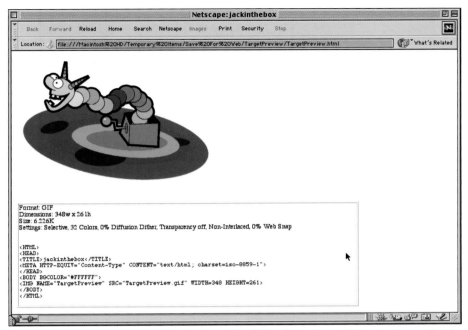

*The square that is highlighted in the **Save For Web** dialog box will be the image that is pre-viewed inside the browser. Notice the table that contains information and HTML code? This contains references to a temporary image and HTML file. If you want to use the HTML that Photoshop generates in final form with path names that work, it's best to save the HTML when you save the file. You will learn to do this in future exercises.*

2. Return to Photoshop. Make sure the image on the upper-right preview is selected and click the **OK** button at last. You'll be prompted to save this image as **jackinthebox.gif**. Save it into your **chap_04** folder and close the **jackinthebox.psd** image, too. When asked if you want to save **jackinthebox.psd**, click **Don't Save**.

You just optimized a Photoshop graphic without altering or saving the original. This can be useful because you can save a master document that remains untouched and save copies as Web graphics. This is ideal because Photoshop documents (.psd) store information about layers, Layer Effects and adjustment layers, while the Web formats GIF and JPEG do not.

Note: The next set of exercises will be in ImageReady.

[IR] 8. Setting Up for Optimization in ImageReady

Because this chapter covers optimization, I want to show you how to do the same processes in ImageReady that you just learned in Photoshop so you know how to do this important task in either application. ImageReady matches Photoshop for optimization capabilities feature for feature. Don't worry about the results being different in these two programs; the underlying code is identical. The only true difference is the location of the windows. In Photoshop, when you choose **Save for Web...**, a single dialog box appears. In ImageReady, the settings are spread across several palettes. I prefer to arrange my palettes in a specific way that groups them together. Here's how I do it.

I. Make sure you're in ImageReady. If your **Optimize** palette is not already visible, choose **Window > Show Optimize**. Click and drag the **Optimize** tab off its palette so it separates as a stand-alone palette. **Hint:** If your palette doesn't offer all the choices shown below, click on the arrow on the top-right corner and choose **Show Options**.

2. Do the same with the **Color Table** palette.

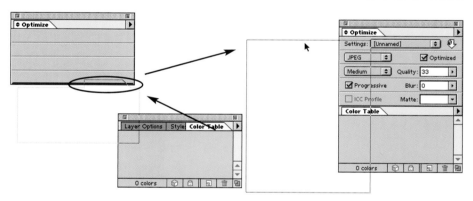

3. Drag the **Color Table** palette by its tab so that it touches the bottom of the **Optimize** palette and turns the bottom dark, as shown above. The two palettes should now be joined when you move them around by the top bar of the **Optimize** palette.

If you ever want to separate them, you can drag either one by its name tab. FYI, sadly, palettes do not join this way in Photoshop. I really like this kind of docking, and I'll recommend you do it with other palettes later in the book whenever it makes sense.

*Why did it make sense to do it just now? Because the only reason you'd ever want to look at the **Color Table** is in the context of saving GIFs.*

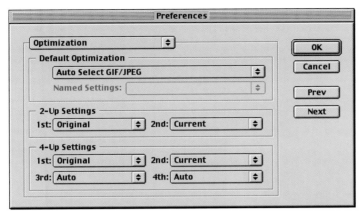

I also like to change the ImageReady Preferences before I start with optimization.

4. Select **File > Preferences > Optimization**.... Change the **Default Optimization** setting to **Auto Select GIF/JPEG**.

This instructs ImageReady to make a best guess for which type of compression format (GIF or JPEG) to select. You can override its guess, but why not have ImageReady make it for you as a good starting point?

5. In the **2-Up Settings**, enter **1st : Current** and **2nd: Auto**. For the **4-Up** Settings, enter **1st: Current** and **2nd: Auto**. Click **OK**.

*Notice that I suggested you change all of your **1st** settings from **Original** to **Current** and everything else to **Auto**? **Original** means that the Photoshop file format would be used, and **Current** means that whatever format you open would be used. Therefore, if you open a GIF or JPEG, it will display as such instead of in the Photoshop file format. **Auto**, as explained before, allows ImageReady to make a best guess for which type of compression to use.*

9. ————————Optimizing a JPEG

Everything in this exercise ought to be pretty familiar to you. ImageReady and Photoshop are almost identical for optimization purposes. I'll show you a few new tricks along the way and you can do them in either application if you want to.

1. Open **orangeflower.psd** again. Notice that it appears in a dialog box that already has tabs that read **Original**, **Optimized**, **2-Up**, and **4-Up**.

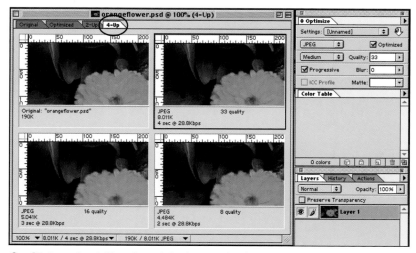

2. Click on the **4-Up** tab and the image should appear in four small preview windows.

*Notice that they all defaulted to JPEG? That's the result of the **Preference** setting you made in the last exercise. ImageReady made a best guess that this photo would best be optimized as a JPEG.*

3. Move the **Optimize** palette over to the right of this window (it should bring the **Color Table** along with it if you completed the last exercise properly).

4. Try all the things we tried in the Photoshop section of this chapter. Change the **Quality** setting, add **Blur**, and see what makes the smallest file size.

You already know how to use this program, because most of it is identical to Photoshop.

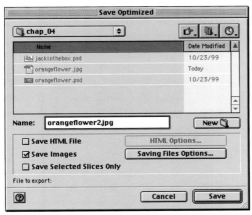

5. When you're ready to save this JPEG, choose **File > Save Optimized**. The above dialog box will appear with the name **orangeflower.jpg** already filled out. Because you already saved a file called **orangeflower.jpg**, change the file name to **orangeflower2.jpg**. Save the file and leave it open for the next exercise.

*This just saved an optimized version of **orangeflower.psd**. Whenever you want to save a Web file, choose **Save Optimized** or **Save Optimized As...**. Whenever you want to save the Photo-shop file, choose **Save** or **Save As...**.*

You might wonder what all the other settings are for in this dialog box. You can save HTML just like from Photoshop, though ImageReady allows you to do much more than that. With ImageReady you can cut apart images (see Chapter 10, "Slicing") and write HTML and compli-cated JavaScript (see Chapter 11, "Rollovers"). You'll get to play with these settings plenty in those chapters!

[IR] **IO.** ——————**Using a Matte Color on a JPEG**

One major difference between Photoshop and ImageReady is that you can edit this image easily in ImageReady, which was not true of the **Save For Web** feature in Photoshop. You would have had to click **Cancel** in the **Save For Web** dialog box to return to Photoshop's image-editing environment. Here in ImageReady, you can edit whenever you want. It's best to click on the **Original** tab, or else ImageReady will try to optimize the graphic while you're working, which can take a long time. In this exercise you will edit the image by erasing the background away from the flower and inserting a new color by using the **Matte** feature.

I. With **orangeflower.psd** still open from the previous exercise, click back on the **Original** tab and click on the **Eraser** tool in the ImageReady toolbar. **Tip:** The shortcut is the letter **E** on your keyboard. Make sure you have the standard **Eraser** selected, as shown above, and not the **Magic Eraser** that has an asterisk next to it (which you will learn about in Chapter 7, *"Background Images"*). If the **Magic Eraser** is selected, click and hold your mouse on it to access a menu of erasers and select the standard **Eraser**, as shown above.

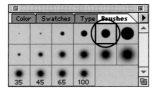

2. Choose **Window > Show Brushes** and select the brush shown above.

3. Use this brush setting to erase all the green leaves of the photograph.

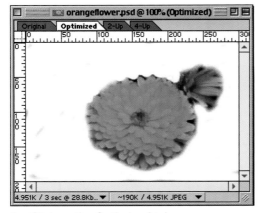

4. Click on the **Optimized** tab.

Notice that the checkerboard background disappeared and turned white? That's because you didn't specify a matte color, and ImageReady defaults to using white. You'll learn how to assign a different matte color in the next few steps.

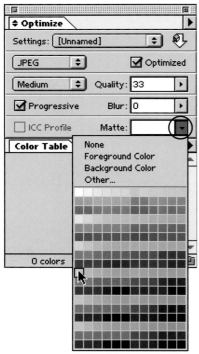

5. In the **Optimize** palette, click on the arrow next to the **Matte:** field and select a color off the pop-up color palette. **Note:** if you don't see the **Matte** field, either click the double-arrow symbol on the left of the **Optimize** tab or click the upper-right arrow of this palette to choose **Show Options**.

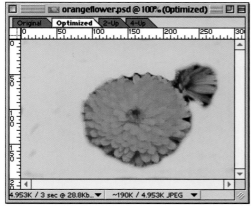

6. The image will now have behind it whichever color you chose. Keep it open for the next exercise.

Previewing and Writing HTML

If you're an experienced Photoshop user, you might be wondering why you would choose to use the **Matte** color to insert a background color into a JPEG. You could have easily made a new layer in ImageReady, filled it with this color, and achieved the same effect. The only advantage is because you used the **Matte** feature, ImageReady now knows to write this same color into the background color element of an HTML page, as well as the image. This exercise will show you how to set **Matte** color for the background color of your Web page.

However, you should note that there are times when the JPEG color will not perfectly match your HTML background color. If this happens to you, it would be better to create a transparent GIF, which you will learn about in Chapter 8, *"Transparent GIFs."*

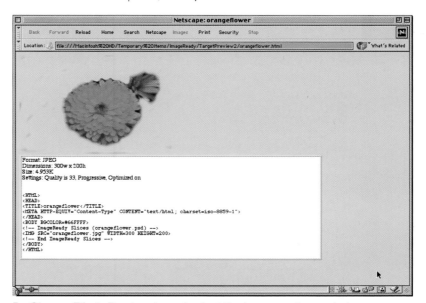

I. Choose **File > Preview In** and select the browser of your choice.

Notice that ImageReady creates a preview in the browser and puts a white box below the image that displays the HTML code that has been automatically written. You can actually copy and paste this code into an HTML editor, if you want. Better yet, you can have ImageReady write the HTML for you. You'll learn to do that next.

2. Return to ImageReady and check your HTML Preferences by choosing **File > Preferences > HTML...** from the menu.

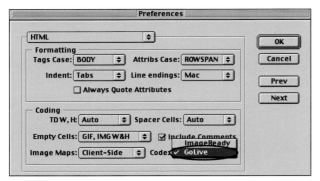

3. Click inside the **Code:** field to access the pop-up menu. If you use GoLive, check that setting. This will enable ImageReady to write HTML code that GoLive will be able to fully understand, edit, and enhance. This is especially important in later chapters when you will be writing HTML and JavaScript. If you are using other editors, such as BBEdit, Dreamweaver, FrontPage, HomeSite, or PageMill (or any other that I failed to mention) choose ImageReady. When you choose this setting, you're choosing to have ImageReady write generic HTML code that will work anywhere. It would even work in GoLive, but not as fluidly as if you checked the GoLive setting. Once you choose whichever setting is right for you, click **OK**.

4. Choose **File > Save Optimized As....**

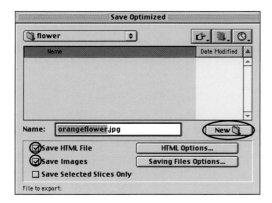

5. In the **Save Optimized** dialog box that will appear, make sure that **Save HTML File** and **Save Images** are checked. Create a folder for this artwork named **flower** by clicking **New** (Mac) or the yellow icon **Create New Folder** button (Windows). **Note:** Windows users should open the new folder **flower** after you create it and before clicking **Save** in the **Save Optimized** dialog box. A separate folder is not required however, it helps to keep your files organized.

*You can save an HTML file in Photoshop, too, by clicking the **Save** button, and then checking **Save HTML** file in the second dialog box that appears.*

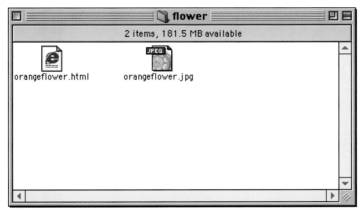

6. Look on your hard drive for the folder **flower** or for the directory where you chose to save the **orangeflower.jpg**. Notice that there are two files, an **HTML** file and the **JPEG** file?

7. Double-click on the **HTML** file, and you'll see the page open in the browser without the white information box that the preview generated before. It also contains references to the real file names instead of the temporary names that were assigned in the white information box.

This page can be opened in any HTML editor or uploaded directly to the Web. If you wanted to format it differently, such as to center the picture or put a headline at the top, you could easily add to the HTML in an editor or, if you know how, code HTML by hand.

8. Return to ImageReady. Leave the image open for the next exercise, which is the last one in this long chapter!

12.————————**Using Lossy Compression**

You already learned the nuances of saving a GIF in Photoshop. All the same techniques you used before will work in ImageReady identically. Because last time you saved a graphic image as a GIF, I didn't show you how to apply **Lossy** compression. You can apply **Lossy** compression to graphics in small amounts but you'll only see a minimal file savings, if any. Where **Lossy** compression really shines is when you add it to a GIF that is photographic in nature, such as the **orangeflower** image you should have left open. Here's how.

I. Revert the image so it's not transparent anymore. You can do this by choosing **File > Revert** and clicking **Revert** (Mac) or **Yes** (Windows).

2. Click on the **Optimized** tab and choose **GIF** as the file format in the **Optimize** palette. Set the palette to **Selective** and **Colors: 64**. Uncheck the **Transparency** checkbox (you'll learn all about transparency in Chapter 8, *"Transparent GIFs")*.

*The image is about 24K at this point. In the past this was the best you could have done. That was before Adobe introduced **Lossy** compression!*

3. Click on the arrow next to the **Lossy:** field and start moving the slider up until you don't like the effect it's having on the image. ImageReady won't calculate the new image size or preview the results until you release the slider.

*I settled at a **Lossy** value of **24**. The GIF is almost half the file size now at 13K! As I mentioned early on in this chapter, there are a few instances when you would want to save a photographic style image as a GIF, such as when you make animated or transparent GIFs. Most of the time, you'd save an image like this as a JPEG and it would be just fine. For those few instances when you do have to save this type of image as a GIF, **Lossy** compression simply rocks.*

4. Close the file, congratulate yourself for doing so much in this chapter, and take a break.

Note | **A GIF with Lossy Compression Is Still a GIF**

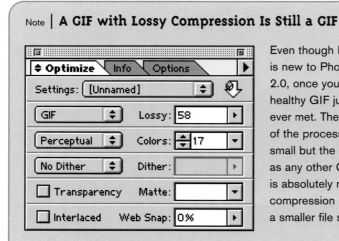

Even though **Lossy** compression in GIF files is new to Photoshop 5.5 and ImageReady 2.0, once you write the GIF it is a normal healthy GIF just like any other GIF you've ever met. The **Lossy** compression was part of the processing you used to make the file small but the GIF format is just the same as any other GIF format on the Web. There is absolutely no penalty to using **Lossy** compression – in fact, the only penalty is a smaller file size and faster download.

Photoshop Versus ImageReady

Which application should you use to optimize graphics? If you have not started to wonder why you would use ImageReady for optimizing graphics now that Photoshop 5.5 is so great, I will remind you to wonder now. To be perfectly honest, there is no reason to use one over the other except for convenience. When I am in Photoshop and want to optimize a graphic, I do so there, and when I am in ImageReady, I do so there.

The bigger question is, which program should you use for which tasks? Here's a chart based on my experiences with these applications and personal preferences.

Context-Sensitive Properties		
Task	**Photoshop 5.5**	**ImageReady 2.0**
Adjustment Layers	●	
Animation		●
Background Images		●
Batch-Processing	●	●
Color Profiles	●	
Color Swatches	●	●
Custom Brushes	●	
Editable Type	●	●
Filters	●	●
Image Maps		●
Importing Vectors	●	●
Layer Effects	●	●
Layers	●	●
Masking	●	
Optimizing Graphics	●	●
Rollovers		●
Slices		●
Styles		●
Transparency	●	●
Web Photo Gallery	●	

5.
Web Color

Web-Safe Color	Hexadecimal Color
Information Palette	Copying Color	Dithering
Preserve Transparency	Color Palette Web Settings

chap_05

Photoshop 5.5 / ImageReady 2.0
H•O•T CD-ROM

Photoshop 5.5 and ImageReady 2.0 offer great tools for working with Web-safe color, from palettes to swatches, to hexadecimal readouts in the **Info** palette. If you don't know what those terms mean, then this chapter will help a lot. You'll get the lowdown on Web color – what Web-safe color is, why you need to care about it, when to use it, and how to use it in Photoshop and ImageReady.

Aside from Web-safe color, there are numerous techniques for manipulating color in these two applications. In this chapter I share my favorite tips for picking, editing, and changing colors. You will learn how to load swatch palettes, convert RGB to hexadecimal, limit the **Photoshop Color Picker** to Web-safe colors, change the **Color** palette to Web-safe colors only, copy HTML color, shift non-safe colors to Web-safe ones, work with hybrid colors, and use **Preserve Transparency** to color artwork. Color has probably never sounded so scary and technical before, but Photoshop 5.5 and ImageReady 2.0 make this process as fun and creative as possible by offering the best Web-color picking tools around.

What Is Web-Safe Color Anyway?

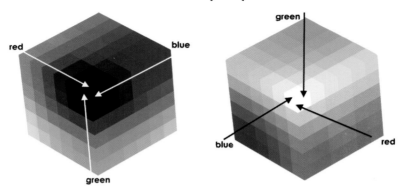

If you've been around the Web for a while, you might have heard the term Web-safe color. Perhaps you've heard other terms, too, such as browser safe, Web palette, 216 palette, the 6 x 6 x 6 cube, Netscape cube, Explorer colors, Web colors, etc. These all refer to the same 216 colors whose numerical definition forms a mathematical cube. I don't know about you, but my mind doesn't think in mathematical cubes, so when I first learned of this concept I was more than confused.

You probably have never thought that color was mathematical before now and if you are mathematically challenged, as I am, I am certain that you will not welcome this news. I'll do my best to explain it, but before I do, let me assure you that you don't have to understand the math to use and benefit from Web-safe color picking. Photoshop and ImageReady take the pain out of understanding this math and make it easy to choose Web-safe colors visually and intuitively. This section of this chapter is really here to give you an understanding of the what, whys, and wherefores of Web-safe color. If you prefer to skip over this background information about Web-safe color, you won't offend me in the least.

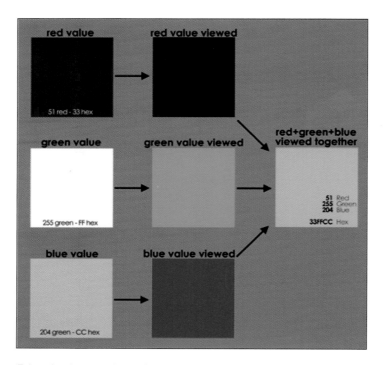

Printed colors are formed from pigments that combine cyan, magenta, yellow, and black (CMYK). Screen colors are formed from three colors of light: red, green, and blue (RGB). Because the focus of this chapter is Web color, understanding how pixels create color is the first step toward comprehending this stuff.

A computer forms a pixel by projecting three lights to a single location on your screen. The lights go from on or off, measured in 256 steps from 0 to 255. This color process is also sometimes called additive light, because it involves adding these three colored lights together. When the lights of all three colors (red, green, and blue) are fully on, white is created. When all lights are off, black is created. Colored pixels are created by various combinations of these three lights.

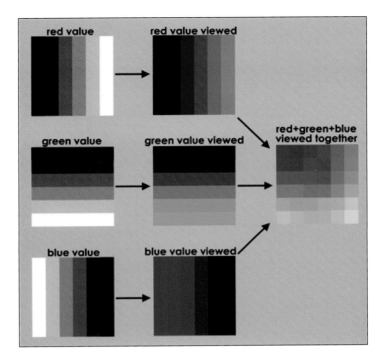

Web-safe colors are derived from distinct values from light to dark, by dividing the potential values of these lights into six equal parts for each of the red, green, and blue elements. By dividing the red scale into six equal parts, it works out to be 0, 51, 102, 153, 204, and 255. If you translate this mathematical formula into percentages, it works out to be 0%, 20%, 40%, 60%, 80%, and 100%. Web-safe colors are created by mixing six values of red, six values of green and six values of blue. The number of 216 colors exists because that is the total number of combinations of 6 x 6 x 6; or six reds times six greens times six blues.

Is Web-Safe Color So Important?

When you publish your images to the Web, people's computer screens, in effect, are your printing press. Your images are subjected to whatever type of monitor and color card your audience is using. If one part of your audience can see your Web site in millions of colors, another audience sector can see your site in thousands of colors, and another part in hundreds, your site is going to look different to different audiences. Welcome to the frustrating world of Web color.

Web-safe color specifically deals with color limitations on 8-bit systems. This term, 8-bit, refers to the number 256, and in the past many computer systems shipped with the limitation of only being able to display 256 colors.

Today, you would be hard pressed to buy a computer that was limited to 8-bit color. When the Web became popular about four to five years ago, this was a much bigger issue. At that time, you couldn't buy a laptop that had thousands or millions of colors (it's still not uncommon to see 8-bit laptops) and you had to buy special video cards and monitors that would support more colors. Many desktop systems didn't have 16-bit (thousands of colors) or 24-bit color cards (millions of colors) like they do today.

Even though most laptop and desktop systems today include color cards that can show more than 256 colors, many of them are set to 256 colors when you buy them at the store. This is not true of Macintosh computers, but it is true for Wintel computers. Most consumers buy computers for word processing, spreadsheets, database work, and games. It is not necessary that these systems view more than 256 colors, so many people never even know to check their settings to change from 256 colors to thousands or millions.

Regardless of all the warnings I'm raising here, the truth is that the number of people with 8-bit systems decreases every year. There will come a day when Web-safe color will be a thing of the past. In fact, many people believe that day is already here. I am not one of them.

While the 8-bit audience is much smaller than it used to be, it's not that difficult to make pages that look just as good to them as to the more fortunate audiences with newer machines and more colors. If you know that your audience is composed mostly of people with newer computers, or you are designing an Intranet for systems that you know can see millions or thousands of colors, then you can ignore all the problems with 8-bit color and not be concerned about Web-safe palettes. If you want to have maximum control over how your pages are seen, even on poorer systems than your own, then you will benefit by using these colors.

What happens if you don't use Web-safe colors and someone with an 8-bit color limitation views your pages? Colors will shift to ones that you didn't choose and might have unwanted dots all over them. If that doesn't concern you, then you could skip to the next chapter.

I am not here to judge whether you should or should not use Web-safe color. If you make the informed decision not to use these colors in your work, you will not be alone. I know many Web designers who choose to do this. My job is simply to inform you of the issues. Your job is to know whether the issues are pertinent to your publishing needs or not. I believe that creative professionals are judged by how good our images look. If your images shift to a color that you didn't choose or appear with unwanted dots all over them, and I could have taught you something that you could have done to avoid those problems, then I did not do my job.

What Is Hexadecimal Color?

When you specify color in HTML, you cannot use decimal values or the base 10 math that we all grew up learning. HTML requires that you convert the decimal values to hexadecimal values, or base 16. Therefore, the Web-safe RGB decimal values of 0, 51, 102, 153, 204, or 255 need to be converted for use on the Web. This handy chart shows how this conversion works.

RGB Color Translation Values		
Decimal	**Percentage**	**Hexadecimal**
0	0%	00
51	20%	33
102	40%	66
153	60%	99
204	80%	CC
255	100%	FF

Fortunately, Photoshop and ImageReady don't require that you use math to create Web-safe color. This chart is here merely to explain this concept.

The numeric values of RGB are represented in hexadecimal because that's the way HTML requires it. Hexadecimal is a base-16 number system. Just as the decimal system that you are already familiar with uses 10 digits (0, 1, 2, 3, 4, 5, 6, 7, 8, and 9), the hexadecimal system uses 16 digits (0, 1, 2, 3, 4, 5, 6, 7, 8, 9, A, B, C, D, E, and F). Letters are used for the digits over 9. Base 10 is natural for humans, who have a total of 10 fingers with which to count, and hexadecimal is natural for computers, which readily work with multiples of two.

RGB Color Translations															
Decimal Digits															
0	1	2	3	4	5	6	7	8	9	10	11	12	13	14	15
Hexidecimal Digits															
0	1	2	3	4	5	6	7	8	9	A	B	C	D	E	F

What Happens If You Don't Use Web-Safe Color?

Two big problems occur to your images if you don't use Web-safe colors. The first has to do with the hexadecimal values that are used in the **BODY** tag of HTML pages. The **BODY** tag specifies which colors are used for the background color, text color, link color, active link color, and visited link color of Web pages.

If you don't use Web-safe colors, then the colors you choose for the **BODY** of your Web pages will shift on systems that are limited to 256 colors. I've had people write to me who published their pages and then didn't understand why they couldn't see the colored links or text that they specified. Their link or text color had shifted to the same color as their background color, rendering their text unreadable! This is a potential penalty of using any color in the spectrum on a Web page. If you stick to Web-safe colors, your colors will not be unexpectedly shifted on 8-bit systems. If you don't use Web-safe colors, you run the risk of not knowing what color the browser will use for those colors you specified in the **BODY** element of your HTML.

You won't need to program the **BODY** tag in HTML in this book because Photoshop 5.5 and ImageReady 2.0 will write all the code for you. You'll learn more about this in Chapter 7, *"Background Images."* The thing is, within Photoshop and ImageReady you'll have the choice of whether or not to choose Web-safe colors for these aspects of HTML. My suggestion is to always use Web-safe colors for the purpose of background colors in HTML, to avoid unexpected color shifting on 8-bit systems.

Graphic viewed in 24-bit.

Same graphic viewed in 8-bit.

Close-up 24-bit.

Close-up 8-bit.

The second problem has to do with color in images. If you don't use Web-safe colors on certain types of images, unwanted dithering can occur. Here are some examples of what that looks like.

Notice the unwanted dots in the image viewed in 8-bit? They're the result of dithering, and they only happen because the color of the eye and skin tone were not chosen from Web safe colors. If the colors chosen for this illustration were Web safe to begin with, they would not dither at all, regardless of whether they were viewed in 24-bit or 8-bit.

The only time not to use Web-safe colors in Web graphics is with photographs or continuous-tone content. When the browser views these types of images, it converts them to 8-bit on the fly and does a better job than if you'd converted them yourself. The following images demonstrate what I'm talking about.

JPEG image viewed on 24-bit or 16-bit system.

JPEG image viewed on 8-bit system.

*GIF image saved with a **Perceptual** palette in Photoshop or ImageReady viewed on 24-bit or 16-bit system.*

*GIF image saved with a **Perceptual** palette in Photoshop or ImageReady viewed on an 8-bit system.*

*GIF image saved with **Web** palette in Photoshop or ImageReady viewed on 24-bit or 16-bit system.*

*GIF image saved with **Web** palette in Photoshop or ImageReady viewed on 8-bit system.*

If you look at the right column of the images to your left, all three rows look identical. If you look at the left column, the bottom image looks the poorest. This demonstrates that the browser does just as good a job of converting the photograph on an 8-bit system as you could if you forced the image to a Web palette. I never use Web palettes on photographs for this reason. The browser does just as good a job as I could, and if I leave the image in a 24-bit or adaptive format, it will look better on systems that can view it in 24-bit or 16-bit. You might recall from Chapter 4, *"Optimization,"* that **Perceptual**, **Selective**, and **Adaptive** are "adaptive" style palettes.

To summarize:

• Web-safe color is something you use to make your images look best on 8-bit systems.

• 16-bit and 24-bit systems can see any color you publish without dithering or shifting color.

• Use Web-safe colors for your hexadecimal **BODY** elements in HTML.

• Use Web-safe colors for areas of solid colors in your graphics.

• Never use Web-safe color palettes for photographic or continuous-tone artwork.

I. _____Changing the Info Palette

The Info palette in Photoshop 5.5 offers a lot of valuable feedback about your image's colors. In past versions of Photoshop, this palette has only listed CMYK and RGB color values. Now, you can change the setting to offer RGB and hexadecimal readouts so that you can read the values of your color images in the context of the Web.

I. Launch Photoshop and click on the **Info** tab on your screen, or choose **Window > Show Info** if it isn't visible. Click on the upper-right arrow to select **Palette Options...** from the pop-up menu. The **Info Options** dialog box will appear.

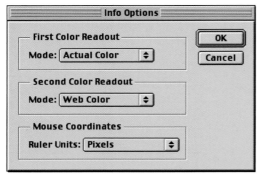

2. Make sure that your **Info Options** match the settings shown here and click **OK**.

3. Open **color.gif** from the **chap_05** folder you transferred to your hard drive from the **H·O·T CD-ROM**.

Note | **The Info Palette in ImageReady 2.0**

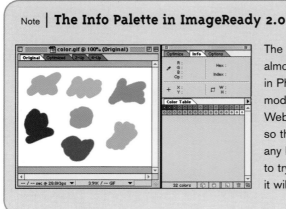

The **Info** palette in ImageReady is almost identical to the **Info** palette in Photoshop, except it cannot be modified, and it ships with proper Web settings right out of the box so that you don't have to change any **Preferences**. **Note:** Feel free to try this exercise in ImageReady; it will work there as well.

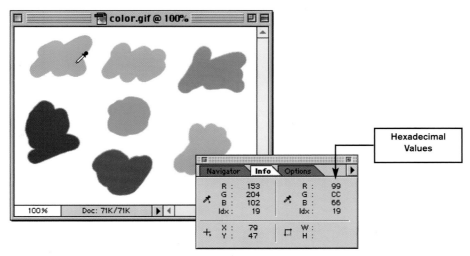

Hexadecimal
Values

4. Choose the **Eyedropper** tool (the shortcut is the letter **I** on your keyboard) and move it over the colors in this image. Look at the **Info** palette and notice that it is giving you the hexadecimal values of each RGB color.

In this example, the RGB value is **R:153**, **G:204**, **B:102**, *and the hexadecimal value is* **99CC66**. *The readout for* **Idx** *(under the RGB column) stands for* **Index**. *An indexed graphic is one that contains a maximum of 256 colors, and the* **Idx** *number is the mathematical position of each color in the* **Color Table**. *I know of no use for the* **Idx** *values readout, except that it alerts you to the fact that you are working with an index-mode graphic. In fact, whenever you are editing a 256-color document in Photoshop, it is referred to as "Indexed" color mode.*

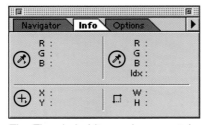

Tip: *The circled items above contain pop-up menus which offer alternative access to the* **Info Options** *settings in Photoshop. This is not available in ImageReady.*

2. ——————— Copy Color as HTML

If you want to get the hexadecimal value of a color from Photoshop into an HTML or text editor, you might find Photoshop's **Copy Color as HTML** feature useful. This feature converts an RGB color value to a hexadecimal color value in text (for example, **#663300**) and puts whichever color value you copy into your computer's clipboard so you can paste it as text into other applications. This is a handy feature if you are writing HTML from scratch and want to quickly and easily get a color value from Photoshop into your code.

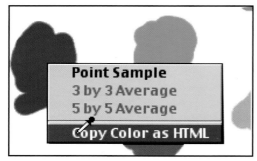

I. This exercise takes place in Photoshop and does not work the same way in Image-Ready. To copy the hexadecimal color of a Photoshop image into an HTML editor, select the **Eyedropper** tool from the toolbar (**I**) and **Ctrl+click** (Mac) or **right-click** (Windows) on a color in a document and select **Copy Color as HTML**. **Note:** The **Eyedropper** tool must be selected for this to work.

2. When you go to paste this color into another program, it will look like this: COLOR="#336633".

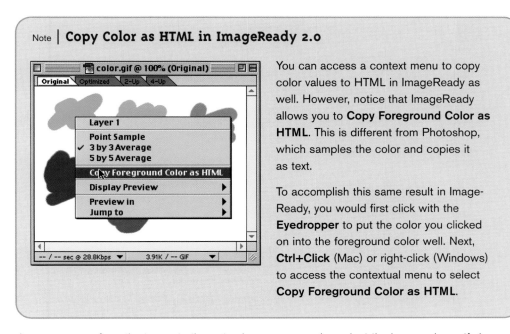

Note | **Copy Color as HTML in ImageReady 2.0**

You can access a context menu to copy color values to HTML in ImageReady as well. However, notice that ImageReady allows you to **Copy Foreground Color as HTML.** This is different from Photoshop, which samples the color and copies it as text.

To accomplish this same result in Image-Ready, you would first click with the **Eyedropper** to put the color you clicked on into the foreground color well. Next, **Ctrl+Click** (Mac) or right-click (Windows) to access the contextual menu to select **Copy Foreground Color as HTML.**

As you can see from the image in the note above, you can also select the layer and specify how the **Eyedropper** samples.

• **3 by 3 Average** is sampling 3 pixels by 3 pixels.

• **5 by 5 Average** is sampling 5 pixels by 5 pixels.

If you opened ImageReady to try this, please return to Photoshop for the next exercise.

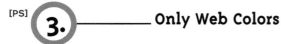

Only Web Colors

In past versions of Photoshop, it's been difficult to choose a Web-safe color from the **Color Picker** without manually typing in Web-safe RGB values. This hassle has been removed in Photoshop 5.5, because the native **Color Picker** can now be set to **Web Only** colors. Here's how.

Note: The same **Color Picker** you'll learn about in this exercise also exists in ImageReady 2.0. The only exception in ImageReady is that there are no **L.a.b.** and CMYK color, and no shifting to the nearest print color. However, everything related to Web color is the same.

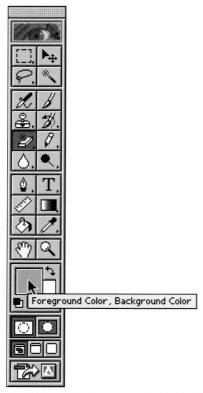

I. Click on the **foreground** color in the Photoshop toolbar. This will open the Photoshop **Color Picker**.

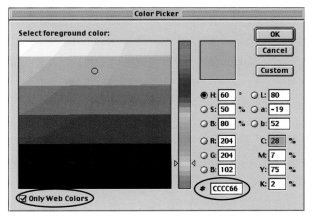

2. Make sure that you check **Only Web Colors** in the lower left corner of this dialog box.

Notice that Photoshop now includes a hexadecimal readout on the right? If you move the arrows up the hue slider you'll see the colors on the screen change.

*H, S, and B stand for **H**ue, **S**aturation, and **B**rightness. The above **Color Picker** is set to view by hue. All the different radio buttons offer different ways of seeing and picking colors. You may find that these different choices help you find interesting colors more quickly. It's very interesting to see how Web colors spread across the spectrum if you actively move the slider when exploring these different settings of **H, S, B, R, G, B**, or **L, a, b**.*

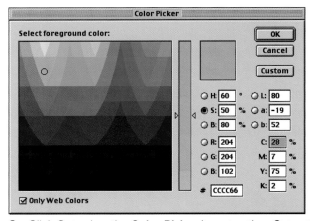

3. Click **S:** to view the **Color Picker** by saturation. Saturation is the measure of color intensity. Try moving the vertical slider or clicking on a different color in the rainbow area to view Web-safe colors by this criteria. Move the slider arrows up to view more highly saturated Web colors, and down to view the desaturated ones.

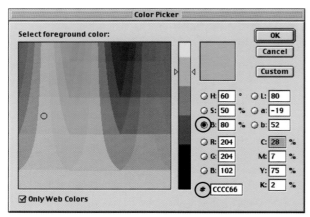

4. Click **B:** to view the **Color Picker** by brightness. Brightness is the measure of light to dark values. Try moving the brightness slider or clicking on a different color in the rainbow area to view Web-safe colors by this criteria. Move the slider arrows up to view brighter Web color values, and down to view darker ones.

*Try clicking on the **R:**, **G:**, and **B:** buttons as well. These stand for **R**ed, **G**reen, and **B**lue. Click on the **L:**, **a:**, and **b:** buttons next. These stand for **L**ightness, **a** Axis (green to magenta), and **b** Axis (blue to yellow). Aside from the psychedelic color experience, these methods offer some other interesting color formations from which to view or pick Web colors.*

5. Click **Cancel** to get out of the color-picking mode, and move on to the next exercise to learn more about Web-color picking options.

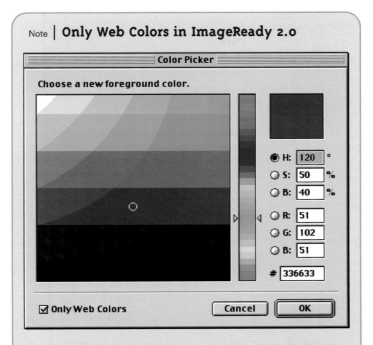

Note | **Only Web Colors in ImageReady 2.0**

The **Color Picker** in ImageReady 2.0 is almost identical to that of Photoshop 5.5, except that it lacks feedback about **L.a.b.** or CMYK color. This is because Photoshop has a dual purpose – it can be used for print or Web. ImageReady was developed for screen graphics only.

[PS]

4. _____ Snapping to Web Colors

The thing about Photoshop is that there are often numerous ways to achieve the same goal. Instead of viewing Web Only colors, you can use the standard **Color Picker** and then snap a non-Web-safe color to a safe one. This feature is also available in ImageReady 2.0.

I. This exercise takes place in Photoshop. Click on the foreground color in the toolbar again to access the Photoshop **Color Picker**.

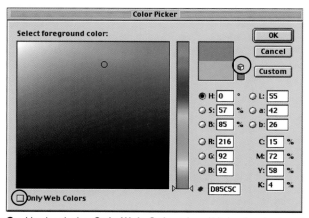

2. Uncheck the **Only Web Colors** box if it is checked and move your cursor around inside the red area. Notice the cube icon that appears to the right of the color preview? The cube alerts you when you've selected a color that's not safe for the Web. If you click on the cube, the color selection will jump to the closest Web-safe color and then the cube will disappear.

3. Click **OK** and the Web-safe color will appear in the foreground color area of your toolbar. **Note:** This feature works identically in ImageReady. If you decide to try it out in ImageReady now, be sure to return to Photoshop for the next exercise.

Setting the Color Palette to Web Colors

There are yet more ways to access and view Web-safe colors from Photoshop. How do you know which way to use? It's often a matter of convenience and/or habit. Sometimes, you'll find yourself intuitively wanting to click on the foreground color to access the Photoshop **Color Picker**, as you just did in Exercises 2 and 3. Other times, it's more convenient to pick a color more quickly. The **Color** palette is a great alternative to using the **Color Picker** because it can stay open on the screen all the time and is faster to access. Here's how to set it to Web-safe colors.

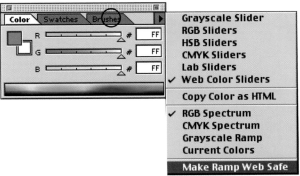

1. Locate the **Color** palette on your screen. If it is not visible, choose **Window > Show Color**. Click on the upper-right arrow to select **Web Color Sliders** from the pop-up menu. Make sure that **RGB Spectrum** is also selected. If it isn't, click on the upper-right arrow again to select it.

2. Click on the upper-right arrow again to choose **Make Ramp Web Safe**.

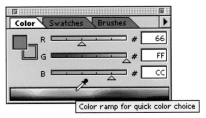

3. Try moving the sliders and you'll see them snap to the Web-color markers. If you move your mouse over the color ramp and click around, you'll see the sliders move to different Web-safe colors.

That's the end of this exercise. You can leave the **Color** palette set this way until you choose to change it. **Note:** ImageReady's **Color** palette looks and functions identically.

6. Setting the Swatches Palette to Web Colors

The last way I'll show you how to set Web colors is in Photoshop 5.5's **Swatches** palette. This palette defaults to displaying the system palette: if you are on a Mac, it will show the Mac system palette; if you are on Windows, it will show the Windows system palette. However, it's possible and preferable to load in Web-safe palettes, and that's just what you'll learn to do next.

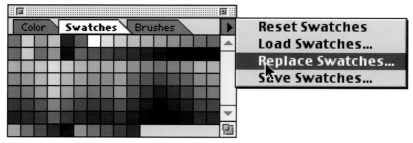

I. This exercise takes place in Photoshop but would work in ImageReady the same way. Click on the **Swatches** tab and then choose **Replace Swatches...** from the upper-right arrow pop-up menu.

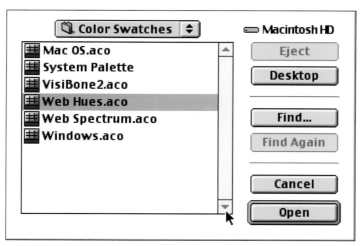

2. Navigate to the Adobe® Photoshop 5.5 folder on your computer and choose **Goodies > Color Swatches > Web Hues.aco**. Click **Open**.

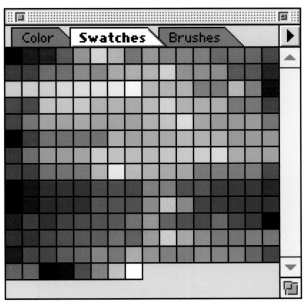

*The **Web Hues** palette will replace the Photoshop default system palette. I stretched the **Swatches** palette by clicking and dragging on the lower-right window handle.*

3. You can leave the **Swatches** palette set up this way. Next time you open Photoshop, it will still be set. **Note:** You can follow this identical procedure in ImageReady and it will function the same as Photoshop.

7.————————— **Loading the lynda.com Swatch**

My husband Bruce Heavin and I wrote a book together in 1997 called *Coloring Web Graphics*, which is now in its second edition. Bruce developed a series of Web-color swatches for that book which he organized aesthetically for picking Web colors. I've included one of these palettes inside the **chap_05** folder of the **H•O•T CD-ROM** for you to try. **Note:** It will be expected in future exercises that you have loaded this **Swatch** into both Photoshop and ImageReady, so be sure to load it in both applications.

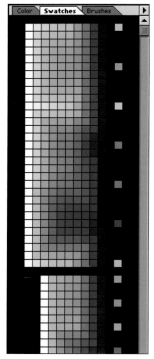

I. This exercise takes place in Photoshop but would work in ImageReady the same way. Click on the upper-right arrow of the **Swatches** palette to select **Replace Swatches....** Navigate to the **chap_05** folder that you transferred to your hard drive from the **H•O•T CD-ROM** and choose **color.aco**. Click **Open**.

2. Drag the **Swatches** palette window as long as it will go, and then use the scroll bar to view the entire swatch document. This swatch is organized by hue (up and down), by value (right to left), and saturation (up and down).

3. Follow the same procedure in ImageReady.

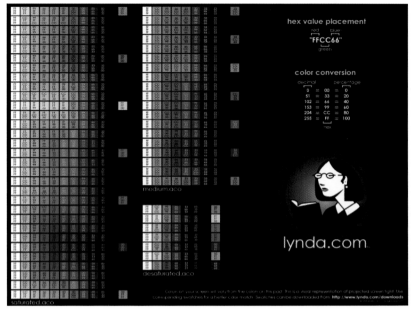

lynda.com sells the mouse pad above, which shows hexadecimal readouts for each color within the color.aco swatch set as well as a conversion chart from RGB to hexadecimal values. You may choose to purchase the pad or just refer to the values printed here when you need to.

Note: Many of the colors are repeated for the sole reason of presenting an array that is organized efficiently for color-picking. It's nice to see all the hues together. If you want to pick a red, for example, you can view the choices easily. It's also helpful to easily see together all the dark colors and/or colors of equal saturation. Once you use this palette, you will likely never remove it from the **Swatches** palette because it is so useful. Exercise 9 will show you how to use this **Swatches** palette in the context of editing browser dither from a color document.

Note | **Save For Web Repetition**

Some of the exercises in this chapter require that you use the **Save For Web** feature again, just as you did in the last chapter. That's because many of the Web-color controls are located inside the same areas of the applications as the optimization settings. As you grow more comfortable with Photoshop and ImageReady, you'll find yourself using the **Save For Web** and optimization palettes in every kind of image on which you work. It might seem repetitive to the last chapter, but you'll soon grow to understand that color-management and optimization are interrelated arts in Web graphics.

8.————Previewing Dither

Unwanted dithering can look bad but, if you don't have an 8-bit system how can you preview whether your images will have it or not? Both Photoshop 5.5 and ImageReady 2.0 can preview how an 8-bit browser will dither. This exercise shows you how to preview dithering in Photoshop.

I. Make sure you are in Photoshop. Open **nonsafe.psd**. It contains non-Web-safe colors. On your system, it probably doesn't show any dithering.

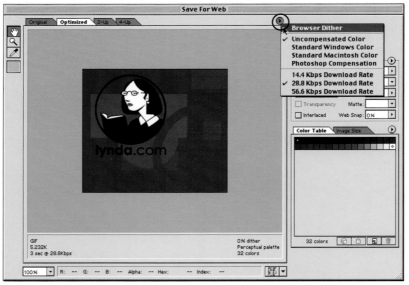

2. To preview how this file will appear on an 8-bit system, choose **File>Save for Web...**. Click on the upper-right arrow to access the menu and select **Browser Dither**.

Yuck! Look at how awful the preview looks. Even though you don't see the image this way on your system, this is the way some people will view it. The next exercise will show you how to fix the image so the colors will look good on anyone's system, regardless of color bit depth.

3. Leave this image and the **Save For Web** dialog box open for the next exercise.

Note | **Previewing Dither in ImageReady 2.0**

There are two ways to preview dither in ImageReady. If you are on the **Optimized** tab in the document window and you've selected the **Eyedropper** tool, select **View > Preview > Browser Dither**. You can also hold down the **Control** key and click on the document (Mac) or right-click (Windows) on the document to access the contextual menu. Select **Display Preview > Browser Dither**.

9. _____Fixing a Non-Safe Image

Not everyone knows to create graphics with the 216 colors in the first place, so it's likely that a day will come when you'll have to doctor up a graphic that was made with colors that will appear yucky when displayed on an 8-bit system. Both Photoshop and ImageReady allow you to shift the colors to Web safe easily. Here's how to do this in Photoshop's **Save For Web** dialog box.

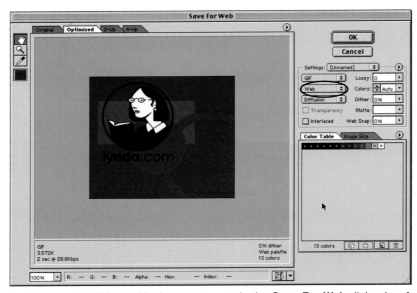

I. You should still have this document open in the **Save For Web** dialog box from the last exercise in Photoshop. Change the palette settings to **Web**. The image stopped dithering, but it also lost a lot of colors. There's a better way. Change it to **Perceptual** and all the colors will reappear, but so will the unwanted dithering.

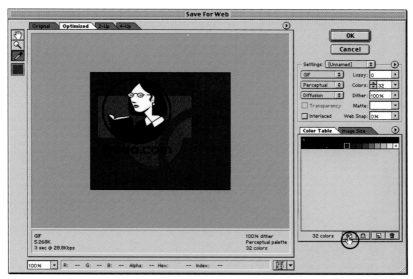

2. Click on the **Eyedropper** on the **Save For Web** dialog box and select a green in the upper-right square of color that is dithered. Notice that the **Color Table** has a single color that is highlighted. Click on the cube icon to shift the color to the closest Web color. In this instance, the closest color is very similar to that of the background color. Not good!

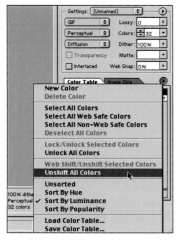

3. A lot of times, clicking on the cube icon works just fine, so this is usually my first strategy. In this case, the color Photoshop picked for me was not a good choice. However, **Command+Z** or **Control+Z** will not undo the change. To undo the shift, click on the arrow to the right of the **Color Table** and select **Unshift All Colors** (Mac) or **Unlock All Colors** (Windows).

Eyedrop on the dithered color.

Double-click on the resulting color in the Color Table.

4. Select the same color again with the **Eyedropper**, but this time instead of clicking on the cube icon, double-click on the color that is highlighted in the **Color Table**.

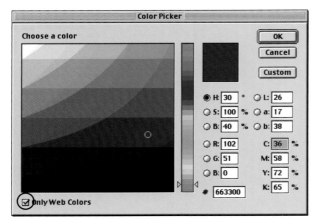

5. The **Color Picker** will open. Make sure that you check **Only Web Colors**. Fish around for a color that you like to replace the color that is dithering. I moved the hue slider up slightly to pick the color you see here. Click **OK**.

6. Notice that the color is no longer dithering? Turn the **Browser Dither** preview off and on and you'll see that this color will not dither regardless of whether it is viewed on your system or on an 8-bit system.

*Also notice that the color you changed appears in the **Color Table** with a diamond and a little white box in the lower-right corner? The diamond signifies that the color is now Web safe, and the white square signifies that the color is locked. Locking is helpful if you decide to lower the number of colors again, because it ensures that Photoshop (or ImageReady) will not throw this particular color away when downsampling the **Color Table**.*

7. Make sure that the **Browser Dither** preview is on again and repeat this process on all the colors that are dithering. This is how you can fix colors that aren't Web safe to begin with.

8. Click **OK** when you're ready. Photoshop will prompt you to save this document as **nonsafe.gif**. Click **OK**. Now you can close the document in Photoshop to go on to the next lesson. If you are prompted to save changes to **nonsafe.psd**, click **No**.

*The beauty of Photoshop's **Save For Web** feature is that you can adjust the image you plan to optimize and never alter the original **.psd** file.*

Note | **Fixing a Non-Safe Color in ImageReady 2.0**

The process of fixing color in ImageReady is almost identical to that of Photoshop, with the following differences.

1. Open **nonsafe.psd**. Be sure that you are on the **Optimized** tab and have set the file in the **Optimize** palette to the same settings as Step 1 of Exercise 9 (GIF, Perceptual). **Tip:** If you're having trouble seeing your image under the **Optimized** setting, go to the top-right corner of the **Optimize** palette and make sure that **Auto Regenerate** is checked off in the pull-down menu.

2. Choose **View > Preview > Browser Dither**.

3. Use the **Eyedropper** tool and click on a color in the image that is dithering. Double-click on any of the dithering colors inside the **Color Table** to bring up the ImageReady 2.0 **Color Picker**. Everything else is the same!

4. Close the document when you're finished. Return to Photoshop because the next exercise will take place there.

[PS] **10.**_____**When Dithering is Good**

So far, dithering has gotten a bum rap in this chapter. You might think that it should always be avoided, but that's really not true. Sometimes a dithered image looks better than a non-dithered one. The rule of thumb is that dithering looks bad in solid colors (like what you witnessed in the last exercise) but it is required on areas of an image that contain glows, drop shadows, blurs, or anything that produces a gradient. This next exercise will demonstrate when to use dithering.

I. This exercise takes place in Photoshop. Open **glow.psd**, choose **File>Save for Web...**, and click on the **Optimized** tab.

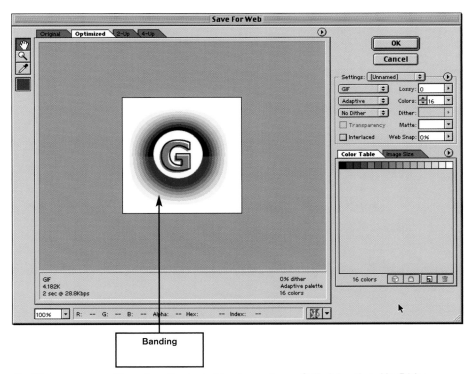

Banding

2. Change your settings to reflect what is shown here: **GIF**, **Adaptive**, **No Dithe**r, **Lossy: 0**, **Colors: 16**.

This particular image would look better and be smaller as a JPEG but if you have to save an image like this as a GIF (for reasons of animation or transparency) you will need to understand how dithering can help things out. Notice the banding in the image? Even though the file is small (approximately 4K), it doesn't look good.

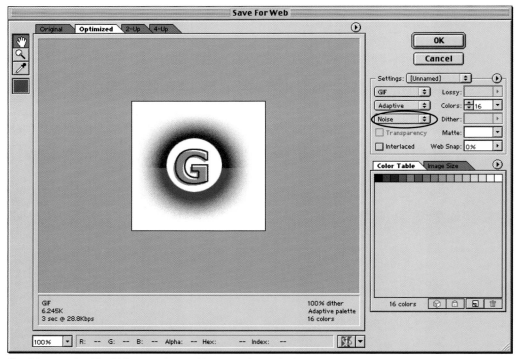

3. Change the **No Dither** setting to **Noise** and watch the image improve.

The file size also increased to 6.24K, but the image looks so much better now that the increase was necessary.

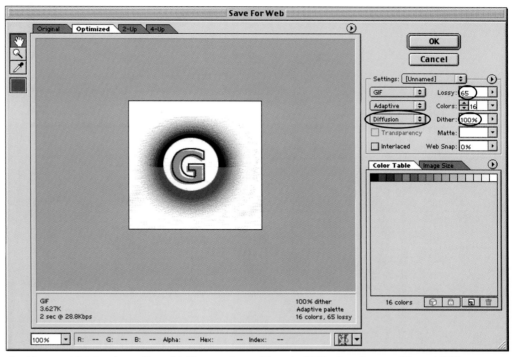

4. I have a trick to share, though! Change the settings to **Diffusion**, **Lossy: 65**, and **Dither: 100%**. The image is now around **3K** and the dithering looks good.

5. Click **OK**. You'll be prompted to save the file as **glow.gif**. Do so and close it, as you will not need it for the next exercise. You should also save and close **glow.psd**.

*Note: This exercise will work identically in ImageReady, except that you would click on the **Optimized** tab instead of choosing **Save For Web...** first.*

II. Preserve Transparency

Now that you've learned how to view Web color in a variety of different ways within Photoshop, how do you make images that use these colors? You could use a brush and paint with any of these colors at any time. You could also use fill tools to color artwork. This next exercise focuses on the **Preserve Transparency** feature of Photoshop, which allows you to easily recolor layered documents with any color you want.

1. This exercise takes place in Photoshop but will work identically in ImageReady. Open **logo.psd**.

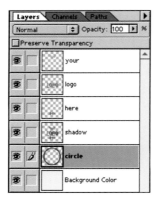

2. Look at the **Layers** palette (**Window > Show Layers**) and you'll notice that this document is composed of multiple layers.

*It's helpful to set your files up with separate layers like this and give them names, so you can color each layer separately and keep track of them. **Tip:** If your palette doesn't display like the one above, simply drag from its bottom-right corner to make it larger.*

3. Right now, this document is colored using greens, browns, and yellows. To change this color scheme to blues, greens, and purples, select the **circle** layer.

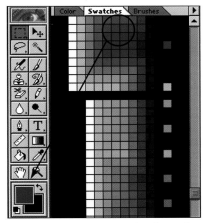

4. Choose a blue from the **Swatches** palette that you loaded in Exercise 7. If you put your mouse over any color and click, that color will be selected in your foreground color in the toolbar.

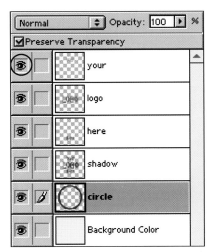

5. With the circle layer selected, click on **Preserve Transparency** in the **Layers** palette. **Tip:** The shortcut key to toggle **Preserve Transparency** on or off is the **?** key.

Preserve Transparency *means that Photoshop will protect the transparent areas of this layer. When you fill the layer with a new color, which is what's coming next, Photoshop will only fill the area of the layer with an image in it and preserve the transparent areas.*

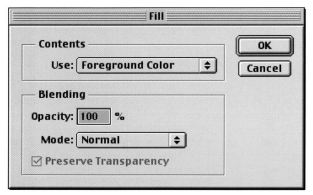

6. Choose **Edit > Fill**, and make sure the settings are the same as what you see above. Click **OK**.

The circle will fill with blue. I'll walk you through this for a couple of more layers, and then you should get the hang of how this process works.

7. Click on the **Move** tool in the toolbar or press the letter **V** on your keyboard to activate it.

8. This time, you'll select the layer with the word "**LOGO**" on it, but through the contextual menu instead of the **Layers** palette. To access this menu, position your mouse over the word "**LOGO**" and...

- (Mac) Press the **Control** key and click your mouse. This brings up a contextual menu that has the name of the layers that are near your mouse. If you're not getting all three choices, try nudging your mouse closer to the word "**LOGO**." Select **logo** from the list.
- (Windows) Right-click. This brings up a contextual menu that has the name of the layers that are near your mouse. If you're not getting all three choices, try nudging your mouse closer to the word "**LOGO**." Select **logo** from the list.

*This is a great way to select layers in any layered Photoshop document. The key to this technique is having the **Move** tool active.*

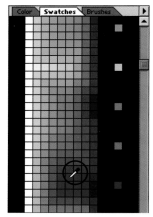

9. Pick a different shade of blue by clicking on the **Swatches** palette.

You could also pick a color through any of the other means this chapter covered, but I prefer the swatch set my husband Bruce created because all the blues are organized so they're close together and easy to compare.

IO. This time, you'll fill the color through a shortcut.

- (Mac) Hold down the **Option** key and then press **Delete**. The layer will change to the new blue you selected.
- (Windows) Hold down the **Alt** key and then press the **Delete** or **Backspace** key (either will work). The layer will change to the new blue you selected.

*The color should change to the foreground color that you've picked without making a trip up to the **Edit** menu! However, the entire layer filled instead of the word "**LOGO**." Why? That's what happens if you don't click **Preserve Transparency** and you fill a layer.*

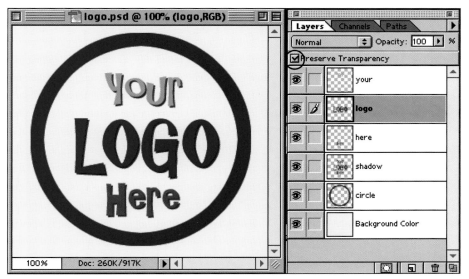

II. Choose **Edit > Undo Fill** (or **Cmd+Z** on Mac, **Ctrl+Z** on Windows). Click **Preserve Transparency** on the selected layer (**logo**). Use the shortcut you learned in the last step again. This time, only the word "**LOGO**" should change to this new blue.

12. This time, change the word "**your**" by combining all the shortcut techniques you just learned. Here are the steps.

• Make sure the **Move** tool is selected (press the letter **V** to select it).
• Position your mouse on the word "**your**" and select the layer by using the contextual menu technique (**Ctrl+click** on Mac, **right-click** on Windows).
• Make sure **Preserve Transparency** is checked on the **your** layer.
• Pick a new blue color.
• **Option+Delete** (Mac) or **Alt+Delete** (Windows) to fill with a new color.

13. Repeat this procedure for the word "**Here**" so it is also filled with another blue color.

14. Chose **File > Save**. Leave this file open for the next exercise.

Note: The steps in this exercise will work identically in ImageReady.

I2. ————————**Filling with DitherBox**

There are going to be times when you want a color that isn't Web safe, but you still want it to look good on systems that are limited to 8-bit colors. Photoshop 5.5 and ImageReady 2.0 include a great filter **DitherBox™** that fills with a hybrid of Web colors by creating a checkerboard pattern of two or more Web colors. By putting two or more colors so closely together, this filter achieves the effect of a secondary color that isn't present in the Web-color palette.

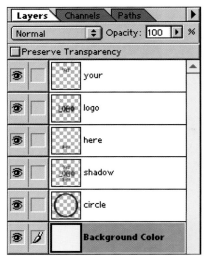

I. This exercise in Photoshop will work identically in ImageReady. With **logo.psd** still open from the last exercise, select the **Background Color** layer.

*You don't have to check **Preserve Transparency** on this layer to change its color because the content fills the entire screen and doesn't have any transparent areas that need preservation.*

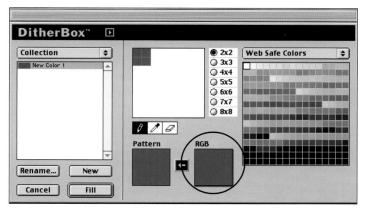

2. Choose **Filter > Other > DitherBox™....** When the **DitherBox** dialog box appears, click inside the **RGB** square shown above.

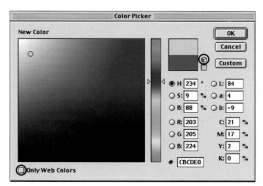

3. This takes you to the **Color Picker**. Make sure that **Only Web Colors** is **unchecked** and select a light blue color.

*You can tell that the color is not Web safe because it has a cube symbol next to it. That's good. You want to pick a non-safe color on purpose. The idea of the **DitherBox™** filter, which you are about to use, is to take non-safe colors and mix a combination of two safe colors to simulate non-safe color.*

4. Click **OK**.

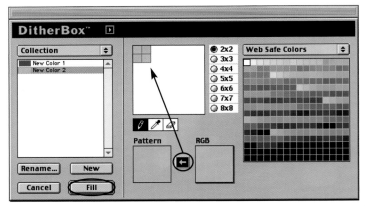

5. Click on the arrow that is circled above to create a pattern of two Web-safe colors. The pattern is composed of two different Web-safe colors that appear above. Click the **Fill** button.

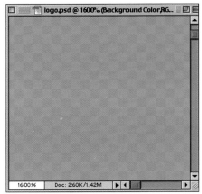

6. The image's background will fill with a light blue. If you click the **Zoom** tool and zoom into the image as tight as possible, you will see that it is filled with a checkerboard pattern. This pattern is not visible when shown at 100%, yet it produces the illusion of a secondary color that is not within the Web-safe spectrum. **Tip:** To zoom back out to 100%, hold the **Option/Alt** key down as you click the **Zoom** tool on this image.

7. Save and close this file.

Note: This exercise will work identically in ImageReady.

I3._____Previewing Gamma

As if dithering problems and color-picking techniques weren't enough to think about in Web publishing, there's another cross-platform issue to consider – gamma. Gamma refers to the midpoint values on a computer system. Pure black and pure white are identical on all the systems, but the intermediary grays appear lighter on Macs and darker on Windows. In general, Mac and Unix systems tend to have lighter displays than Windows. There's nothing that you can do about this sad fact, but at least Photoshop and ImageReady allow you to preview how this will appear differently on the opposite platforms. This exercise will show you how.

I. This exercise takes place in Photoshop and works a little differently in ImageReady (the next exercise will demonstrate this). Open **dinoset.psd**.

2. Choose **File Save for Web...**. Make sure you select the **JPEG** setting so the color stays true to the original.

3. Click on the upper-right arrow to access the menu. You can preview the image with four kinds of color: **Uncompensated Color**, **Standard Macintosh Color**, **Standard Windows Color**, and **Photoshop Compensation**. Try each setting and notice the differences.

4. Click **Cancel** to exit the **Save For Web** dialog box.

5. You can also preview gamma without being in the Photoshop **Save For Web** dialog box. Choose **View > Preview > Macintosh RGB**, **Windows RGB**, or **Uncompensated RGB**.

6. Close this file.

Note: Previewing color is slightly different in ImageReady. It is covered in the next exercise.

Note | **What Do the Four Color Settings Mean?**

You may be wondering what these settings mean. First of all, these are previews only. If you leave one of these previews checked, it will not affect how the image is stored once it is saved, only how it is previewed. Here's what each means.

• **Uncompensated Color:** Color without any alteration.
• **Macintosh Color:** How the image will appear on a Macintosh.
• **Windows Color:** How the image will appear on Windows.
• **Photoshop Color:** If you had any color profiles set (* which I hope you don't!) the settings would affect this preview.

[IR]

————Previewing Gamma in ImageReady

You learned how to preview gamma in Photoshop's **Save For Web** dialog box earlier. It's possible to do this in ImageReady as well, only it differs just enough to warrant its own exercise. Here's how it's done.

I. Launch ImageReady and open **dinoset.psd**. Click on the **Optimized** tab and make sure that your **Optimize** settings are set to **JPEG**.

2. Choose **View > Preview > Standard Macintosh Color**. Try all the preview settings to see how this same image will display on different platforms.

*There's not a lot that you can do about the gamma shifts, but the ability to preview these changes is helpful in showing you whether you need to adjust your image so it is lighter or darker. If you did want to permanently make your image lighter or darker, you would choose **Image > Adjust > Levels...** and move the slider to lighten or darken your image accordingly.*

3. Save and close this file. You're finished with this chapter.

Bet you never knew there was this much to Web color before now!

6.
Type

Editing Type in Photoshop	Jump To Settings
Rendered Versus Editable Type	Preserve Transparency
Layer Effects and Styles	Stroking Text
Clipping Groups	Painting Type

chap_06

Photoshop 5.5 / ImageReady 2.0
H•O•T CD-ROM

Text on the Web can be a touchy subject for professional designers because HTML affords very little typographic control. Fortunately, this isn't a book about HTML, it's a book about Photoshop and ImageReady, a set of programs with unsurpassed typographic control. Many Web designers avoid the limitations of HTML type by making artwork for type instead of relying on code. If you're gonna make artwork that contains typography, you're gonna love what Photoshop 5.5 and ImageReady 2.0 can do for you.

This chapter covers the many aspects of type, including anti-aliasing, kerning, spacing, baselines, color treatments, special effects, button creation, and styles. I have a huge smile on my face as I imagine how happy you will be once you learn the techniques this chapter covers. Type is one of my favorite subjects, and it's likely to add great visual appeal to the sites you design.

Differences in Type in Photoshop 5.5 and ImageReady 2.0

Almost all the exercises in this chapter work in either Photoshop or ImageReady except when noted otherwise. There is one huge difference between the two applications: Photoshop type is edited via a dialog box and ImageReady type is edited on screen. This results in a slight difference in filling and changing colors, which will be described in detail in this chapter. In Photoshop, when you click on your screen with the **Type** tool active, you type into a separate dialog box. In ImageReady, when you click on your screen with the **Type** tool active, you type directly on the screen.

Another byproduct of this difference is that a tiny blue line appears under any type that you create in ImageReady. If you are an Adobe Illustrator user, this might be a familiar sight. Actually, when it comes to type, ImageReady resembles Illustrator much more than it does Photoshop. I prefer the way ImageReady handles type over how Photoshop handles it, except for the fact that there is no good way to deselect the blue line when you're working. The only way, in fact, to turn it off is to click in the **Layers** palette on a layer other than a type layer. Conversely, the only way to format the type is to select the type layer, which causes the blue underline to reappear. This is a bummer, but at least you know the solution now.

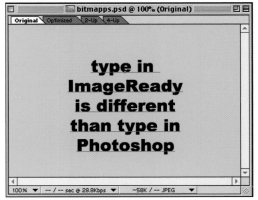

In ImageReady, a tiny blue line appears under editable text.

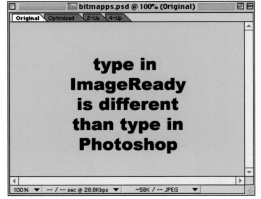

To make the blue line disappear, click off the type layer in the **Layers** palette.

Before getting into advanced type treatment features, it's a good idea to understand how the **Type** tool works for typesetting. This exercise will cover features such as size, kerning, tracking, baseline, leading, color, anti-aliasing, and setting faux bolding and italics.

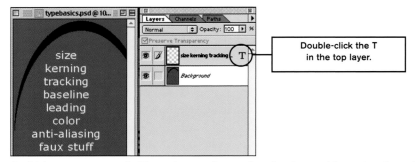

I. Make sure you are in Photoshop and open **typebasics.psd** from the **chap_06** folder that you transferred to your hard drive from the **H•O•T CD-ROM**. If your **Layers** palette is not visible, choose **Window > Show Layers**. Notice that one of the layers contains a **T** on it? Double-click on the **T**. The **Type Tool** window will open.

*Note: If you do not have **Verdana** or **Georgia** installed, other fonts will be substituted. You can download these fonts for free from the Microsoft Web site (**http://www. microsoft.com/typography/fontpack/default.htm**) if you'd like, or work with whatever fonts are automatically substituted for you.*

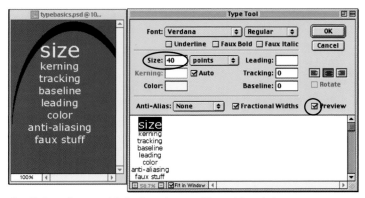

2. Select the word "**size**" and enter **Size: 40 points**.

*You should see the change appear on your screen if you have the **Preview** box checked. You can change the size of any character or word, even if it's within a paragraph.*

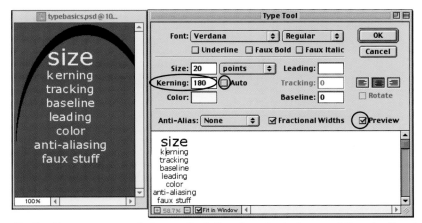

3. Position your cursor between the letters **k** and **e** in the word "**kerning**" and click so the insertion bar appears. Uncheck **Kerning: Auto**. Hold down the **Option** (Mac) or **Alt** (Windows) key and press the right or left arrow on your keyboard. Notice how the space between the two letters expands and contracts? Change the setting to **180** so it matches the example above.

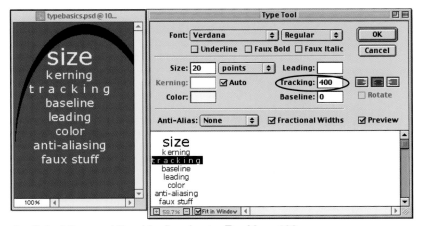

4. Select the word "**tracking**" and enter **Tracking: 400**.

Notice how all the letters in the word expand? Kerning affects the space between two characters, while tracking affects the space between all the selected letters.

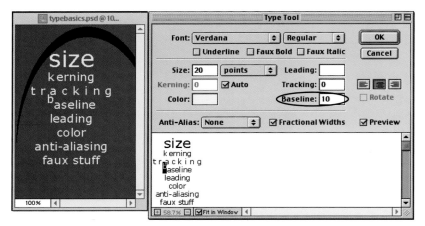

5. Select the letter **b** in "**baseline**" and enter **Baseline: 10**.

Notice the letter "b" appears above the baseline of the rest of the word? If you use a negative number, the letter will drop below the baseline. Baseline adjustments can be applied to entire words or individual characters.

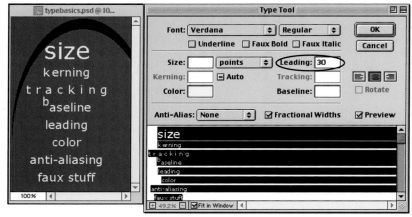

6. Select all the words in the list and enter **Leading: 30**.

Notice that all the lines of type expand so there is more vertical space between them? Leading affects the space between each line of type. The term refers to the olden days of typesetting, when foundries would use actual pieces of lead to physically separate each line of type. I wonder if some old typesetters are turning in their graves watching this process?

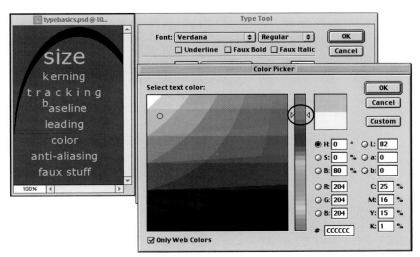

7. Deselect the words and click in **Color:** to access the **Color Picker**. Try moving the slider around and clicking on different colors. They should preview instantly. Unfortunately, you cannot color the words or characters separately in this interface. You will learn how to do this in a later exercise. Click **OK** once you pick a new color.

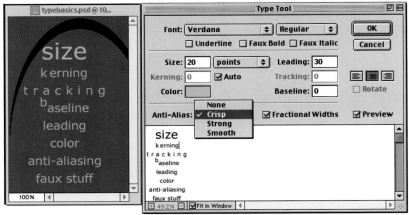

8. Click on the pop-up menu next to **Anti-Alias:** and select **Crisp**, **Strong** and **Smooth**, too.

*Previous versions of Photoshop did not have these many choices for anti-aliasing. This is a great feature for Web work, because different levels of anti-aliasing work best depending on the font and size you are using. If you design for print, these issues are not as important because you would typically print your work at high resolution. Because the resolution of the Web is so low, you have to judge if your type looks good on the screen. I usually choose **None** for type that is under 14 points, and I experiment with **Crisp**, **Strong**, and **Smooth** for larger type.*

Note | **What is Anti-Aliasing, Anyway?**

Anti-aliasing is a term that refers to how the edges of artwork look. In the context of this chapter, aliased type looks jaggy, while anti-aliased type looks smooth. Most of the time you'll choose to anti-alias the type in your Web graphics, though sometimes on very small point sizes, aliased type is more readable.

Aliased   *Anti-Aliased*

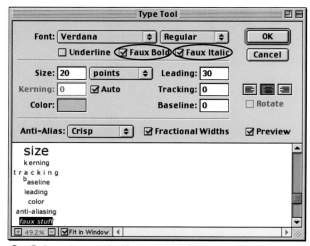

9. Select the words "**faux stuff.**" Click the checkboxes for **Faux Bold** and **Faux Italic**.

This is great for fonts that don't include italic or bold styles.

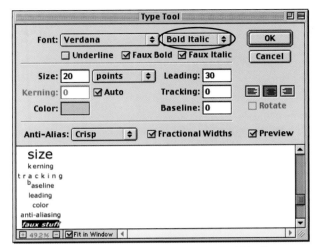

10. Change the **Font:** from **Regular** to **Bold Italic**.

*If the font you use does have a **Bold**, **Italic**, or **Bold Italic** setting, the **Faux Bold** and **Faux Italic** causes the type to be even bolder and more italicized.*

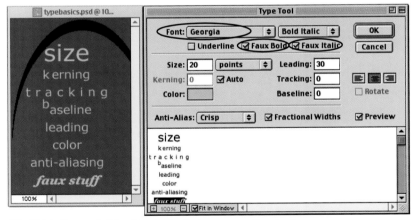

11. With "**faux stuff**" still selected, choose another font.

*In this example I chose **Font: Georgia**. You can change the font on a character or word basis.*

12. Click **OK** and choose **File > Save As...** and name the file **pstypebasics.psd**. Leave the file open for the next exercise.

2. _____Jump To

ImageReady's text tools are a little different from Photoshop's. In order to see the differences, it will be interesting to view in ImageReady the file you just completed in Photoshop. You could quit Photoshop and launch ImageReady and open the file you just saved, or you could more easily use a neat shortcut, using the **Jump To** button in Photoshop which is preset to open ImageReady. This does require that you have enough RAM. If you don't, you can always quit Photoshop and open the file inside ImageReady instead.

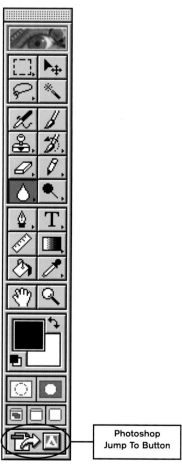

Photoshop
Jump To Button

I. You should still be in Photoshop, but you're about to switch to ImageReady. With **pstypebasics.psd** open, click on the **Jump To** button at the bottom of the Photoshop toolbar. This will open the document inside ImageReady.

2. Select the **Type** layer by clicking on it in the **Layers** palette. Notice the blue underline? The only way to turn this blue underline off is to select a different layer. Don't do that now though, because you're going to need the **Type** layer selected for the next step.

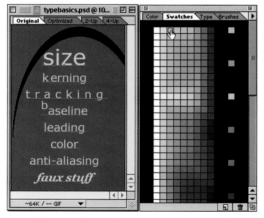

3. Click the **Swatches** tab to make its palette active, or if you can't find it choose **Window >
Show Swatches**. Click on a color. The type should change color instantly.

*Changing the color of type this way offers an advantage over Photoshop, which requires filling
the color with the **Fill** command or accessing the **Type Tool** window.*

4. Settle on a color you like before advancing to the next exercise. It's very important that you do
not save this file yet, so you can learn about the **Update** feature in the next exercise.

[PS/IR] **3.**————————**Changing the Update Feature**

If you have enough RAM in your computer to use the **Jump To** buttons in Photoshop and ImageReady, then there is a **Preference** that you should change in both applications. The Preference relates to whether the programs prompt you to update changes or update them automatically. I prefer to disable the **Update** prompt because I find it annoying, and I'll show you why. Because this is an easy change to make, I thought you might like to know how to disable it, too.

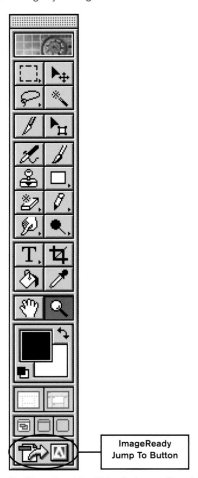

ImageReady
Jump To Button

1. You should still be in ImageReady, but you're about to switch to Photoshop. Now that you've made a change to the color in this document in the last exercise, click on the **Jump To** button in ImageReady to go back to Photoshop.

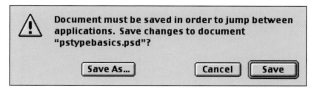

2. You will be prompted to save the document. Click **Save** to write over the existing document and jump over to Photoshop.

*If you were to pick **Save As...**, you would be able to save a new version of this document instead of writing over the existing one. Sometimes this might be your choice, especially if you wanted to keep track of different versions in different states of editing.*

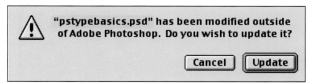

3. Since the document was already open in Photoshop in its original state when you were in Exercise 1, before you made the color change in ImageReady in Exercise 2, you will be prompted to update the file in Photoshop. Click **Update**.

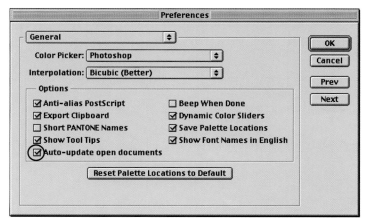

4. If you jump back and forth between Photoshop and ImageReady often, this **Update** dialog box will get annoying. To disable it, jump back to ImageReady and choose **File > Preferences > General...** and check **Auto-update open documents**. Click **OK**. Jump back to Photoshop.

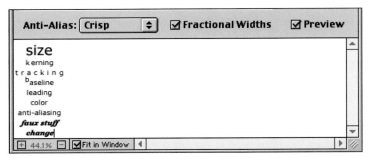

5. Double-click the **T** on the type layer in the **Layers** palette to access the **Type Tool** window. Inside the window, click your cursor after the words "**faux stuff**" and press the **Return** key. This makes a new line of type. Write the word "**change**" and click **OK**.

6. The word "**change**" appears cut off at the bottom of the screen. That's OK because you can move it up easily. Click the **Move** tool in your toolbar (or press the letter **V** on your keyboard, which is the shortcut I always use). With the **Move** tool selected, click and drag up on the type in the document window and it will move up.

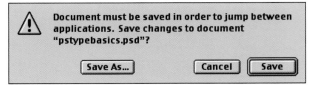

7. Now that you've made some changes in Photoshop, click the **Jump To** button to go back to ImageReady. You will be prompted to save the open document. Click **Save**.

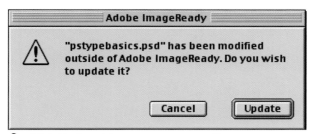

8. Click **Update**. The next few steps will show you how to disable this dialog box from appearing every time you make a change to the file.

It's not that updating the image is bad, it's necessary! The issue I have with this process is that since I have to update in order to continue working on the document, I would prefer to have ImageReady and Photoshop update the file for me, so I don't have to click on this dialog box every time I jump between them. You've already disabled this in Photoshop, and the next step will show you how to disable it in ImageReady.

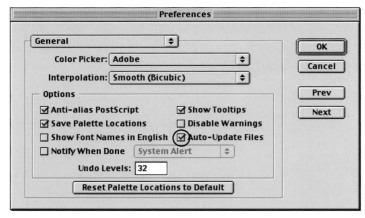

9. Once again, choose **File > Preferences > General...**, check **Auto-Update Files** and click **OK**.

IO. Leave this file open for the next exercise.

*The purpose of this exercise was to show you how to jump between the two applications and how to turn off in both that pesky **Update** warning. FYI, the warning is intended to alert you to the fact that you are writing over the file each time you jump.*

[IR] 4. _____ **Editing Type**

You've learned how to edit type in Photoshop, now we'll examine the same features in ImageReady.

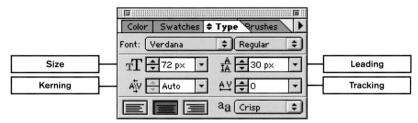

Size	**Leading**
Kerning	**Tracking**

1. You should be in ImageReady. To edit the type you created in Photoshop, you'll need to work with the **Type** palette on **pstypebasics.psd**. You can access it by double-clicking on the **T** on the ImageReady toolbar or by choosing **Window > Show Type**.

The **Type** palette is similar to the **Type Tool** window in Photoshop in functionality but not in appearance. Again, if you are familiar with Illustrator, you might notice a lot more similarities between ImageReady and Illustrator's **Type** palette than Photoshop's.

2. Click the **T** in the toolbar (or press the **T** key on the keyboard), and select the word "**size**" on the screen. In the **Type** palette, change the size setting to **72 px**.

There is no need to double-click on the **T** in the **Layers** palette as you did in Photoshop. Instead, in ImageReady you actually edit the words right on the document itself.

3. Click between the **k** and the **e** in "**kerning**" and change the setting to **0** as shown above. **Tip:** Sometimes you must press the **Enter** key for the change to take place.

4. To view the **baseline** and **faux** settings, you'll need to expand the **Type** palette. Click on the upper-right arrow and select **Show Options**. Notice that the baseline setting appears at the bottom of the palette. **Note:** You can also expand this palette by double-clicking on the double-arrow to the left of the word "**Type**" on the **Type** palette.

Movie | **ir_type.mov**

To learn more about viewing the **Type** settings inside Image-Ready 2.0, check out **ir_type. mov** from the **movies** folder that you transferred to your hard drive from the **H•O•T CD-ROM**.

5. Select the "**b**" in the word "**baseline**" and change the value in the **Type** palette's **baseline** setting to **0**. **Note:** Sometimes you must press the **Enter** key for the change to take place. The **Faux** settings are available under the same menu.

6. Save and, finally, close the file. Leave ImageReady open for the next exercise.

5. ─────────**Rendering Type**

It's wonderful that type is editable in ImageReady and Photoshop because you can change your mind at any time about spelling, font, color, kerning, tracking, size, anti-aliasing, etc. There are certain things, however, that cannot be done with editable type. This exercise will show you how to render the type so it can be recolored on a character or word basis, or treated with a **Layer** Effect in either ImageReady or Photoshop.

I. You should be in ImageReady. Open **pullquote.psd**.

*There are two things that you cannot do with this type — color individual characters or run **Filter** effects. Notice that the **Filter** menu is grayed out and that if you select a word or character and then try to change the color, the entire text block changes. This is a job for rendered type! This is true of both ImageReady and Photoshop.*

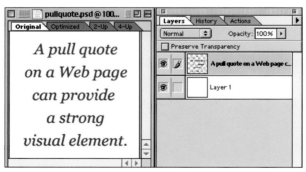

2. Make sure the **Type** layer is selected in the **Layers** palette and choose **Layer > Type > Render Layer**. The blue underline will disappear because the type is no longer editable.

Choosing to render a type layer converts the type from editable text to non-editable text. It freezes the type into pixels, and it is no longer editable as type but is now fully editable as an image. This enables the features that are disabled when the type is editable.

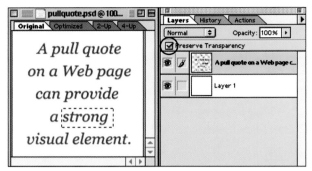

3. In the **Layers** palette, make sure that the top layer is selected and check **Preserve Transparency**. Drag a selection region around the word "**strong**" using the **Marquee** tool at the top-left corner of the toolbar (the shortcut for the **Marquee** tool is the letter **M** on your keyboard).

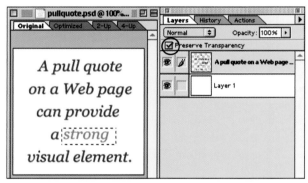

4. Select a color other than dark blue, and press **Option+Delete** (Mac) or **Alt+Delete** (Windows) to change the color.

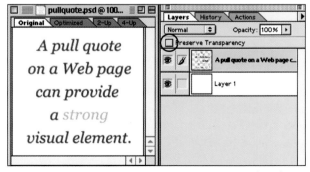

5. Deselect the selection by pressing **Cmd+D** (Mac) or **Ctrl+D** (Windows). Uncheck **Preserve Transparency**, to allow a **Filter** Effect to expand beyond the shape of the type itself.

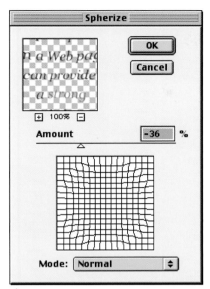

6. Choose **Filter > Distort > Spherize**. Drag the **Amount** slider to **-36%** and click **OK**.

The result should look like this.

7. Choose **File > Save As…** and name it **pullquote2.psd**. Once the file is saved, close it because you won't be needing it again. Leave ImageReady open for the next exercise.

*Note: This exercise would work identically in Photoshop 5.5. Saving the file as **pullquote2.psd** effectively saves a copy with your changes and leaves the original **pullquote.psd** untouched, so you can try this exercise in Photoshop if you want to.*

> ### Note | **Rendering Type and Preserve Transparency**
>
> Be aware that it would have been impossible to color the word "**strong**" without first render-ing the type layer. It was also necessary to check **Preserve Transparency** in order to fill a single word of type with a different color. It would have been impossible to apply the **Filter** effect with the **Preserve Transparency** feature turned on, so you turned it off before applying the filter. I often toggle **Preserve Transparency** on and off many times in the course of color-ing and applying **Filter** effects to type (and other artwork too!).

What Is Preserve Transparency?

You are probably wondering what the heck **Preserve Transparency** is and why I am suggesting you toggle it on and off. **Preserve Transparency** preserves the transparent areas of a layer and allows you to edit only the pixels that are turned on.

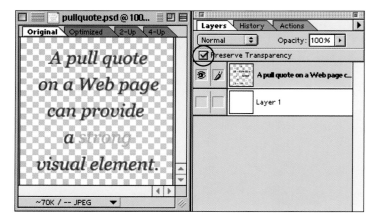

Unless every pixel on a layer is turned on, there are areas of transparency and areas of non-trans-parency. The checkerboard pattern in ImageReady indicates where the areas of transparency are in a layer. If you want to edit a layer that contains transparency, the **Preserve Transparency** option allows you to select the active pixels in the layer while "preserving" the transparent pixels. This is a form of masking that doesn't require any selection on your part. I can't tell you how many students I see who try to select a layer with the **Magic Wand** tool, not realizing that **Preserve Transparency** would give them a much better selection since it is based on which pixels are turned on and off on the layer.

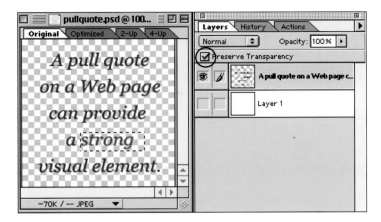

With **Preserve Transparency** turned on, you can recolor artwork without making a selection with a selection tool. Alternatively, if you have **Preserve Transparency** active, you can make a selection with the **Marquee** tool, and it will serve as a compound-mask, that is, two masks at once. That is what happened when you only recolored the word "**strong**" in the last exercise.

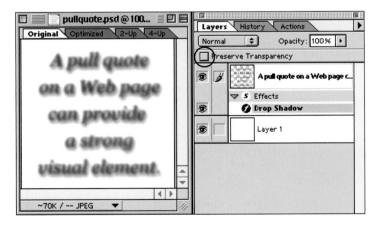

It's necessary to turn **Preserve Transparency** off when you want to run filters on a layer, since the resulting mask would prohibit any transparent pixels from being edited. In the above example, I ran the **Gaussian Blur** filter on the layer without **Preserve Transparency** checked. Filters will likely have no effect if you leave **Preserve Transparency** on. I typically turn it on when I want to recolor artwork, and turn it off when I want to filter artwork. This is a feature I use often in Photoshop and ImageReady and I feel it is important to teach since it is a superior method to masking than any other of which I know.

6. Setting Up Artwork for Buttons

Buttons are one of the most common page elements in Web design. Now they are easier to draw because ImageReady introduced a new tool in its toolbar that does not exist in Photoshop, called the **Shape** tool. It contains a rectangle, ellipse, and rounded rectangle for creating button objects. This exercise teaches how to use the **Shape** tool, shows you how to set up your layers from scratch for buttons, as well as how to name and color them.

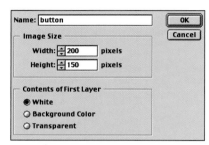

I. You should be in ImageReady. Choose **File > New**. Fill out the settings to match those above. When you're finished, click **OK**.

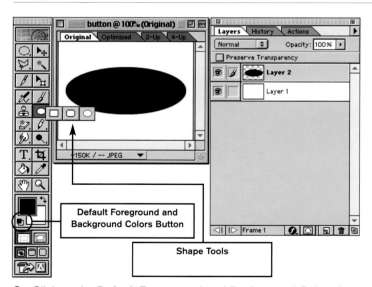

2. Click on the **Default Foreground and Background Colors** button to switch the palette to solid black and white.

*This assigns black as the **Foreground Color**. ImageReady and Photoshop default to using the **Foreground Color** whenever you use a drawing tool.*

3. Hold your mouse down on the **Rectangle** tool to see the other **Shape** tool choices. With your mouse depressed, slide over to the **Ellipse** tool. With the **Ellipse** tool selected, draw a shape on to the screen by placing your cursor in the upper-left corner of the document window and dragging to the right. **Tip:** If you'd like the shape to originate from the center, hold the **Shift** key before you click and drag the shape.

*This new tool in ImageReady is very helpful for creating primitive shapes that are used in buttons. The tool also has the advantage of automatically creating a new layer in the **Layers** palette. Notice that the color of the button is the same color that you set earlier as the Foreground swatch on the toolbar.*

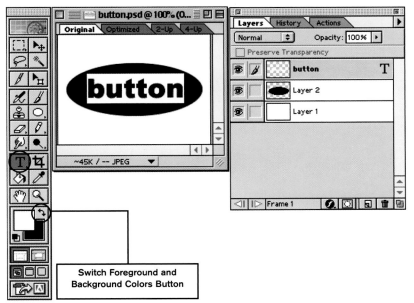

4. Click the **Switch Foreground and Background Color**s button to put white into the **Foreground Color** area. Click the **Type** tool, or press **T** to activate it, and click on the **Ellipse** on the screen to type the word "**button**."

*This also produces its own layer automatically, just as the **Ellipse** tool did.*

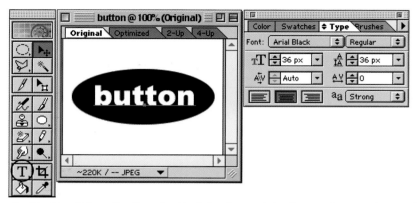

5. Double-click on the **Type** tool to bring forward the **Type** palette, and enter the settings that you see above. If you don't have the font **Arial Black**, choose another extra bold font.

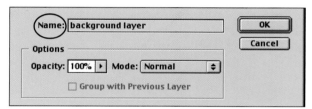

6. In the **Layers** palette, double-click **Layer 1**. This brings up the **Layer Options** window. Type **Name: background layer**. Click **OK** (Mac) or press **Enter** (Windows) and you'll see that the layer appears with the new name in the **Layers** palette. Follow the same directions for **Layer 2** and name it **ellipse shape**.

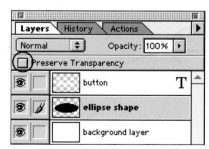

7. Your **Layers** palette should look like this. With the **ellipse shape** layer selected, click on the **Preserve Transparency** checkbox. Pick a new color from the **Swatches** palette (choose **Window > Show Swatches**) and use **Option+Delete** (Mac) or **Alt+Delete** (Windows) to fill it.

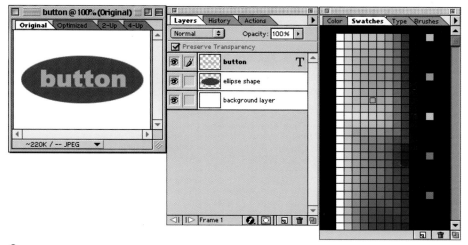

8. Select the **button** layer in the **Layers** palette, and pick a new color from the **Swatches** palette. It will change as well.

Why didn't I instruct you to create the shapes in color to begin with? Because I wanted to show you how flexible ImageReady and Photoshop are once you separate elements on to their own layers. You are never locked into any color if you work this way.

9. Choose **File > Save** and the name **button.psd** will fill in automatically. This is because you gave the new document this name in Step 1 of this exercise. Leave this file open for the next exercise.

Note | **What's a Layer Effect?**

Making artwork convey that an object is clickable can be a challenge. There are certain button-artwork conventions that are seen all over the Web — bevels, drop shadows, and/or inset type. **Layer Effects**, which were first introduced in Photoshop 5.0, can help you make button artwork, because they offer many of the effects found under the **Filter** menu, such as **Blur** or **Offset**. **Layer Effects** actually combine multiple **Filter** effects once and offer the added convenience of being editable. A **Layer Effect** for a drop shadow, for example, can be altered at any time, meaning that the angle of the shadow, the intensity, or the amount of blur is always adjustable. **Layer Effects** weren't in ImageReady 1.0, but they've made their way into Image-Ready 2.0 in a big way. Once you add a **Layer Effect**, you can always change your mind about its appearance, which is not true of filters.

[IR] 7. _____Layer Effects

If you have never worked with these critters before, you're bound to be quite enthralled. While ImageReady and Photoshop both offer **Layer Effects**, each application handles them a little differently. The next series of exercises will reveal the power and differences of **Layer Effects** in each program. I'll begin with ImageReady, which is where I do most of my **Layer Effects** work because I prefer the way they work here versus in Photoshop.

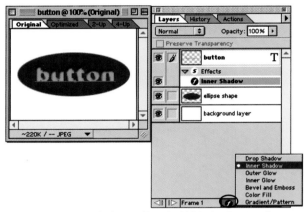

I. You should be in ImageReady. With the **button** layer selected in **button.psd**, which you should still have open from the previous exercise, click on the *f*-shaped **Layer Effect** icon at the bottom of the **Layers** palette. This will access the pop-up menu, from which you should select **Inner Shadow**. This will cause the **Layer Effect** to appear on its own sub-layer beneath the **button** layer.

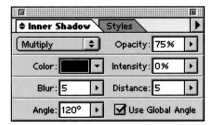

*Tip: Choosing **Inner Shadow**, or any other **Layer Effect**, ought to bring forward the **Layer Effect Options** palette for that **Layer Effect**. If it doesn't, there are two other ways to bring it up: Double-click on the **Inner Shadow** icon below the **S Effects** area on the **button** layer (**S Effects** stands for **Style Effects**), or choose **Window > Show Layer Options/Effects.***

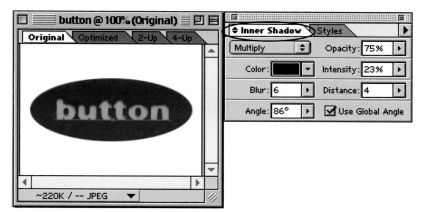

2. In the **Inner Shadow Options** palette, try changing the **Color**, **Blur**, **Intensity**, and **Distance** settings. You're sure to be impressed by this flexibility, and you can change your mind at any time.

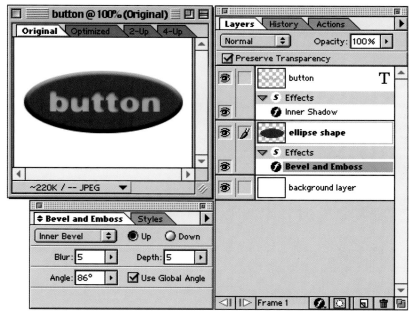

3. Select the **ellipse shape** layer and click on the *f*-shaped **Layer Effect** icon at the bottom of the **Layers** palette. Choose **Bevel and Emboss**. The **Bevel and Emboss Options** palette should be active now, and you can try some different settings for this effect as well.

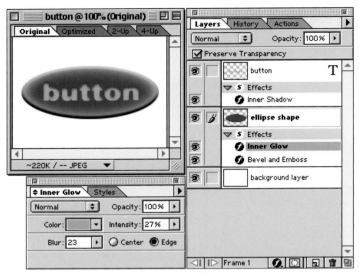

4. You can add two or more **Layer Effects** to each layer in ImageReady. With the same layer selected, click again on the *f*-shaped **Layer Effect** icon at the bottom of the **Layers** palette and select **Inner Glow** from the pop-up menu. I've changed the settings so this effect is much more obvious than it is with its default settings.

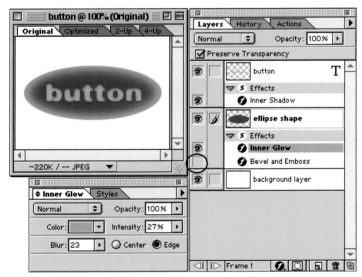

5. You can selectively turn on and off **Layer Effects**. On the **Layers** palette, click the eye icon to the left of the **Bevel and Emboss** setting to turn it off. You can try different combinations this way.

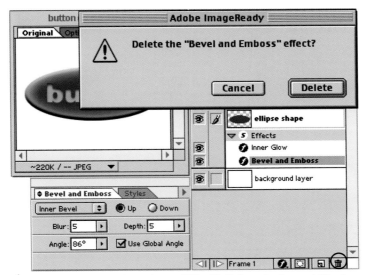

6. What about deleting a **Layer Effect**? Select the **Layer Effect** you want to delete and click on the **Trash Can** icon at the bottom of the **Layers** palette. Select the **Bevel and Emboss Layer Effect** on the **ellipse shape** layer, and delete it this way. **Note:** On Windows you will have a **Yes/No** option on this dialog box. Click **Yes** to delete the **Layer Effect**.

*You could alternately delete in one step, by dragging the layer on to the **Trash Can** icon.*

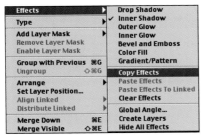

7. You can also copy and paste **Layer Effects** for consistency. Select the **Inner Shadow Layer Effect** that's on the **button** layer. Choose **Layer > Effects > Copy Effects**.

8. Select the **ellipse shape** layer and choose **Layer > Effects > Paste Effects**.

*Both layers now have the exact same **Layer Effect**. This technique of copying and pasting effects can be great for creating consistent appearances between elements of your interface.*

9. Save the file and leave it open for the next exercise.

[PS]

8. _____Layer Effects

Layer Effects are supported a little differently in Photoshop. As I already said, I actually prefer the way they work in ImageReady, so that's where I do most of my **Layer Effects** work. Still, sometimes you find yourself making type in Photoshop and it's great that this same feature is there as well.

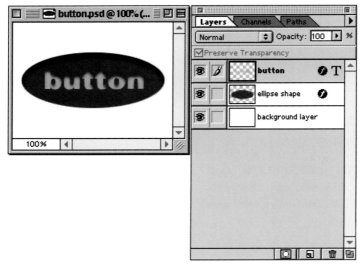

1. You should be in ImageReady, but you are about to switch to **Photoshop**. Click on the **Jump To** button at the bottom of the ImageReady toolbar. This should pop you over to Photoshop and open the same **button.psd** file there.

*Notice that there is no **Layer Effect** icon at the bottom of the **Layers** palette in Photoshop. The circles with the **f** shape in them are visible on each layer they were used on, but without a twirl-down arrow or a name of the effect showing. The appearance is different, but the **Layer Effects** are still visible and working here.*

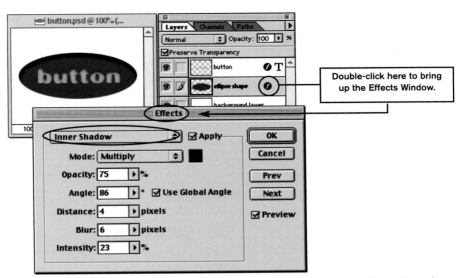

2. In the **Layers** palette, double-click on the **Layer Effect** icon in the **ellipse shape** layer to bring up the **Effects** dialog box. Change a couple of settings and you will see the artwork change. Make sure that **Preview** is checked. Do not click **OK**. You can add multiple **Layer Effects** in Photoshop as well. Click on **Inner Shadow** and you'll access a pop-up menu.

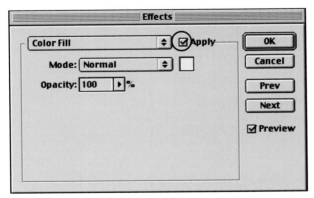

3. Choose **Color Fill** and check on **Apply**. Make sure **Preview** is checked. Click inside the red color swatch to pick another color. Bingo, the layer changes color! Click **OK**.

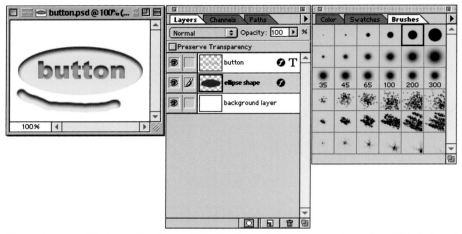

*If you draw on this layer, the **Layer Effect** will apply to your brush strokes. This is true in ImageReady as well. In order to draw on the **ellipse shape** layer, however, you will have to uncheck **Preserve Transparency**. As I mentioned earlier, I use **Preserve Transparency** all the time, but it won't let you edit the layer in its transparent areas. Being able to turn **Preserve Transparency** on and off when you need to is part of its power.*

4. Click on the **Paintbrush** tool in the Photoshop toolbar (the shortcut is the letter **B** on your keyboard) and grab yourself a brush from the **Brushes** palette (**Window > Show Brushes**). Paint a stroke on the artwork.

Whoa! It's the same color with the same effect. Told you so!

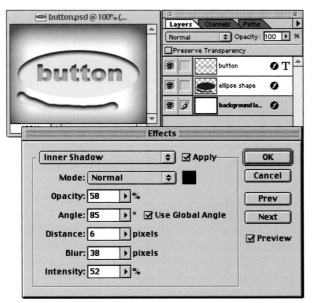

5. Select the **background layer** and choose **Layer > Effects > Inner Shadow...**. I changed the settings so this effect shows up well on the **background** layer. Change your settings to match mine or choose your own settings. When you're finished, click **OK**.

6. You can copy and paste **Layer Effects** in Photoshop, just like you could in ImageReady. You can even selectively turn them on and off if you have multiple effects by checking or unchecking the **Apply** box inside the **Effects** dialog box. Deleting **Layer Effects** is a little different, however. Make sure the **background layer** is still selected and choose **Layer > Effects > Clear Effects**.

7. Save your work and click on the **Jump To** button again to return to ImageReady.

9.——————**The Gradient/Pattern Layer Effect**

There is one **Layer Effect** that exists in ImageReady but not in Photoshop — the **Gradient/Pattern Layer Effect**. This next exercise will show you how to use it, how it disappears in Photoshop, and how to make it reappear in ImageReady.

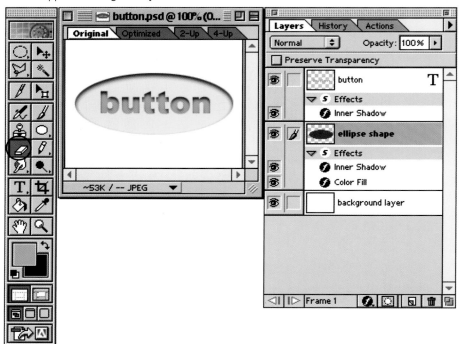

I. The last exercise should have jumped **button.psd** to ImageReady. With that file open, select the **ellipse shape** layer from the **Layers** palette and then the **Eraser** tool from the ImageReady toolbar (the shortcut is the letter **E** on your keyboard). Go ahead and erase the brush stroke you made in Photoshop.

Everything is flexible and changeable between these two programs, so you should never settle for anything that isn't to your liking. This brush stroke showed off an interesting technique, but resulted in something that wasn't very attractive.

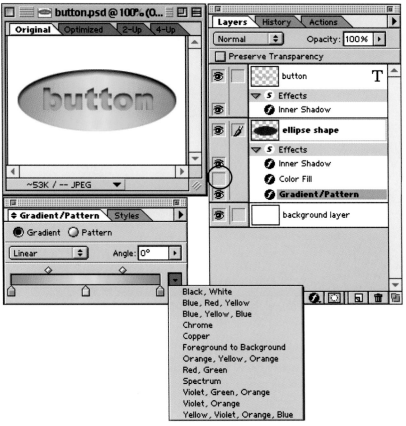

2. With the **ellipse shape** layer still selected, click on the **Layer Effect** icon at the bottom of the **Layers** palette and select **Gradient/Pattern** from the pop-up menu. This effect will not show because the **Color Fill Layer Effect** is hiding it. Turn off the eye icon for the **Color Fill** layer so you can see the **Gradient/Pattern Layer Effect**. Click on the arrow to the bottom-right of the **Gradient/Pattern** palette to access a pop-up menu of gradient effects. The one shown in this example is the **Orange, Yellow, Orange** gradient.

3. Because Photoshop doesn't support this effect, it will be interesting to see how it appears over there, won't it? Click the **Jump To** button to see what happens in Photoshop. Click **Save** when you are prompted.

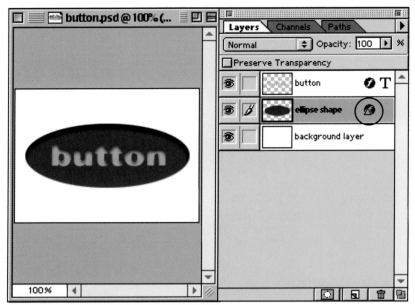

Notice that the gradient isn't visible, but that the **f** symbol to the right of the **ellipse shape** layer has a warning triangle on the icon? That is Photoshop's symbol that the effect exists but the application doesn't support it.

I suspect that the **Gradient/Pattern Layer Effect** exists in ImageReady as a substitute for a true gradient tool or the ability to create pattern fills, both of which are found in Photoshop.

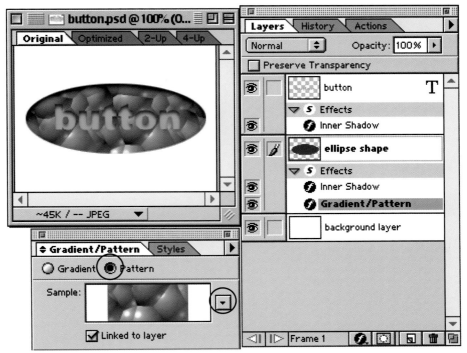

4. Click the **Jump To** button to switch back to ImageReady. Select the **Gradient/Pattern Layer Effect** on the **ellipse shape** layer, and then click the **Pattern** button inside the **Gradient/Pattern Options** palette. If you click on the arrow to the right of the preview, you'll locate a menu listing of other patterns. Try different patterns and go wild until you get bored.

*Note: If you wanted to add a pattern to the button layer, select it first and then add the **Gradient/Pattern Layer Effect** to that layer.*

5. Save and close the file. Leave ImageReady open for the next exercise.

[IR/PS] **10.**————————**Applying Styles**

Styles are the equivalent of **Filter Effects** on steroids. They allow you to apply multiple effects to artwork in one single operation. It's possible to pick from existing **Styles** or you can save your own custom versions. **Styles** are only available in ImageReady, but if you work in Photoshop on a file that contains **Styles** that you created in ImageReady, it will not remove or alter them. This exercise covers how to apply **Styles** that ship with ImageReady. Subsequent chapters will show how to create your own **Styles** and work with them in Photoshop.

I. You should be in ImageReady. Open **typeobjects.psd**. Make sure the **Styles** palette is visible. If it isn't, choose **Window > Show Styles**.

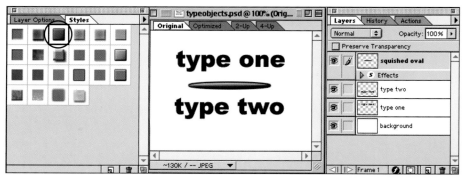

2. With the **squished oval** layer selected, double-click on the third **Style** from the upper left, the dark red square.

3. In the **Layers** palette, click the arrow to the left of the words **S Effects** to view the **Layer Effects** that one single operation just applied. Double-click on any of the **Layer Effects** that appear on this layer, and you'll be able to view the settings to deconstruct the way this **Style** was built.

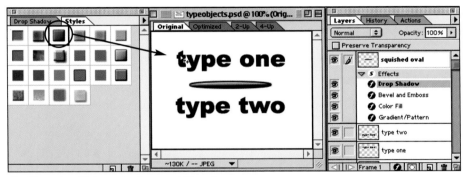

4. Drag the **Style** on to the word "**type**."

*The **Style** will appear on the **type one** layer, even though you didn't select the layer first. Most operations in Photoshop and ImageReady require that you select a layer before it can be edited. **Styles** are different; they can be dragged onto artwork on the screen.*

5. Click the **S Effects** arrow below the **squished oval** layer to the display of each **Layer Effect** so you can see the other layers in the **Layers** palette. Drag the same **Style** on to the **type two** layer and on to the white **background**. **Note:** The tip of the cursor has to touch the artwork for Image-Ready to know what artwork the **Style** is getting dragged onto.

The results of dragging the Style on to each element on the screen.

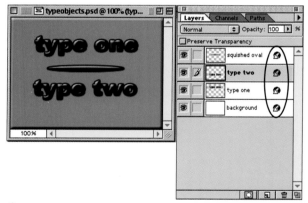

6. Save this file, and click on the **Jump To** button to see how it looks in Photoshop, which, as you know by now, supports **Layer Effects** but not **Styles**. It looks quite different here, right?

*Notice all the **f** symbols with triangles on them? This just means that Photoshop cannot render some of the **Layer Effects** that were part of the **Styles** chosen for this artwork. It looks unsightly, but the good news is that Photoshop won't delete or damage any of the **Styles**. It honors what it cannot display, it just cannot display it.*

7. Press the **Jump To** button to return to ImageReady. Leave this file open for the next exercise.

II. ————————Making Your Own Styles

Styles are very powerful, but the ones that ship with ImageReady might not be your cup of tea. This next exercise shows you how to modify existing **Styles**. It should please you to know that when you create a custom **Style**, as you will learn to do in this exercise, the **Style** becomes part of ImageReady and can be easily used in other documents. It is stored with ImageReady's **Preferences**, so unless those get thrown away the **Styles** you make will be part of ImageReady forever.

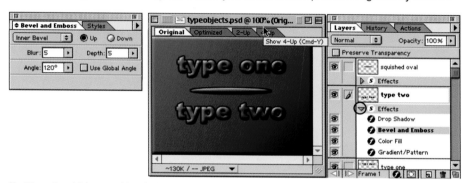

1. You should be working in ImageReady. With **typeobjects.psd** still open from the previous exercise, click on the **S Effects** arrow on the **type two** layer to expand its view of the **Layer Effects**. Double-click on the **Bevel and Emboss Layer Effect**. This will bring forward the **Bevel and Emboss Layer Options** palette.

2. Change the settings to **Blur: 6** and **Depth: 2**. Go ahead and double-click on any of the other **Layer Effects** to modify their settings.

*These are the same exact **Layer Effects** you were working with in earlier exercises. You can learn a lot about **Layer Effects** by simply viewing their settings.*

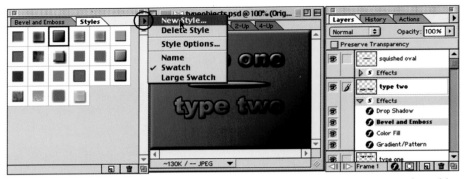

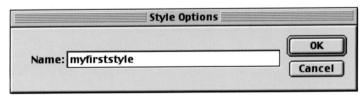

3. Let's say you really prefer the change you just made to this **Layer Effect** and would like to make it a custom **Style** that you could reuse. Click on the **Styles** palette and click on the upper-right arrow to choose **New Style…** from the pop-up menu.

4. You will be prompted to name the **Style**. Once you have given it a name, click **OK**.

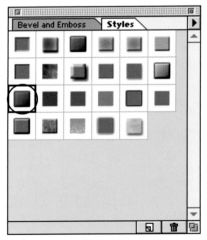

5. The new **Style** will appear and it will be highlighted. Go ahead and drag it on to all the layers again in the **Layers** palette. This **Style** will replace the old Style that you had applied earlier.

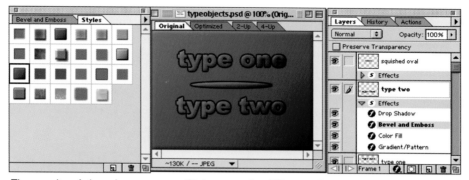

*The results of dragging your new **Style** on to the different elements on your screen.*

6. What if you don't like the color red? Double-click on the **Color Fill Layer Effect** and change the color. Make another new **Style** and drag this one on to the layers.

*See how flexible this system is? You can view the **Styles** by name as well as by swatch.*

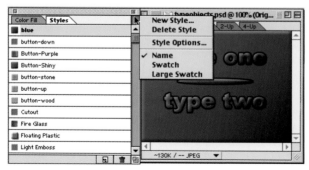

7. Click on the upper-right arrow of the **Styles** palette and choose **Name** from the pop-up menu. This changes the **Styles** display from icons to names.

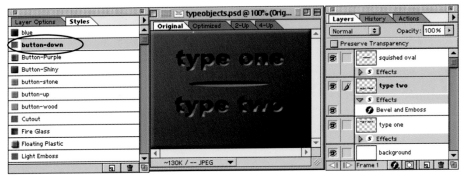

8. Notice how there are a lot of **Styles** in the palette that are gray? Those **Styles** don't have **Color Fill Layer Effects**. Go ahead and drag the **button-down Style** on to the **squished oval**, **type one**, and **type two** artwork.

9. With the **type two** layer selected, add a **Color Fill Layer Effect** by clicking on the **f** symbol at the bottom of the **Layers** palette and selecting **Color Fill**. This **Layer Effect** defaults to being red, but you know how to change all that, right?

Note | **How To Delete a Style or Effect**

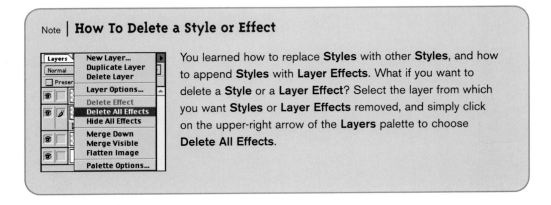

You learned how to replace **Styles** with other **Styles**, and how to append **Styles** with **Layer Effects**. What if you want to delete a **Style** or a **Layer Effect**? Select the layer from which you want **Styles** or **Layer Effects** removed, and simply click on the upper-right arrow of the **Layers** palette to choose **Delete All Effects**.

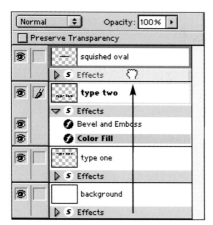

IO. You can also drag the **S Effects** or individual **Layer Effects** to other layers to transfer them via the **Layers** palette.

II. When you're finished playing around with **Styles**, save and close this file.

There are three key points to learn from Exercise 11:

1. When you drop a **Style** on to a layer with an existing **Style**, ImageReady automatically replaces that **Style**.

2. When you add a **Layer Effects** to a **Style**, ImageReady adds another **Layer Effect** and builds on to whichever **Style** has already been applied.

3. Any of the gray **Styles** can be colorized by adding a **Color Fill Layer Effect**. This section is over, though I realize you could probably play with this newfound feature for hours. Feel free! Don't let me stop you. The more you experiment with **Styles**, the better you'll get at using and understanding them.

_____**Stroked Text Using Styles and Filter Effects**

There are a couple of different ways to create stroked (outlined) text in ImageReady and Photoshop. This exercise covers how to use **Styles** and **Layer Effects** for this task. The subsequent exercise will show you how to use selections instead.

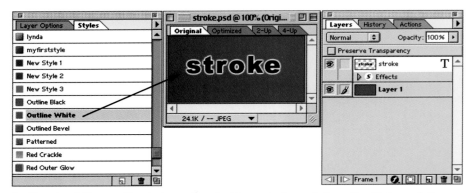

I. You should be working in ImageReady. Open **stroke.psd**. From the **Styles** palette, drag **Outline White** on to the "**stroke**" text.

You don't have to have the **stroke** layer selected when you use the "drag" technique.

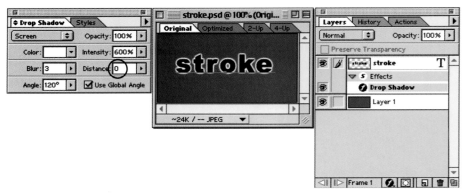

2. To give this type a thicker outline, click on the **S Effects** arrow under the **stroke** layer to expand its contents. Double-click on the **Drop Shadow Layer Effect** to bring forward the **Drop Shadow Layer Options** palette. Notice that the **Distance** is **0**? This lack of a distance offset is why the drop shadow appears as a stroke.

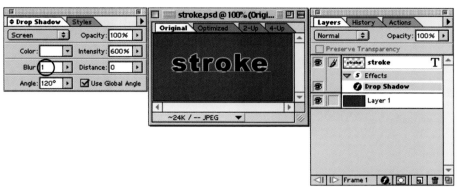

*If you change the **Blur** setting to **1**, the stroke gets thinner.*

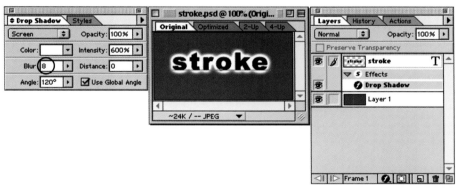

*If you change the **Blur** setting to **8**, the stroke becomes thicker, but it also starts to look blurry which isn't necessarily what you might want.*

3. Put the **Blur** setting back to **3** which is a pretty decent looking stroke.

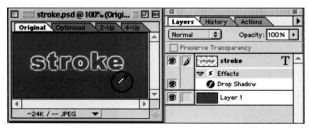

4. To make the type appear as an outline instead of a stroke, select the **stroke** layer and use the **Eyedropper** from the toolbar to pick up the green color in the background. The interior fill of the type will look like it has disappeared, even though it is still there.

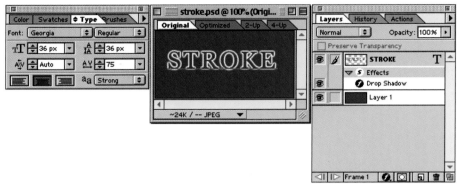

The type is still fully editable, by the way. As I mentioned earlier in this chapter, whenever you see the blue underline in ImageReady, it means you're viewing editable type.

5. Click the **Type** tool (**T**) in the toolbar, select the type on the screen, and retype the word in all capitals. If you choose **Window > Show Type**, you'll be able to view the **Type Options** window. Click on the **Move** tool (**V**) and if you change the font, the change should update instantly on your screen with the stroke intact. Neat stuff.

6. When you're finished, choose **File > Save As...**, name this **irstroke.psd**, and click **Save**.

*Notice that when you saved the file with a new name, ImageReady immediately updated the file name of what is open on your screen? In effect, you've just saved a copy of the original document with a new name. When you choose **Save...** instead of **Save As...** you simply update the existing document. A **Save As...** command saves a copy of the file and lets you work on a copy of the original.*

7. Close the file after it is saved.

_____Stroked Text Using Selections

Using **Layer Effects** for stroke and outline effects is OK, but those techniques have limitations because as soon as you stack more than one type object that contains a stroke or outline, you will not be able to see through to another. These techniques also prevent you from offsetting the stroke from the type. Using selections and making a stroke layer is a much more versatile way to go.

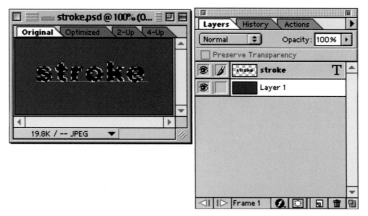

I. You should be in ImageReady. Open **stroke.psd**. It will be a fresh copy of the **stroke.psd** file. Make sure the **stroke** layer is selected and choose **Select > Load Selection > Stroke Transparency**. This loads a perfect selection of the type.

Note | **Select › Load Selection Method**

I watch many Photoshop and ImageReady users try to make a selection of this nature by using the **Magic Wand** tool or other selection tools without realizing that you can always get a better selection by choosing the **Select > Load Selection** method.

This selection process is based on Photoshop and ImageReady's layer transparency, and doesn't rely on threshold methods of other selection tools. (A threshold method means the program looks to how many colors are close to the selection and bases the selection on the color "threshold" that matches the number of colors. The **Magic Wand**, for example, is a threshold selection tool). The **Select > Load Selection** method makes a better selection than any of you could make manually!

A shortcut for this method is to **Option+Click** (Mac) or **Alt+Click** (Windows) on any layer that contains transparency.

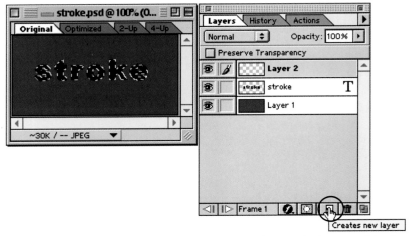

2. With the selection active, click the **New Layer** icon at the bottom of the **Layers** palette. The selection will appear on the new empty layer, which is exactly what is wanted to create a stroke. You'll learn how to do this in the next step.

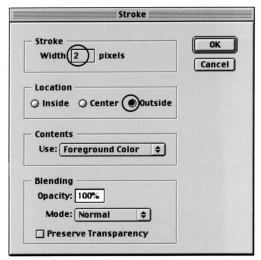

3. Pick a lighter color than what is in your **Foreground Color** swatch (click on the **Foreground Color** swatch in the toolbar to access the **Color Picker**) and choose **Edit > Stroke...** and the **Stroke** dialog box will appear. Fill out the settings as shown above, **Width: 2 pixels** and a **Location** of **Outside** for the stroke. Click **OK**.

The selection is still active, but it's important to turn it off.

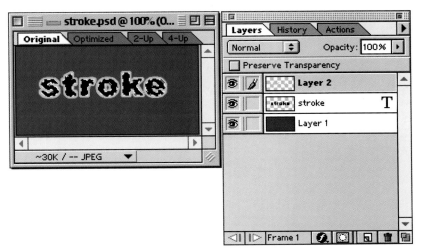

4. Press **Cmd+D** (Mac) or **Ctrl+D** (Windows) and the selection ants will disappear.

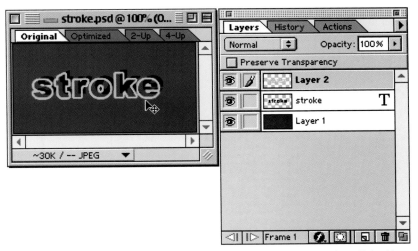

5. Select the **Move** tool (**V**) from the toolbar and move the stroke a little. You can get interesting type effects by having this as a separate layer.

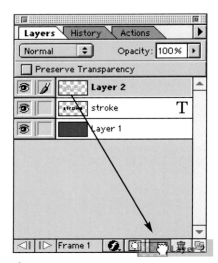

6. Drag **Layer 2** on to the **New Layer** icon at the bottom of the **Layers** palette. This will duplicate the layer.

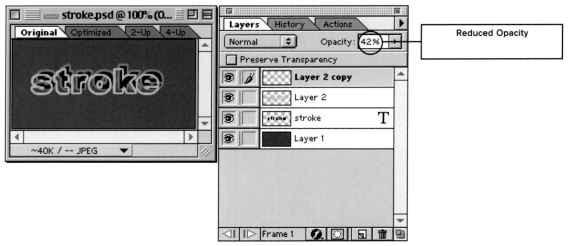

7. Move the duplicate layer so it is offset again and lower the opacity. You have total control over this effect because the stroke is on its own layer.

8. Choose **File > Save As…** and save this as **stroke2.psd**. Close the file.

14.————**Clipping Groups**

I'm sure you've probably seen type on the Web and elsewhere that contains a photographic image. This technique can be achieved in ImageReady and Photoshop by using **Clipping Groups**. This technique consists of artwork that is used as a mask and content that goes into that mask. In this example, I'm using type, but you can use other kinds of artwork for **Clipping Groups**, too.

1. Make sure that you are working in ImageReady. Open **dinosaurs.psd**.

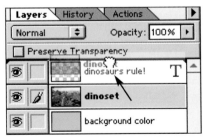

2. Move the **dinoset** layer above the **type** layer in the **Layers** palette by clicking and dragging it to the top position. This will temporarily obscure the **type** layer.

3. Hold down the **Option** (Mac) or **Alt** (Windows) key and move your cursor to the line that divides the **dinoset** and **type** layers. The cursor will change from a hand to the **Clipping Groups** icon. When your cursor is directly over the line click, the photograph will go inside the layer. At the same time, the solid dividing line between the two layers will turn into a dotted line.

4. Make sure that the **dinoset** layer is selected and that the **Move** tool from the toolbar is active. Click on the screen and notice that you can move the photograph independently from the type. Position it where you like it.

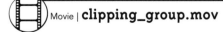

Movie | **clipping_group.mov**

To learn more about setting up Clipping Groups, check out **clipping_group.mov** from the **movies** folder on the **H•O•T CD-ROM**.

5. If you want to move the type and the photo together, select the **dinoset** layer and click on the **Link** field (circled above) in the **type** layer. Now if you use the **Move** tool to move the artwork, both items will move together.

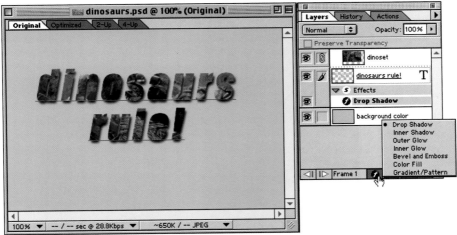

6. You can add **Layer Effects**, too. Click on the **type** layer and then click on the *f* icon at the bottom of the **Layers** palette to select **Drop Shadow**. Sweet! Save and close this file.

This works identically in Photoshop. Because the type is editable, you can still change the font, the size, or the style even though the clipping group is in effect. This allows experimentation with numerous variations.

Note | **Clipping Groups**

A **Clipping Group** involves two or more layers that are separated by the dotted line that appeared in Step 3 of the previous exercise. The dotted line indicates that anything above the line is "clipped" or "masked" within the layer directly below. This is a great technique for inserting content inside a shape. I used to use **Edit > Paste Into** in Photoshop to get this effect, but a **Clipping Group** is a much better method. It's better because it's more flexible — you can still move the layers above the dotted line or alter them where as the older **Paste Into** method could never be edited once it was pasted.

15. Painting Inside Type

You'll start to notice in this book that I love the **Preserve Transparency** technique. This time, instead of filling the type layer using **Preserve Transparency**, you'll learn to paint inside the layer. Woo hoo!

1. Make sure that you are inside ImageReady. Open **painting.psd**. Select the layer **Painting Type** and select the **Airbrush** tool from the toolbar. If you try to paint the type, the brush won't work, because you can't paint on an editable type layer in ImageReady.

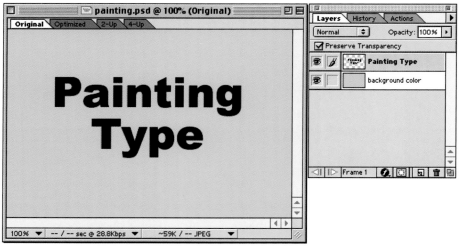

2. Choose **Layer > Type > Render Layer** to make it possible to paint on the **Painting Type** layer. Click the **Preserve Transparency** checkbox to make it active.

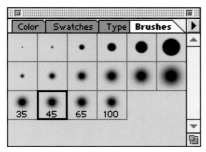

3. Select the **Airbrush** tool (**J**) from the toolbar. Go to the **Brushes** palette (if it is not visible, choose **Window > Show Brushes**) and select the soft-edged brush that is called **45**, which stands for a feather of 45 pixels.

4. Pick a color and start painting the type. There are endless things you can do with this technique — enjoy yourself!

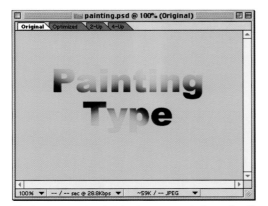

5. When you're finished, save and close the file.

Note: *This exercise would work in either Photoshop or ImageReady.*

7.
Background Images

Size Relationships	Previewing Backgrounds
Magic Eraser	Seamless Backgrounds	Tile Maker Filter
Full-Screen Backgrounds	Directional Backgrounds

chap_07

Photoshop 5.5 / ImageReady 2.0
H•O•T CD-ROM

Designing for HTML is challenging, in that there are really only two layers – a background layer and a foreground layer. In contrast, it's possible to work with unlimited layers in just about every digital design program I can think of, including Photoshop, inDesign, PageMaker, QuarkXPress, Illustrator, FreeHand, etc. Because HTML restricts you to only two layers, the background layer has an added amount of importance, so in this chapter I've put a lot of effort into presenting numerous techniques.

There are workarounds using Style Sheets instead of standard HTML. But this is a book about making Web artwork, not about writing code or using a Web-page editor. For that reason, this chapter focuses on the challenges of and solutions for making effective background images that work with standard HTML. There are two core issues when making a background image – the speed with which it will download, which involves optimization, and its appearance, which involves imaging techniques.

What Is a Background Image?

A background image appears in the background layer of a Web page. By default, it will repeat to fill the size of a browser window. The number of times that a background image will repeat (or, as it's also called, tile) is dictated by the size of the original image and of the browser window in which it is displayed.

A background image starts off in life no different than any other GIF or JPEG. The thing that makes it a background is the HTML code inside the **BODY** tag. The HTML for a tiled background is simple. Here's the minimum code required to include a tiled background image in an HTML document.

```
<HTML>
<BODY BACKGROUND="small.jpg">
</BODY>
</HTML>
```

Tip | **Design Tips for Readability**

When creating artwork for background tiles, it's especially important to pay attention to contrast and value. Try to use either all dark values or all light values. If you combine darks and lights in a single background image, your background might look great on its own, but neither light nor dark type will work consistently against it and your image won't read.

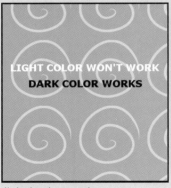

light background   *dark background*   *medium background*

If you are wondering how to pick colors for backgrounds, here are some basic guidelines.

- If you're using a light background, use dark type.
- If you're using a dark background, use light type.
- It's best to avoid using a medium value for a background image or one with a lot of contrast, because neither light nor dark text will read well.

Background Image Sizes

Artwork that is used for a background image can be any dimension, large or small. The size will determine the number of times the pattern will repeat inside a Web browser.

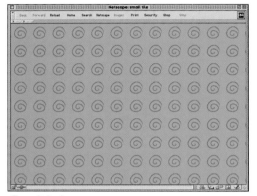

Small *Result in browser*

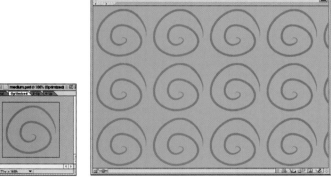

Medium *Result in browser*

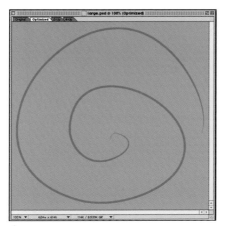

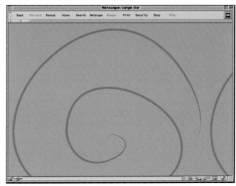

Large   *Result in browser*

As you can see in these examples, a background tile with larger dimensions is going to repeat less often. A tile that measures 40 x 40 pixels will repeat 192 times in a 640 x 480 browser window. A tile that measures 320 x 240 pixels will repeat four times in a 640 x 480 browser window. You can create an image so large that it's only going to repeat once in a standard-size browser window. Basically, the size of the image you choose to make depends on the effect you want to create.

Enlarging a background tile can enlarge its file size as well. If you create a tile that is 50K, it is going to add that much file size to your Web page and adversely affect down-loading speed. One formula I use, though it is not scientifically accurate or measurable, is that each kilobyte of file size represents one second of download time for the average viewer. Therefore, it is just as important to practice good optimization skills in order to maintain small file sizes and fast downloading speeds with background images, as it is with other types of images.

A background image doesn't necessarily have to be big to look big. Later in this chap-ter, you'll learn how to make some very big-looking background tiles that are actually very small in dimensions and file size.

[IR] **I.** ____Defining, Editing, and Previewing a Background Image

Once you've created or opened an image in ImageReady 2.0, the program's **Preview** feature makes it easy to define your image as a background image to see how it will look in a browser. In this exercise, you'll learn to define, edit, and preview artwork as a background image.

I. This exercise takes place in ImageReady. Open **small.psd** from the **chap_07** folder that you transferred to your hard drive from the **H•O•T CD-ROM**.

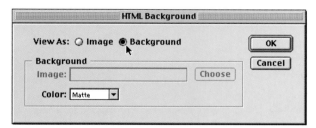

The first step in previewing an image as a background tile is to identify it as an HTML background. This lets ImageReady know that when you preview this image, you want to see it tiled as a background image, not as a foreground image.

2. Choose **File > HTML Background...**, click on the **Background** button, and click **OK**.

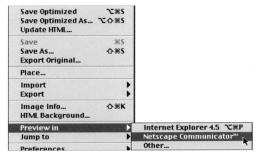

3. Choose **File > Preview in** and select the browser of your choice.

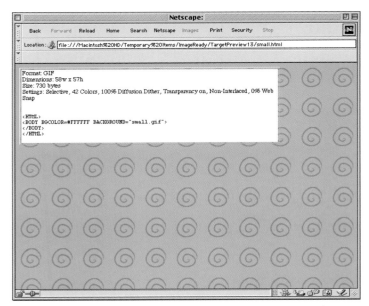

ImageReady will launch the browser (if it isn't already open) and preview this document as a repeating background image. Notice that the preview includes a white text box that contains details about how the image was optimized, as well as the HTML used to define this image as a background. My optimization settings were set to JPEG, but yours might be set to GIF. This doesn't matter for the moment; the point is that this white text box is offering valuable information about the image that is displayed.

The HTML within this white box helps you see the code that ImageReady is generating, as well as information about how the file (or files, in the case of rollovers or sliced documents) is optimized. Later, you'll learn how to have ImageReady write this file as a final HTML document so that the text in this preview would not be part of the document.

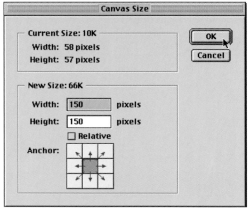

4. The size and content of this image affects its appearance in a browser. Return to ImageReady. Choose **Image > Canvas Size...** and set the canvas size to **150** pixels by **150** pixels, and click **OK**. This will change the size of the canvas around the image to be larger than the image itself.

5. Choose **File > Preview in** and choose a browser again to see how this change in dimensions will affect the appearance of this image.

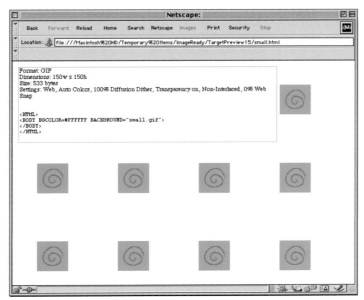

Notice that the areas of the exposed canvas that were transparent have now been changed to a white background around the spiral. That's because ImageReady will substitute a white color for your transparent pixels unless you specify otherwise. In order to change the white border around the spirals, you would need to fill in the transparent pixels with another color.

6. To match the same green that is already in the image, select the **Eyedropper** from the Image-Ready toolbar and click on the green to sample the color. Select the layer **background** from the **Layers** palette (if it's not visible, choose **Window > Show Layers**). Press **Option+Delete** (Mac) or **Alt+Delete** (Windows) to fill the entire background layer with green.

7. Choose **File > Preview in** and select a browser of your choice to see how the change will affect the repeating background image.

Tip | **Shortcut for Previewing in Browser**

Are you getting bored by going to the file menu each time to preview in a browser? If you want to skip ahead for a second, you could look at Chapter 13, *"Automation,"* to learn how to program a shortcut for this previewing task by using **Actions**.

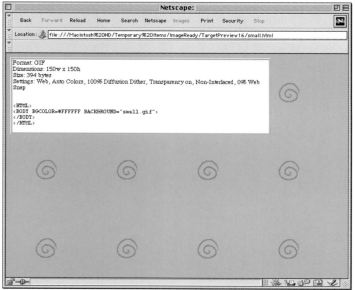

8. Return to ImageReady and leave the file open for the next exercise. Choose **File > Save**.

It's great that ImageReady allows you to preview the image as a background so easily. This allows you to change your mind. In the past, there wasn't a way to preview a background tile from an image editor.

---

2. ————Saving a Background Image

In this exercise, you'll learn to save a background image as a final document instead of just previewing it from ImageReady. When you're working on your own Web projects, this is what you would do after you finished experimenting with how you wanted the background image to look. The image is still in Photoshop format, so it will need to be optimized in order to function properly on the Web. The resulting GIF file will be no different than any other GIF image. The only thing that will make it a background image is the code inside the HTML file that tells the browser to display your GIF as a background image. Fortunately, ImageReady saves images and the necessary HTML code to make this happen! Alternately, you could simply save the optimized image and insert it as a background image inside the HTML editor of your choice.

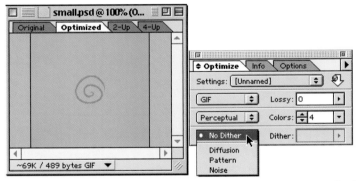

I. With **small.psd** still open from the last exercise, click on the **Optimized** tab in the document window. If the **Optimize** palette isn't open, choose **Window > Show Optimize**. Match your **Optimize** settings to the ones shown above.

Because the image is composed of flat colors, it is going to look best as a GIF.

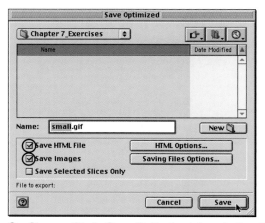

2. Choose **File > Save Optimized As…**. In the dialog box, check both **Save HTML File** and **Save Images**.

When ImageReady saves the file, it will generate both a GIF and an HTML document containing the BODY BACKGROUND *tag that identifies this GIF as a background image. The program knew to include this tag inside the HTML code it generated because you designated this image as a background image in Step 2 of the previous exercise.*

*When you save the file, the **Name:** field defaults to the name of your original image file. You can rename the GIF if you like or keep its default name. Navigate to the **chap_07** folder to see the image and HTML file that were just generated. Next, you'll get to check out the final results by opening the newly created HTML document in a browser.*

> ## Note | **Save HTML or Not?**
>
> I never use the HTML file that ImageReady generates for background images because I prefer to use an HTML editor like GoLive or Dreamweaver when I assemble my Web pages. That's usually because I like to put foreground images on top of background images and position them wherever I want, which the HTML allows with much more control than ImageReady. The only reason I save the image and the HTML is so that I can view the background image without the white preview text readout.

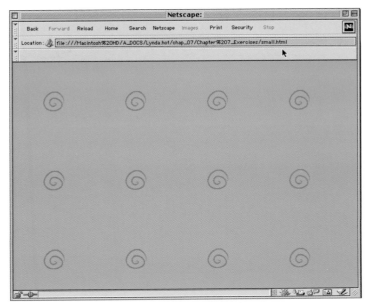

3. Double-click on the HTML file (**small.html**) to open it. If you would prefer to open it in a differ-ent browser, simply open that browser, choose **File > Open** and browse to the HTML file on your hard drive that ImageReady saved automatically.

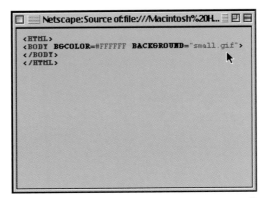

4. If you choose **View > Page Source** you will see the HTML code that ImageReady generated. Return to ImageReady for the next exercise and close **small.psd**.

3. ——————————Recoloring Background Image Artwork

In this exercise, you will learn one way to recolor a black and white image in ImageReady, and how to use the Swatch palette **color.aco** to select colors with similar values. Once you have learned this basic procedure, you can experiment with various combinations of colors to see the impact of choosing colors with similar or contrasting values. You will need to have the custom swatch palette **color.aco** loaded to do this exercise, so if you haven't already done so, follow the instructions in Chapter 5, *"Web Color."*

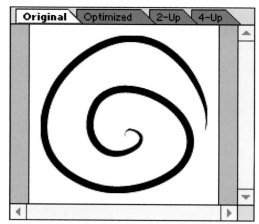

I. Open **bw.psd**.

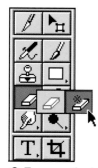 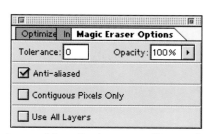

2. To erase the background from the image, you'll use a fantastic new tool called the **Magic Eraser. Note:** If the **Magic Eraser** is not selected (it has a little cluster of dots on its upper left) press your mouse on the **Eraser** tool until a pop-up menu of other tool choices appears and select the **Magic Eraser**. Double-click the **Magic Eraser** icon on the toolbar to open the **Magic Eraser Options** palette. Set the properties to match the settings you see above, **Tolerance: 0, Anti-aliased**.

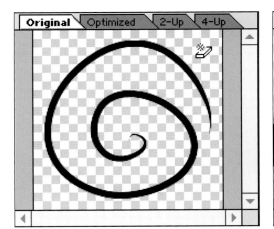 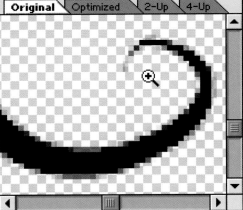

3. Click anywhere on the white background and the background color will be deleted.

4. Choose the **Zoom** tool from the toolbar and click to zoom in and examine the image close up. (The letter **Z** is the shortcut key for the **Zoom** tool at the bottom right of the ImageReady toolbar.) You'll see that the edge of the black spiral shape is anti-aliased. That's going to help you keep smooth edge when you recolor the image. To zoom back out, hold down the **Option** (Mac) or **Alt** (Windows) key and click on the image again with the **Zoom** tool. **Tip:** If you need a refresher on anti-aliasing, revisit Chapter 6, *"Type."*

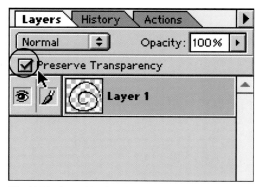

5. With the white background out of the picture, you can now add some color to the spiral. Select the **Layer 1** in the **Layers** palette and check **Preserve Transparency**.

When you fill the layer with a new color in the next step, ImageReady will fill only the layer's image area – the spiral – and will preserve the transparent areas.

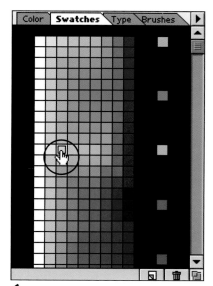

6. Choose **Window > Show Swatches** to bring up the **Swatches** palette. You should still have the **color.aco** palette loaded from Chapter 5, *"Web Color."* This palette is arranged so that colors selected from the same vertical row will have the very similar values. Click on a color to select it, then press **Option+Delete** (Mac) or **Alt+Delete** (Windows).

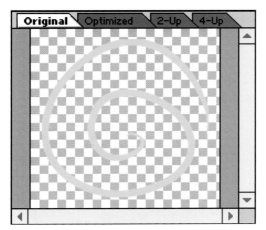

After you select a color, your spiral shape will fill with the color you selected.

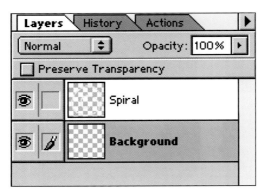

7. Click on the new layer icon at the bottom of the **Layers** palette. Double-click on the layer to rename it. In the **Layer Options** dialog box, name this layer **Background**. Then double-click on **Layer 1** and rename it **Spiral**. Drag the **Background** layer below the **Spiral** layer in the **Layers** palette. You'll see a heavy, dark line below the **Spiral** layer once you drag the **Background** layer into its new position when you do this correctly. Let go with your mouse and it should end up below the **Spiral** layer.

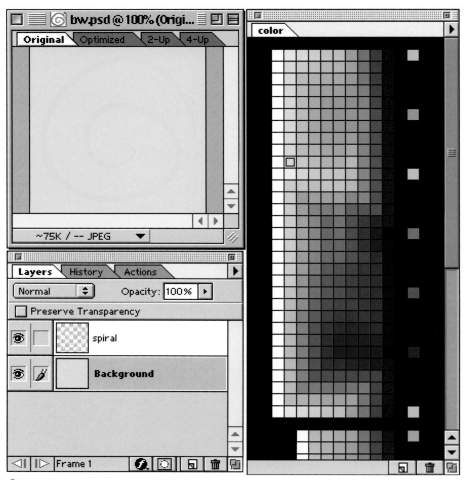

8. Select the **Background** layer. Make sure that the **Preserve Transparency** box isn't checked. Select another color from the same vertical row in the **Swatches** palette and press **Option+Delete** (Mac) or **Alt+Delete** (Windows) to fill the **Background** layer with the second color. Your image's background will be filled with the color you selected.

*The reason I suggested you choose another color from the same vertical row in the **Swatches** palette was because it will have a similar value (lightness or darkness). This swatch set is organized by lights and darks, and if you're looking to match the value you can choose from a vertical row and do so successfully.*

*Note: You didn't need to check **Preserve Transparency** in Step 9 because you filled all the transparent pixels of the **Background** Layer with a color. **Preserve Transparency** is only useful when you want to change the color of active pixels in a layer, as you did in the previous step. In fact, if you check **Preserve Transparency** for a layer that has no active pixels, such as this one, the feature will actually prevent you from filling the layer with color. For more information on **Preserve Transparency**, revisit Chapter 5, "Web Color," where it was first introduced.*

9. Save and close this document, and leave ImageReady open.

Now that you've learned this coloring procedure, you can experiment with different color combinations. It's easy to make color changes when you work in layers, isn't it? As you can see, the colors I've selected are extremely close in value and that makes the pattern effect very subtle. By "value" in this instance, I mean that the colors are of similar lightness. Value is the measurement of light or dark color. If you want, you can preview this image in your Web browser to get a better idea of how this particular color combination performs inside a background tile. If you don't remember how to preview an image as a background image, revisit Exercise 1 in this chapter.

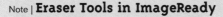

Note | **Eraser Tools in ImageReady**

Standard Eraser

Magic Eraser

There are two eraser tools in ImageReady – the standard **Eraser** and the **Magic Eraser**. The standard **Eraser** subtracts color based on what areas of the image on which you click and drag over. The **Magic Eraser** is a better choice when you want to subtract areas of your image based on color, like in this last exercise. It would have been pretty tricky to exactly erase all the white away from the black with the standard **Eraser**, hence the need for a "Magic" Eraser.

4.————————**Seamless Background Tiles**

The background images you created so far have produced a very obvious-looking pattern once pre-viewed in a browser. In the following exercises, you'll learn how use ImageReady's **Offset** filter to create the appearance of a seamless background effect.

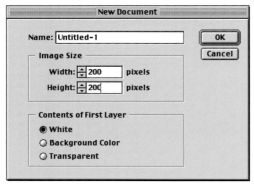

I. Create a new document that is **200 x 200** pixels against a white background. This is just a recommended size; you can make the canvas larger or smaller if you like. Leave it untitled for now.

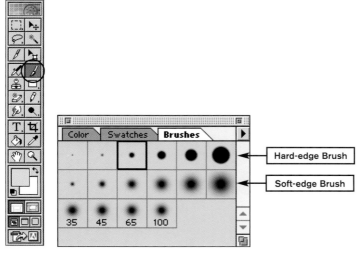

2. Select the **Paintbrush** from the toolbar. You can select a hard- or soft-edge brush from the **Brushes** palette (choose **Window > Show Brushes** if it's not visible).

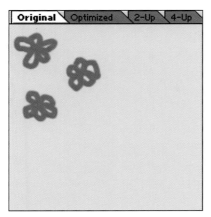

3. Draw an image on your canvas. Make sure that you do not draw to the very edge of the canvas and that your image does not touch the edge of the document window (or in this case, the light green area). I intentionally draw the artwork in one corner, so that I can easily see where I last drew shapes as I apply the **Offset** filter.

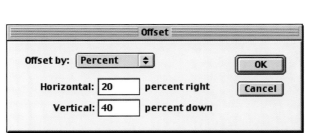

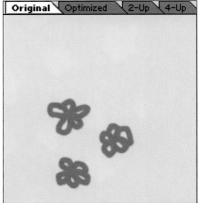

4. Select **Filter > Other > Offset....** In the **Offset** dialog box, enter **Horizontal: 20** and **Vertical: 40**. Click **OK**.

*I usually pick irregular values other than the defaults (which are **50** x **50** percent) to better create a non-symmetrical background. Since a seamless tile should look organic and not predictable, it is better to use irregular numeric values so the offset is less predictable.*

*The **Offset** filter shifts your original image to the right and down, and wraps it so that part of your image will drop off one edge of the screen and appear at the opposite edge.*

5. Continue to draw inside the blank areas of the image.

6. Press **Cmd+F** (Mac) or **Ctrl+F** (Windows) to apply the **Offset** filter again. **Note:** This keyboard shortcut will reapply whichever filter you last applied. This will again shift the pixels and wrap them around the image, opening a blank area on the canvas. Continue to draw, filling in the blank areas without touching the edge of your canvas.

Notice that there is no large unfilled area in this image.

7. Press **Cmd+F** (Mac) or **Ctrl+F** (Windows) to apply the **Offset** filter again. You may need to repeat the **Offset** filter process several times until no large areas of white are visible.

8. To see what this image looks like in the browser, you must first identify it as an **HTML Background** (as you did in Exercise 1, select **File > HTML Background...**, then select **View As: Background** and click **OK**).

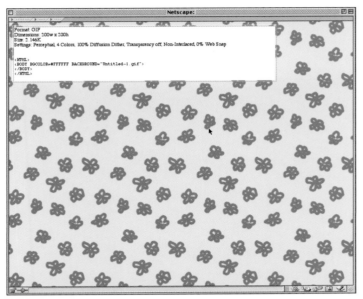

9. Next, preview in a browser (**File > Preview in**).

10. Return to ImageReady and select **File > Save As** to save the original file. Name the file **tilebg.psd** and save it inside your **chap_07** folder.

It's always a good idea to save both a Photoshop document (.psd) and an optimized graphic, so that you can re-edit the image if you ever want to.

11. Check the **Optimize** palette to make sure this image's settings are set to GIF and the number of colors are low, because it is made up of flat colors and is not continuous tone like a photograph. If you need a refresher on how to make the smallest possible GIF, revisit Chapter 4, *"Optimization."*

12. Select **File > Save Optimized As...** to save the optimized file as a GIF. The application will offer to name it **tilebg.gif** for you.

13. Save and close it.

 Movie | **offset.mov**

To learn more about how to use the **Offset** filter to create a seamless background image, check out **offset.mov** from the **movies** folder on the **H•O•T CD-ROM**.

Saving Options in ImageReady

There are many different **Save** options in ImageReady. Here's a handy chart that explains them.

Save Options	
Function	**Result**
Save Optimized	Saves the file with its current optimization settings and file name.
Save Optimized As...	Saves the file with its current optimization settings and enables you to change the file name. It can also overwrite an old file if you save it with the same name. When you use this feature, ImageReady opens the new file with the new file name that you saved.
Update HTML...	Allows you to overwrite HTML that Image-Ready generated. You will get to try this out in Chapter 14, *"Importing/Exporting."*
Save	Saves the file as a .psd.
Save As...	Saves the file as a .psd and enables you to change the name. It can also overwrite an old file if you save it with the same name. When you use this feature, ImageReady opens the new file with the new file name that you saved.
Export Original	Offers other file format options, such as Amiga IFF, BMP, PCX, PICT, Pixar, Quick-Time Movie, Targa, and TIFF.

Copying and Pasting with Offset

There's another way to create a seamless background tile in ImageReady. In this exercise, you'll apply the **Offset** filter after you've copied and pasted existing artwork into a new document.

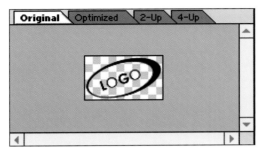

I. Open **logo.psd**.

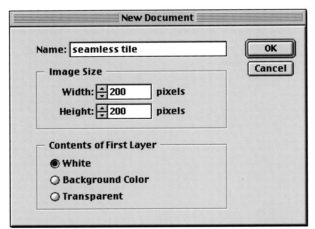

2. Choose **File > New** and create a new document that is **200 x 200** pixels against a white background. Type **Name: seamless tile**. You can make the canvas larger or smaller if you like, but you should make it larger than the artwork you're using. The relationship between the size of the tile you're creating and the size of the source artwork will determine the spacing of the logo on the background tile.

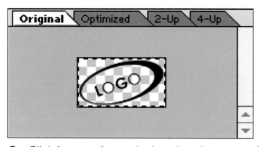

3. Click **logo.psd** to make it active, then press **Cmd+A** (Mac) or **Ctrl+A** (Windows) to select the entire image area.

4. Press **Cmd+C** (Mac) or **Ctrl+C** (Windows) to copy the logo. Click on your new, empty document to make it active and then press **Cmd+V** (Mac) or **Ctrl+V** (Windows) to paste the logo.

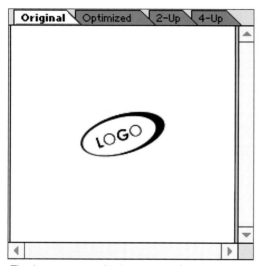

The logo appears in the center of the document. Whenever you paste an element into a document, ImageReady automatically centers it. With the logo in place, you're ready to apply the **Offset** *filter.*

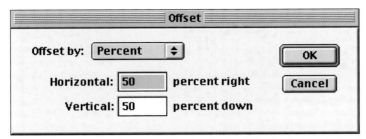

5. Choose **Filter > Other > Offset….** In the **Offset** window that will appear, match the settings to what you see above and click **OK**.

*In this instance, you will be making a symmetrical repeating tile, so leaving the default settings at **50** percent by **50** percent is a desirable thing.*

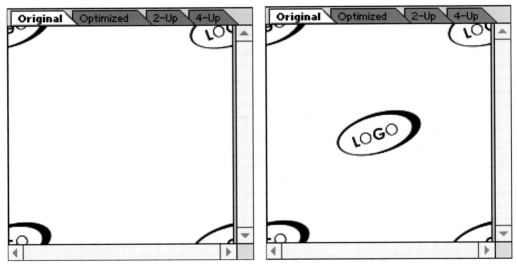

6. The logo looks like it's split into four quarters, which are now positioned at the four corners of the tile. Press **Cmd+V** (Mac) or **Ctrl+V** (Windows) again to paste another copy of the logo into the center.

7. Identify this image as an HTML background (select **File > HTML Background…**, then select **View As: Background** and click **OK**).

Now you're ready to preview your seamless background tile in a browser to see the results of your labor.

8. Choose **File > Preview in** and select a browser.

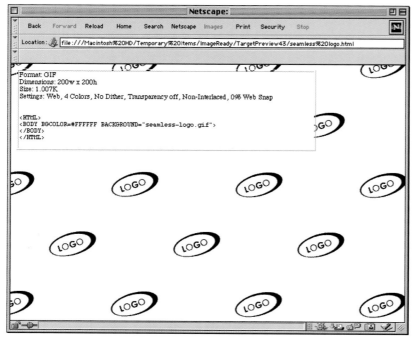

Here are the results of the preview. The first logo you pasted, which was offset by **50** percent using the **Offset** filter and split to the four corners of the tile, is flawlessly reassembled in the browser window when the image is tiled as a background.

This background effect is very symmetrical and formal. Each repeat of the logo is an equal distance from all the others. That's because you started with a square image, pasted both logos to the document's center, and set both the **Horizontal** and **Vertical** offset values to **50** percent. You can also use the **Offset** filter to create a range of less symmetrical effects, by adjusting the offset percentages.

Now that you've previewed this document, you can go back and experiment with adjusting the **Offset** filter settings or try doing the exercise over with a smaller or larger tile size. You could also recolor the logo or the background, using the techniques you learned in Exercise 3.

8. When you're finished playing, save the file. See if you can remember how to save it as both a .gif and a .psd. **Tip: File > Save Optimized As...** and **File > Save As....** When you've saved the file, close it because it won't be needed again in this chapter.

Ways to Access the Offset Filter in ImageReady

You might have noticed that there are two different ways to access the **Offset** Filter in ImageReady. Here's a chart to explain the differences.

Offset Filter	
Option	**Result**
Filter > Other > Offset...	This is the way to access the **Offset** Filter when you want to enter new settings.
Filter > Offset...	This is the way to access the **Offset** Filter when you want to reapply the **Offset** Filter with the same settings as before.

Note | **The Offset Filter in Photoshop**

Offset
Horizontal: 0   pixels right   [OK]
Vertical: 0   pixels down   [Cancel]
Undefined Areas   ☑ Preview
○ Set to Background
○ Repeat Edge Pixels
● Wrap Around

If you want to use the **Offset** Filter in Photoshop, it can be accessed by choosing **Filter > Other > Offset**. Photoshop uses a slightly different interface than ImageReady for the **Offset** Filter. It doesn't have a percent option and it offers non-wraparound options (such as **Set to Background** and **Repeat Edge Pixels**). You can make seamless tiles in Photoshop using the **Wrap Around** setting. The major drawback to creating background images in Photoshop is that they cannot be previewed in the browser.

6. _____Seamless Photographic Background Images

Seamless background images are not limited to graphics. With ImageReady 2.0's **Tile Maker** Filter, photographs can be the source of beautiful seamless background images. This filter overlaps and blends the edges of an image, which creates a convincing seamless pattern effect. Consider this approach if you are looking for ways to incorporate seamless photographic backgrounds into your Web design.

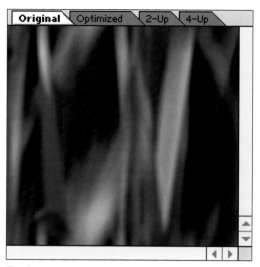

I. Open **grass.psd**.

2. Choose **File > HTML Background....** In the dialog box, change **View As:** to **Background**, then click **OK**.

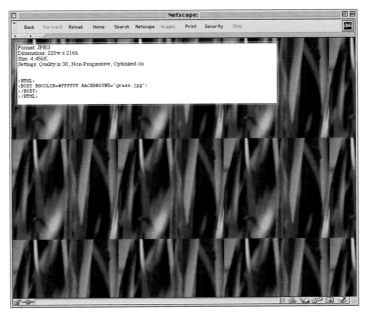

Format: JPEG
Dimensions: 220w x 216h
Size: 4.456K
Settings: Quality is 30, Non-Progressive, Optimized on

```
<HTML>
<BODY BGCOLOR=#FFFFFF BACKGROUND="grass.jpg">
</BODY>
</HTML>
```

3. Choose **File > Preview in** and select a browser .

Notice the obvious edges from the seams of the source image? The **Tile Maker** *Filter will fix those in a snap.*

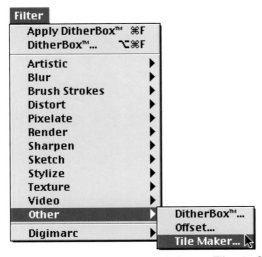

4. Return to ImageReady and choose **Filter > Other > Tile Maker....**

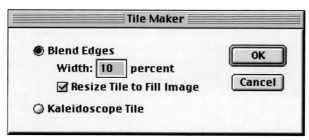

5. The **Tile Maker** dialog box will appear. Above, you see the default settings – **Blend Edges** selected, **Width: 10** percent, and **Resize Tile to Fill Image** checked. Click **OK**.

Tip: Kaleidoscope Tile can also give you some beautiful abstract effects, so you might want to experiment with it later.

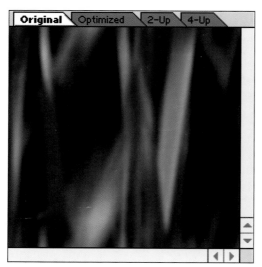

Here's what the image will look like after you apply the filter. You can see it's a little magnified, but the true difference is easier to see when you preview it.

6. Choose **File > Preview in** and then choose whichever browser you prefer.

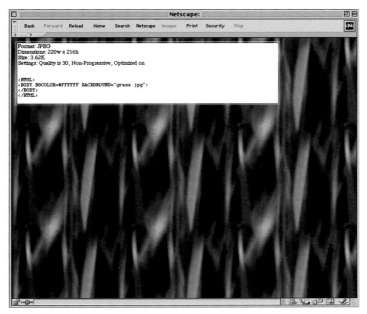

In a browser, the background has become a little softer and the edge blending has hidden the sharp edges where the grass blades run off the image.

Tip: If you want to preview just the background without the HTML information box displayed, generate an HTML document by choosing File > Save Optimized As... and in the dialog box check both Save HTML File and Save Images. If you need a refresher on saving and previewing, revisit Exercise 2.

Although this image is attractive and has no seams, it contains too much contrast to read with text over it. The next step will show you one of my favorite methods for modifying an image's brightness and hue.

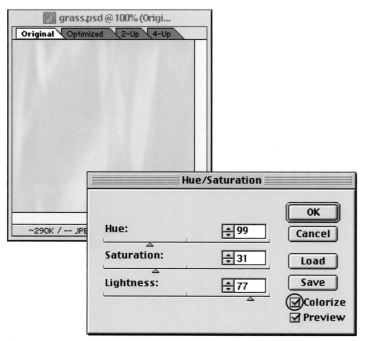

7. In ImageReady, choose **Image > Adjust > Hue/Saturation...** Try the settings that you see here or pick some you like better. Notice that **Colorize** is checked? That's what's making the image turn from full color to monochromatic. You can uncheck it if you want to keep the natural colors of the image. Click **OK**.

8. Optimize and preview the results. This background image would be much easier to work with if you were trying to make text read over it.

9. Close the file. If you want to save it, revisit the previous exercises that have described how to do so. Keep ImageReady open for the next exercise.

Which Program Is Best for Background Images?

It is challenging to remember which program is best for creating background images, when each program can perform certain functions but not others. Here's a handy chart to refer to when you question which is best.

Creating Background Images Program Choice		
	Photoshop 5.0	ImageReady 2.0
Offset Filter	•	•
Tile Maker Filter		•
Make Custom Brushes	•	
Save Custom Brushes	•	
Load Custom Brushes	•	•
Preview Backgrounds in Browser		•

7. ————Full-Screen Background Images

Using a full-screen graphic as a background image can produce an impressive effect. If optimized properly, a full-screen graphic doesn't have to be too large to download efficiently, particularly if you limit your colors and use large areas of flat color. I recommend that you make all your full-screen background images at least **1024 x 768**, even if you are designing your site to work at a smaller resolution. It's important that the background looks good when viewed at all sizes, from **640 x 480**, to **800 x 600**, all the way up to **1024 x 768**. Feature film directors face this problem when they shoot a wide screen film that will also come out on video. Most directors try to frame their shots to look good in both the wide-screen theatrical screen size and your home TV. You can use the same idea to design a flexible full-screen graphic background that looks good in a variety of browser windows.

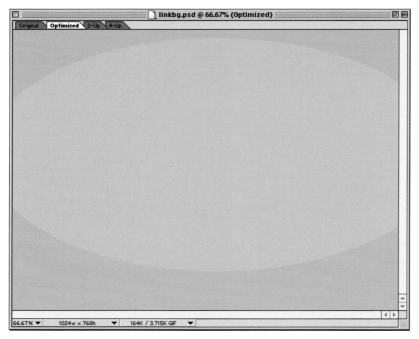

1. Open **linkbg.psd**.

This is the background image from the Links page of our lynda.com Web site. It's a big file – 1024 x 768 pixels – but when optimized as a GIF with four colors its file size is less than 4K. Images with large areas of solid colors like this optimize unbelievably well. Downloading speed won't be an issue, but how will this graphic look when viewed at different resolutions?

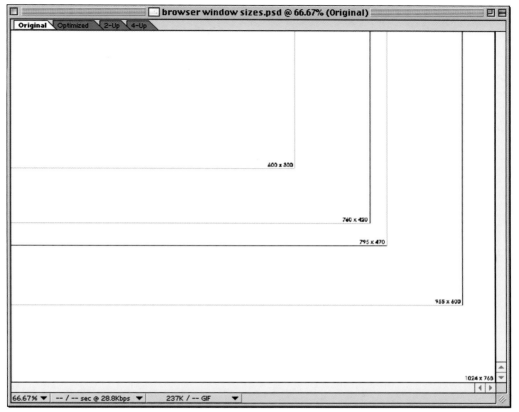

2. Open **browser window sizes.psd**. This Photoshop file can be used as an overlay for full-screen background images. It will help you to understand exactly how the image will be cropped at different resolutions.

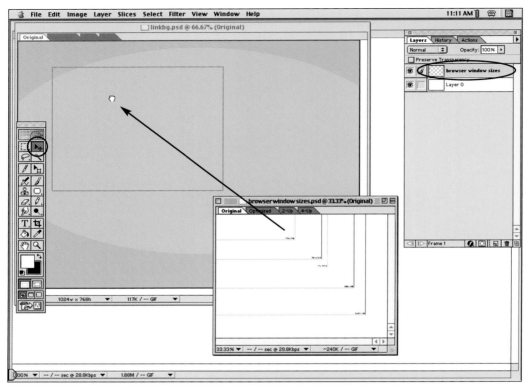

3. While in **browser window sizes.psd**, select the **Move** tool from the toolbar, make sure the layer labeled **browser window sizes** is selected, and click and drag the file into the open **linkbg.psd**.

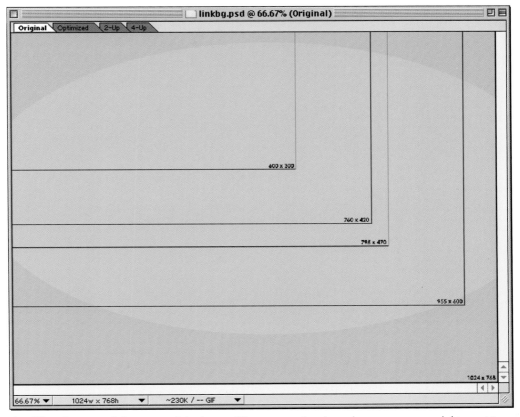

4. Align the upper-left corner of the layers. These are rather large images, so you might want to zoom in to fine-tune the alignment.

*Tip: To get the two aligned just so, you might want to go back and forth between the letters **Z** and **V** (the **Zoom** tool and the **Move** tool). Remember that to zoom back out, you'll need to hold down the **Option** (Mac) or **Alt** (Windows) key and click on the image again. We move this overlay document into our full-screen background images all the time at lynda.com to visualize how background images will look at different sizes.*

Movie | **dragginglayer.mov**

To learn more about how to drag a layer from one document into another, check out **dragginglayer.mov** from the **movies** folder on the **H•O•T CD-ROM**.

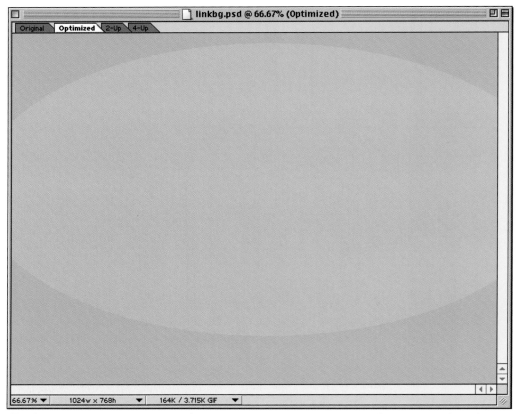

5. When you're ready to create a GIF of the image, be sure to turn the **browser window sizes** layer off by turning off its visibility with the eye icon. If you need a refresher on how to optimize this as a GIF, revisit Chapter 4, *"Optimization."*

6. Close both files.

The point of this exercise was to show you how to use an overlay to visualize how a large image would look in smaller browsers. You don't actually want to publish the graphic with the overlay; it's just there for your reference only. Feel free, in fact, to steal this overlay and use it on all your large background images. We find it useful and I hope you do too.

[IR]

8. Large-Screen Photographic Background Images

In addition to working with large graphics for background images, it's also possible to work with large photographs. The key is to compress the photograph so that it's small enough to download at a reasonable speed on most browsers. This exercise will allow you to explore some of the optimization options for large-screen photographic images.

I. Open **purpleorange.psd**. Click on the **Optimize** palette and choose the **JPEG** format. With the settings above, I was able to reduce the image size to around 33K.

*Tip: If you recall, there are a few other ways to make a photograph smaller. One thing that would make it smaller and easier to read text over it, would be to reduce the contrast and saturation. Be sure to click back on the **Original** tab before making these adjustments, otherwise the program will slow down because it will try to optimize the image with each change you make.*

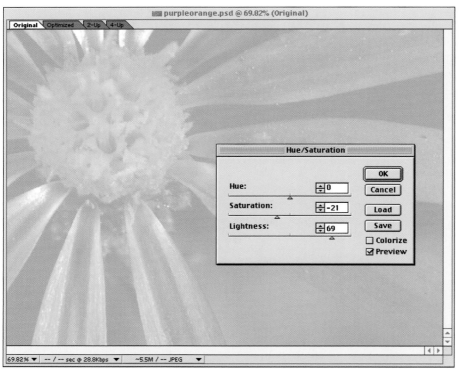

2. Choose **Image > Adjust > Hue/Saturation....** Match the settings shown above or experiment with your own. Click **OK** when you're happy with the results.

3. Click on the **Optimized** tab again to see if the file size got smaller. The changes I made brought the image down to 13K.

4. When you are ready to preview the image, choose **File > HTML Background...**, click on **View As: Background**, and preview in a browser. Once you're happy with the results, you can chose to **Save Optimized As...**, which will save a JPEG version of this document, or **Save As...**, which will save a **.psd** file. Either way, close the file.

9. Directional Tiles

A wonderful trick that's widely used on the Web is to make what are called directional tiles — graphics that are narrow and tall or wide and narrow before you preview them, but that expand into full screen images when repeated as background images. You can create the illusion of a big full-screen graphic background with a tiny tile. A tall, skinny directional tile like the one below will repeat from left to right across the browser window and create a background of broad horizontal stripes.

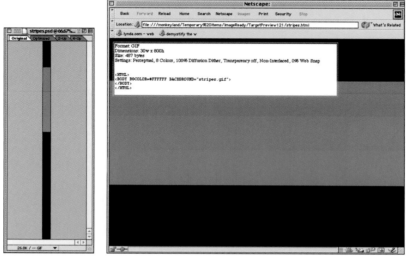

I. Open **stripes.psd** and identify it as an HTML background (choose **File > HTML Background...**, choose **View As: Background** and click **OK**). Choose **File > Preview in** and select a browser. Notice the effect of the long and narrow tile — it repeats in a horizontal fashion.

2. Return to ImageReady and rotate the artwork by choosing **Image > Rotate Canvas > 90°CW**.

*The **CW** stands for clockwise, so this will rotate the image to the right. **CCW** stands for counter clockwise.*

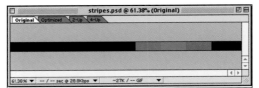

3. Resize the window to make it horizontal by dragging it from its bottom-right handle.

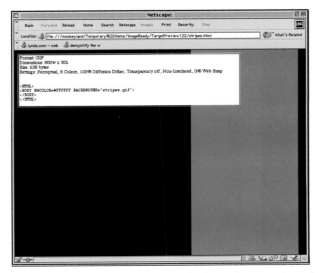

4. Choose **File > Preview in** and select a browser from the list again.

This ought to give you an idea of how these directional tiles work. Try changing the image inside this graphic, and watch the results. Fill it with a different color scheme or select and fill a new area for a new stripe. The sky's the limit now that you know how images repeat inside browsers and you have ImageReady's great preview options at your disposal!

5. Save and close the file. You've finished another chapter, folks!

8.

Transparent GIFs

Problems with GIF Transparency	Transparency Terminology
Creating and Previewing Transparency	Fixing Bad Edges
Pitfalls of Backgrounds	Saving Transparent GIFs	GIF89a Export

chap_08

Photoshop 5.5 / ImageReady 2.0
H•O•T CD-ROM

By default, all images made on the computer are in the shape of a rectangle or square. The only way to make an image appear in a different shape is to apply a mask which hides the square or rectangular nature of the document. At the moment, GIF is the only format in wide use for the Web that supports the ability to mask. Unfortunately, masking is very limited in this format and can produce unwanted fringing and halos around transparent GIF images. That's the bad news. The good news is this chapter describes this problem in detail and offers solutions.

Photoshop 5.5 and ImageReady 2.0 both have marvelous support for creating transparent GIFs. The two applications counter the problems that are inherent to transparency in the GIF format with a set of excellent tools. This chapter's exercises are designed to help you master these tools.

Problems with GIF Transparency

Any time you create an image in Photoshop (or ImageReady) that contains a drop shadow, soft edge, or even an anti-aliased edge, you are using 8-bit transparency. Photoshop uses 256 levels of opacity to create drop shadows, glows, or soft, feathered edges.

Sadly, the GIF format only supports 1-bit masking (pixels are on or off) instead of the beautiful 8-bit masking that Photoshop supports. Whenever an image contains anti-aliasing, glows, or soft edges of any kind, the GIF transparency poses a challenge because of its 1-bit limitation.

Photoshop Anti-Aliased Edge

Photoshop Glow

Photoshop and ImageReady use up to 256 levels of Opacity when layering artwork. This is called 8-bit transparency.

GIF Anti-Aliased Edge

GIF Glow Edge

The GIF file format is limited to 1-color masking, and can't display or support any transparent pixels when layering artwork over background images. This is called 1-bit masking. The problem is that 1-bit masking produces halos around the edges of transparent GIF graphics. You will learn how to control this problem in this chapter.

What Does Anti-Aliasing Look Like?

Anti-aliasing is a common computer term that describes an edge of a graphic that blends into a neighboring color. Most computer graphics programs offer this ability, which hides the jagged nature of pixel-based artwork.

An Anti-Aliased Edge

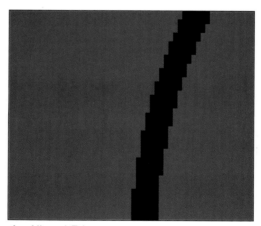

An Aliased Edge

How to Recognize a Transparent Layer

In order to create transparent GIF files in Photoshop or ImageReady, your artwork must be first created on or converted to a Photoshop transparent layer. How can you tell if your Photoshop or ImageReady document uses a transparent layer? If you see a checkerboard background behind the image, it's a transparent layer.

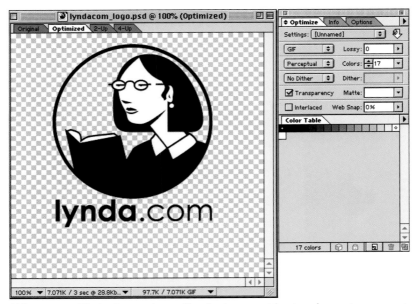

Whenever a Photoshop or ImageReady document is stored on a transparent layer, you will see a checkerboard pattern in the background. If you have other layers turned on that prevent you from seeing the checkerboard background, turn them off before you save the image as a transparent GIF. You'll find this process described in detail in this chapter.

Offset Problems in Browsers

You might wonder, why the fuss with all this transparency stuff? Couldn't you simply make a foreground image with the background image incorporated and lay that over the same background image? Good question. Here's why you can't. Because foreground and background images don't line up in browsers, you'd end up with an unwanted offset, as shown below.

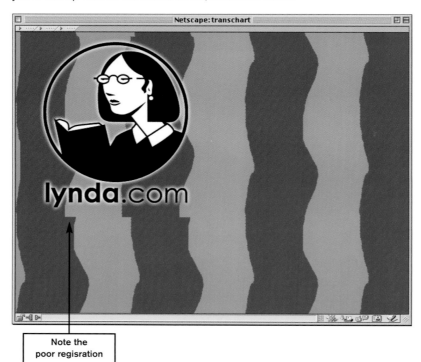

Note the
poor regisration

You can't forgo transparency layers and just lay foreground and background images together, because foreground and background images don't line up in browsers. This method would not ensure good registration between the two elements. You can do better than this by learning the methods described in this chapter.

Transparency, Masks, and GIFs

Here's a helpful chart to explain some of the terminology used in this chapter.

Transparency Terminology	
Term	**Definition**
Mask	A mask hides parts of an image from being visible. In the case of a transparent GIF file, the mask is what hides the transparent areas of the image, but the mask itself is not visible to the end user.
Transparent Photoshop Layer	The checkerboard pattern on a Photoshop layer indicates that there is a mask in effect. When you draw a shape on a new layer in Photoshop, an invisible mask (called the **Transparency Channel**) is invoked.
Transparent GIF	A transparent GIF includes an invisible mask and is seen by the Web browser in shapes other than square or rectangle. This chapter shows you how to mask out parts of GIF images.
GIF	A GIF can be transparent or not. The only thing that makes it transparent is if you specify the transparent setting in Photoshop or ImageReady.

I. _____Creating and Previewing GIF Transparency

You can create transparent GIF files in either Photoshop or ImageReady. I prefer to do this task in ImageReady because its previewing capabilities are superior to Photoshop's. This first exercise will teach you how to set GIF transparency and how to preview the results in a browser.

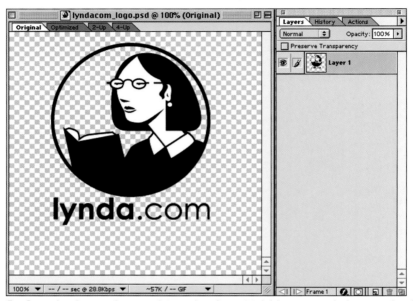

I. Open **lyndacom_logo.psd** from the **chap_08** folder you copied to your hard drive from the **H•O•T CD-ROM**.

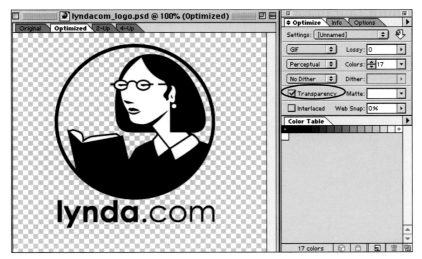

2. Click on the **Optimized** tab and make sure that the **Optimize** and **Color Table** palettes are visible. If they are not, choose **Window > Show Optimize** or **Window > Show Color Table** to open them. In the **Optimize** palette, match the compression settings to what you see above: **GIF**, **Perceptual**, **Colors 17**, **No Dither**. Make sure that you can see the **Transparency** checkbox on the **Optimize** palette, and that it is checked. **Tip:** If you don't see this setting, expand the palette to display all its options by clicking on its upper-right arrow and selecting **Show Options**.

3. Choose **File > HTML Background....** In the **HTML Background** window that will appear, choose **View As: Image**.

This lets ImageReady know that when you preview this image, you want to see it displayed as a foreground image.

4. The **HTML Background** window is also the place where you specify the background image or color you'd like to see your transparent foreground image displayed over. Click the **Choose** button and navigate to the **chap_08** folder of the **H•O•T CD-ROM**. Select **fine_bg.gif** and click **Open**. You will be returned to the **HTML Background** dialog box, and the path name to the file should appear inside the **Background Image** field. Click **OK**.

5. Choose **File > Preview in** and select a browser. The **lynda.com** logo will appear over the background image you selected.

You can see that the transparent settings are working, but notice the white fringe around the edges of the image? You'll learn to eliminate that problem in the next exercise. The white box with HTML text is a product of the preview; in order to get rid of it you would need to choose **File > Save Optimized As** *and save the images and the HTML. You learned how to do this in Chapter 7, "Background Images." You may want to revisit it for a refresher on saving HTML.*

6. Return to ImageReady and leave the same document open for the next exercise.

[IR]

2.————————**Fixing Bad Edges**

In the last exercise, you learned to specify transparency and preview the results against a patterned background. This resulted in an unwanted edge that is commonly referred to as a "fringe," "halo," or "matte." This next exercise shows you how to eliminate this bad edge so that the resulting preview will look good.

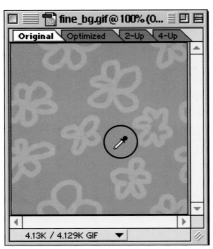

1. With the **lyndacom_logo.psd** file still open, choose **File > Open** and select **fine_bg.gif**. Select the **Eyedropper** from the toolbar, and click on the orange background to sample the color.

*The reason why I asked you to select this color is so you could specify it as the **Matte** color for your transparent GIF. You'll learn how to do this in the next step, but the important thing is to first get the color into the **Foreground Color** swatch of the toolbar.*

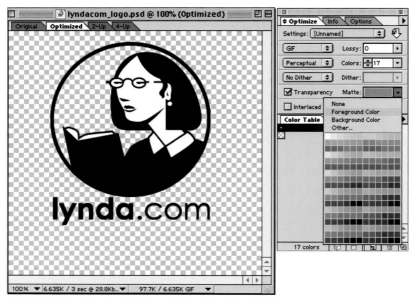

2. Return to the **lyndacom_logo.psd**, which you should still have open from the last exercise. (You can simply click on it, or select **Window > lyndacom_logo.psd**.) Click on the **Optimized** tab in the document window. In the **Optimize** palette, click on the down-pointing arrow to the right of the **Matte:** field. Select **Foreground Color** from the pop-up menu. The same orange color that you just put in the toolbar will appear inside the **Matte:** field. **Note:** If you look closely at the edge of the image, you might also see that the same orange color was put underneath the anti-aliased edge of the graphic.

Movie | **setting_mattecolor.mov**

To learn more about setting **Matte** color, shown in Step 2, check out **setting_mattecolor.mov** inside the **movies** folder you transferred to your hard drive from the **H·O·T CD-ROM**.

3. Check this out in a browser (**File > Preview in**).

*The background image is still specified from the last exercise, so you will see the foreground image laid over the **fine_bg.gif** again, only with its new orange edge. With a fine-toothed background pattern like this, even though the background is busy, the matte color produces a nice, clean edge.*

4. Return to ImageReady and leave **lyndacom_logo.psd** open for the next exercise. You won't need **fine_bg.gif**, so close it.

3. ——————— Adding a Drop Shadow

On a simple anti-aliased edge, changing the matte color to match the background image did the trick. What if the edge of your foreground image contains a drop shadow or soft edge? This next exercise will show you what to do.

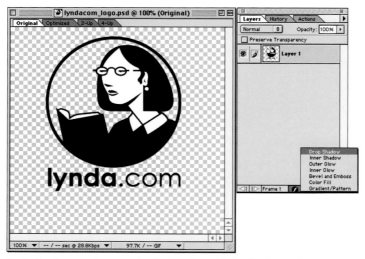

I. In **lyndacom_logo.psd**, click on the **Original** tab to add the **Drop Shadow Layer Effect**. Add a **Layer Effect** to the **Layers** palette (**Window > Show Layers)** by clicking on the **Layer Effect (f)** icon at the bottom of the palette and selecting **Drop Shadow** from the pop-up menu. You can leave this **Layer Effect** at its default settings for this exercise.

*Tip: I typically like to edit images when I'm on the **Original** tab, otherwise ImageReady tries to optimize the graphic as I'm editing it, which slows things down. When you're on the **Original** tab it's also possible to perform editing tasks (such as drawing or typing) that are not allowed when the document is set to the **Optimized** tab.*

2. Click on the **Optimized** tab again. The image will appear with a gangly orange border around it because of the matte color you assigned to it.

While it looks extremely yucky here, it will look just fine against the background image in a browser, which you'll get to preview in the next step.

3. Check this out in a browser (**File > Preview in**).

If you look closely you can see the trick, but this technique will be acceptable on the Web, and it sure beats having unwanted colored edges around your images.

4. Return to ImageReady and leave the file open. Don't worry about saving it just yet. The next exercise will show you a situation where the technique you just learned won't work.

[IR] **4.** ——————**The Pitfalls of Broad Backgrounds**

The reason the orange matte worked so well in the previous exercises is because the specified background image contained a fine-tooth pattern that contained the same orange you assigned as the matte color. This technique does not work in every scenario, as you'll see when you switch background images in this exercise.

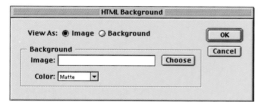

I. With **lyndacom_logo.psd** open, choose **File > HTML Background...**. In the **HTML Background** window, click **Choose** and select **broad_bg.gif** from the **chap_08** folder. Click **Open**. Back in the **HTML Background** dialog box, click **OK**.

2. Preview this in a browser (**File > Preview in**). Ugh... the results are not pretty.

*This is a case when matching the **Matte** to the background image will not work, because the color changes in the background image are too broad. If you changed the matte color to green it would show up in the orange areas; if you changed it to orange it would look as it does here. The solution is to remove the drop shadow effect, the orange matte color, and the anti-aliasing along the edge.*

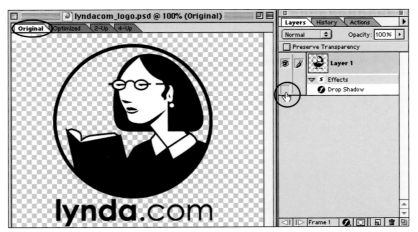

3. Return to ImageReady and click on the **Original** tab. Turn off the **Layer Effect** that was added in the last exercise by clicking on the eye icon to its left.

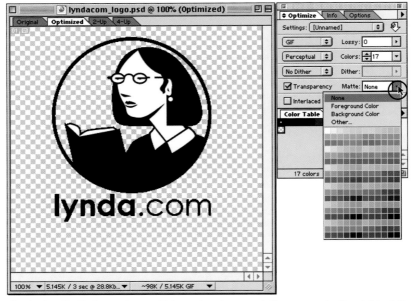

4. In the **Optimize** palette, click on the down-pointing arrow to the right of the **Matte:** field, and choose **None** from the pop-up menu. This removes all the anti-aliasing from the edge of the logo.

*The nice thing about using **Matte: None** is that it only removes anti-aliasing from the edges of the graphic. Anti-aliasing within the logo is still preserved.*

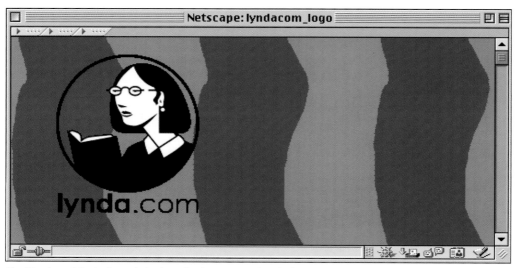

5. Preview this. It doesn't look so bad anymore, but it doesn't contain the drop shadow either.

Actually, there is nothing you can do to save the drop shadow except to use a different background like the fine tooth pattern that was used before. On broad backgrounds you can't use any matte color because the illusion will be broken over the changing colored image. This is a limitation of the GIF file format, and not ImageReady or Photoshop's fault.

6. Return to ImageReady and keep the same image open.

5. ————————**Saving Transparent Images**

So far, you've learned to preview transparent GIF images over background images, but you haven't saved anything yet. This exercise will focus on saving techniques in ImageReady.

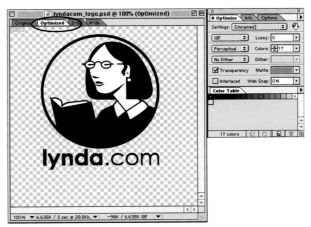

1. Click on the **Optimized** tab of the **lyndacom_logo.psd** document window to ensure that the transparency settings are configured how you want. Decide whether or not to choose a **Matte** color or none, based on all the previewing techniques you have learned.

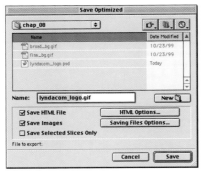

2. Choose **File > Save Optimized As...**. ImageReady will insert the .gif extension at the end of the file name. **Note:** The file you are saving will carry all of the settings that are inside the **Optimize** palette. If you want to save the HTML, which specifies the background image as well, check **Save HTML File** as well as **Save Images**. This choice depends on whether you would like ImageReady to build your page or work within an HTML editor such as GoLive or Dreamweaver. Either way, click the **Save** button.

3. Close the file.

6. _____Transparency in Photoshop

I mentioned earlier in the chapter that transparency could be specified from within Photoshop as well. I said that I preferred ImageReady because of its preview capabilities. As you might now realize, being able to preview the transparent foreground image against a background image can help you understand which **Matte** technique to use. Still, there are times that it will be more convenient to work inside Photoshop, so this next exercise will teach you how to create transparent GIFs there.

1. Open Photoshop. Choose **File > Open** and navigate to **lyndacom_logo.psd** inside the **chap_08** folder.

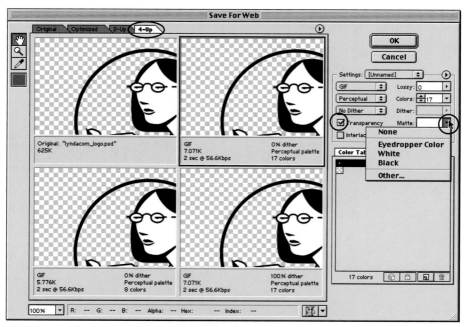

2. Choose **File > Save for Web...** and the file will open inside the **Save For Web** dialog box. If you are not in the **4-Up** view, as shown above, go ahead and click on the **4-Up** tab so you can compare optimization settings. It's important that **Transparency** is checked, and that your preferred optimization settings are selected in the **4-Up** display.

3. Click the arrow to the right of the **Matte:** field, and you'll see that you have similar choices to those that you had in ImageReady, except there is no color swatch. If you want to pick a color, you can choose **Other...** from this pop-up menu.

Note: You don't need to choose anything in this step; you're just looking at the differences between doing the exercise in Photoshop versus ImageReady.

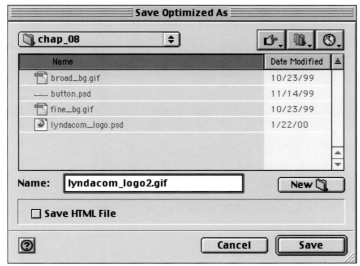

4. Click **OK**. You'll have the choice to save it with or without the HTML file. Because you can't specify a background image inside Photoshop, there would be little reason to save the HTML, so do not check the **Save HTML File** checkbox. Because you saved an earlier version of **lyndacom_logo.gif** from the last exercise, change the name to **lyndacom_logo2.gif**.

5. Click **Save**. That's all there is to creating a transparent GIF in Photoshop! Close the file.

7. Transparent Layer Versus Transparent GIF

Though you've worked so far on the **lyndacom_logo.psd** in this chapter, you might not realize that it was created against a Photoshop transparent layer and then made into a transparent GIF. Why is this important for you to know? Because it's impossible to create a transparent GIF unless your Photoshop document contains transparent areas. This exercise should help you learn how to turn off layers so you can access a file's transparent layers.

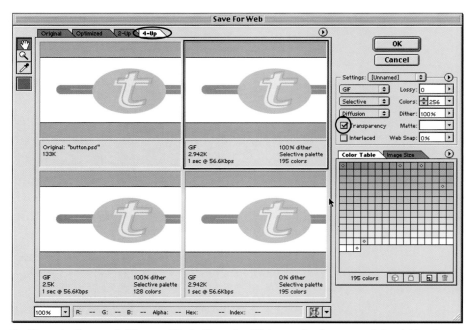

I. Open **button.psd**. Choose **File > Save for Web...** and select one of the **4-Up** views with the GIF format. Click the **Transparency** checkbox on and off.

*Notice that nothing happens. You cannot create a transparent GIF on a document that doesn't display any Photoshop layer transparency. Photoshop and ImageReady look at the document in a flattened state even if it contains a lot of layers like this one. It's essential that the Photoshop transparent layer (indicated by a checkerboard pattern) be visible. Even though the layer has transparency, Photoshop cannot access the necessary information because the **background** layer is turned on in the **Layers** palette. The next step will show you what to do.*

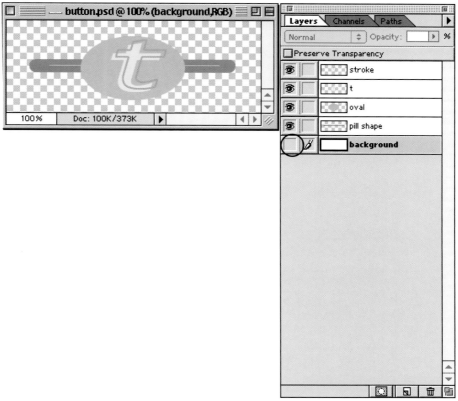

2. Click **Cancel** to return to the document window. In the **Layers** palette (**Window > Show Layers**), turn off the visibility of the **background** layer by clicking off the eye icon. Now you will see the checkerboard pattern that indicates Photoshop layer transparency. Choose **File > Save for Web...** again.

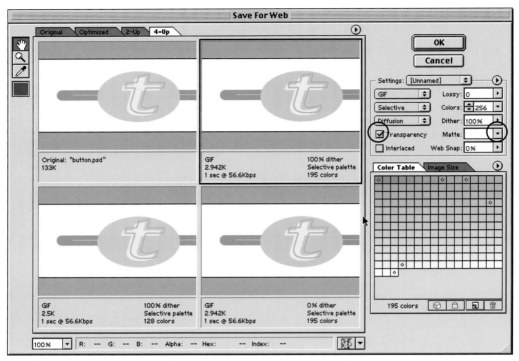

3. Now when you turn on the **Transparency** checkbox, you should see the preview of the transparent GIF change. Play around with this for awhile. Select different **Matte** colors and watch the edge color change.

Click **OK** *when you've arrived at the settings you like. The file* **button.psd** *will still be open, which is fine because it will be used again in the next exercise.*

This exercise alerted you to a potential problem in Photoshop and ImageReady: You cannot make a transparent GIF unless layer transparency is visible in a document.

[PS]

8. _____GIF 89a Export

In past versions of Photoshop, the way to make transparent GIF images differed from what I've taught in this chapter. However, you can still use this alternate way of making transparent GIF images. The only penalty is that you will not be able to influence the **Matte** color, which I think is critical to good-looking transparent GIF images. One advantage to this older method, however, is that you do not need to show any Photoshop layer transparency for it to work.

I. With the **button.psd** image open, choose **File > Export > GIF 89a Export....**

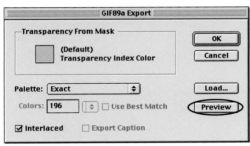

2. Click on the **Preview** button.

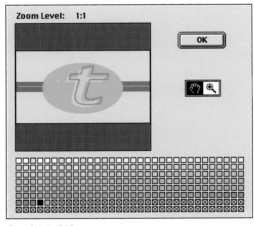

3. Click **OK**.

*You don't have any control over the **Matte** color this way, but Photoshop knows to knock out the white background. This method offers far less control than what the exercises in this chapter taught, and, for that reason, I don't recommend you use it.*

4. Close the file. You've completed another chapter. Onward ho!

9.
Image Maps

| Server-Side or Client-Side | What is an Image Map |
| Making an Image Map | Using Invisible Layers |

chap_09

Photoshop 5.5 / ImageReady 2.0
H•O•T CD-ROM

Most buttons and navigation bars on the Web are composed of individual images that link to individual URLs. An image map is called for when you want a single image to link to multiple URLs, such as a map of the United States in which each state is linked to a different URL.

In the past, image maps were not made in image editors, but in HTML editors or standalone image map-editing software. ImageReady 2.0 makes it easy to create image maps without the need for other applications. While it isn't possible to do the same thing in Photoshop 5.5, if you open a .psd document saved from ImageReady that contains an image map, Photoshop will retain the information until you return to ImageReady.

Server-Side or Client-Side Image Maps?

There are two types of image maps — server-side and client-side. In the early days of the Web, it was only possible to create server-side image maps. When Netscape 2.0 was released, the ability to work with client-side image maps was introduced.

What do those terms mean? Anything that is server-sided resides on the Web server and is accessed through a CGI (**C**ommon **G**ateway **I**nterchange). A CGI is a type of script that can be written in Perl, C++, AppleScript, or other programming languages. CGI scripts reside on the Web server. Typically, most Internet Service Providers supply their subscribers with a CGI script that can activate server-sided image maps. It's then a matter of linking to the script and uploading a map definition file that should also be stored on the Web server. To further muddle the issue, there are two types of Web servers — those that follow the conventions of CERN (**C**onseil **E**uropéen pour la **R**echerche **N**ucléaire — where Tim Berners-Lee conducted research at the time the Web was being developed) and those that follow the NCSA (**N**ational **C**enter for **S**upercomputing **A**pplications). If you decide to create a server-side image map, you will need to check with your Web-hosting company to see if they are CERN or NCSA compliant.

Sound complicated? It is, in fact, much more complicated to create a server-side image map than a client-side image map. Anything client-sided means that it is performed on the client. What is a client? Why, it's a Web browser, silly. You mean you weren't born knowing that? Don't fret, neither was anyone else. The Web browser that you use on your hard drive is your very own Web client. Bet you never thought of it that way, but now you can have two kinds of clients in your life — those who pay the bills, and those who display your Web pages!

The deal is that a client-side image map is performed by the browser and doesn't involve the server at all. Client-side image maps are always easier to work with because you don't have to fuss with CGI scripts, map definition files, and knowing what kind of Web server your hosting company uses.

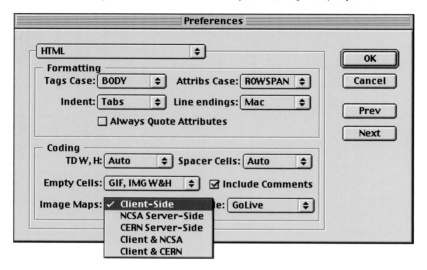

Most Web sites today only use a client-side image map, and that's what this chapter will cover. If you want to create a server-side image map in place of or in addition to a client-side image map, then visit your ImageReady **Preferences** and change the **Image Maps:** setting to reflect your choice. The default is **Client-Side**, so if that's what you plan to create you won't need to change your **Preferences**.

What Does an Image Map Look Like?

A client-side image map contains the **MAP** and **USEMAP** tags as well as all the
coordinates for the image map regions. The coordinates plot the dimensions
and location of the "hot" regions.

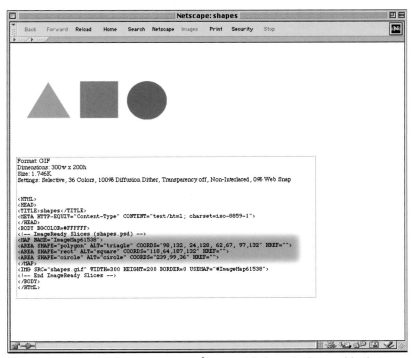

*This is an example of an image map (the graphic is a single graphic that
contains all three shapes – the triangle, square, and circle) and of how
ImageReady will write the HTML code. Notice there are three types of* **AREA
SHAPE** *elements – a polygon, a rect (rectangle), and circle. After those you'll
see a listing for* **COORDS** *(coordinates) followed by a lot of comma-separated
numbers. Those numbers describe the coordinates of the shape regions
around each shape.*

[IR]

I. _____Making an Image Map

In the past, creating an image map involved manually tracing around the regions of the image that you wanted to assign a URL. What's revolutionary about the approach that ImageReady 2.0 takes is that you don't have to do any tracing. The program does it for you! If you have your artwork separated on different Photoshop layers, ImageReady is smart enough to know where the regions of that layer are. Making an image map in ImageReady is as simple as double-clicking, checking a box, and selecting from a menu.

I. Open **shapes.psd** in the **chap_09** folder you transferred to your hard disk from the **H•O•T CD-ROM**.

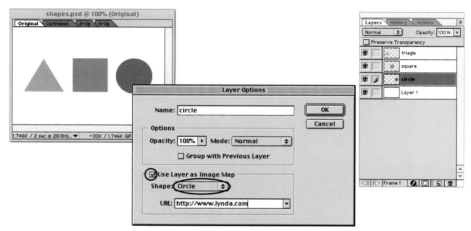

2. In the **Layers** palette (if it's not visible, choose **Window > Show Layers**) double-click the layer named **circle** to access the **Layer Options** dialog box. Check the box **Use Layer as Image Map**, from the **Shape:** pop-up menu select **Circle**, and enter the URL of your choice. **Note:** If you are not online when you test the preview or final file, this link will not work.

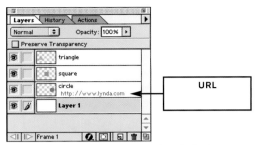

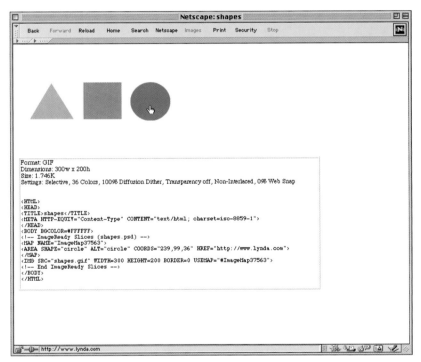

3. Click **OK** and click off of the **circle** layer to see clearly that a URL has been listed inside that layer. This is an indication that ImageReady has stored image map information with this layer.

4. Choose **File > Preview in** and select a browser of your choice. When you place your cursor over the circle previewed in the browser, a hand will appear, indicating that this is a link. In the code, notice that there is a line that reads: `<AREA SHAPE="circle" ALT="circle" COORDS="239,99,36" HREF="http://www.lynda.com">`. This is telling the browser to recognize an image map in the shape of a circle, with the coordinates of 239, 99, 36, and to link it to lynda.com.

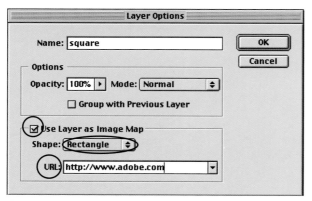

5. Return to ImageReady. Double-click the layer named **square**, and in the **Layer Options** dialog box that will appear, check **Use Layer as Image Map**. Change the **Shape:** to **Rectangle** and enter a different URL. Click **OK**.

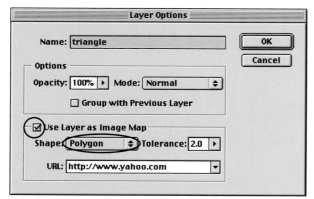

6. Double-click the layer named **triangle** and check **Use Layer as Image Map**. Change the **Shape:** to **Polygon**, **Tolerance: 2.0**, and enter a different URL. Click **OK**.

7. Choose **File > Preview in** and select a browser. If you are online, you can even test the links and they should work, assuming that you entered them correctly.

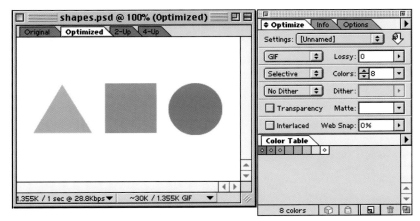

8. So far, you have only previewed the image map. Return to ImageReady to save a final version. Click the **Optimized** tab and create appropriate settings inside the **Optimize** palette (if it's not visible, choose **Window > Show Optimize**) **GIF**, **Selective**, **No Dither**, **Colors: 8**.

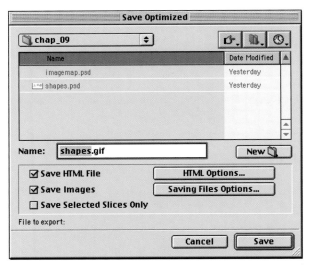

9. Next, choose **Save Optimized As...**, make sure you check **Save HTML File** and **Save Images**.

This GIF file is just like any other GIF file. The only thing that makes this GIF an image map is the HTML file that it creates, which tells the browser the coordinates of the linked regions.

IO. Click **Save** and close the **shapes.psd** file.

Note | **External Versus Internal URLs**

If you are linking to a Web site other than where this document will be uploaded, then you must include the entire http://www header information. If, for example, I was uploading this image to lynda.com and wanted to link to classes.html, then I wouldn't need the http://www header information. The link to an outside URL is called an external link and the link to the interior URL is called an internal link. If you are going to use internal links, it's really important to know the exact directory structure of your site. Here are some examples.

• If I stored the HTML file for this image map inside the same folder as the HTML pages to which it linked, then I could specify the URL like this:
  classes.html

• If I stored this image map inside an images folder and the HTML to which it linked inside an html folder, then I would specify the URL like this:
  ../html/classes.html

• If I stored this image map inside an images folder and the HTML to which it linked inside a folder named html that was inside the images folder, then I would specify the URL like this:
  html/classes.html

Many HTML editors, including GoLive and Dreamweaver, have site-management features, which help you manage these links. It's easiest to link to an external URL because you don't have to know the location of the file and how it relates to where the image map is stored. If you plan to link to internal pages, it might be best to set the actual links inside your HTML editor.

---

2. ——————Making an Invisible Layer an Image Map

The last exercise demonstrated how easy it is to make an image map inside ImageReady. What if you want a different shape than what already exists on the layer? This next exercise will show you what to do.

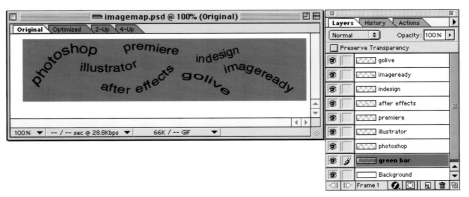

I. Open **imagemap.psd**. This is a layered Photoshop document that contains some type set in Adobe Illustrator. You'll learn how to import Illustrator artwork in Chapter 14, *"Importing/Exporting."*

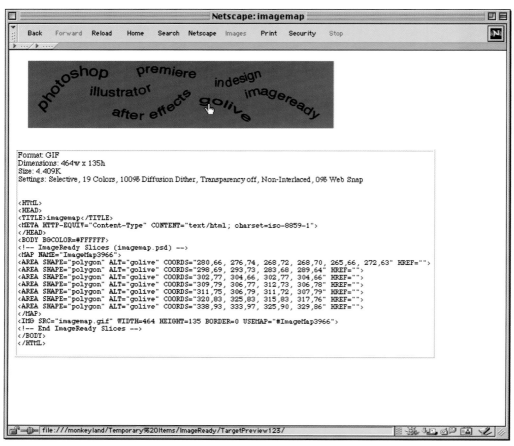

2. In the **Layers** palette, double-click the layer named **golive** and, in the **Layer Options** dialog box, check **Use Layer as Image Map** using a **Polygon**. Click **OK**. (You don't have to assign a URL in ImageReady for the image map to work.)

3. Choose **File > Preview in** and select a browser. Run your mouse over the letters for **golive**.

Notice how close this image map region is to the letters? Also, notice how many coordinates ImageReady generated for the code? This is not good. The image map is too hard to access and the code is too verbose. What to do? Make a bogus layer.

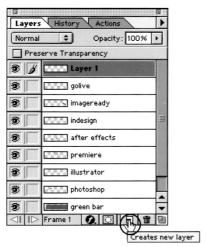

4. Return to ImageReady. Make sure you're still on the **golive** layer and click the **New Layer** icon. This should add a new empty layer above the **golive** layer.

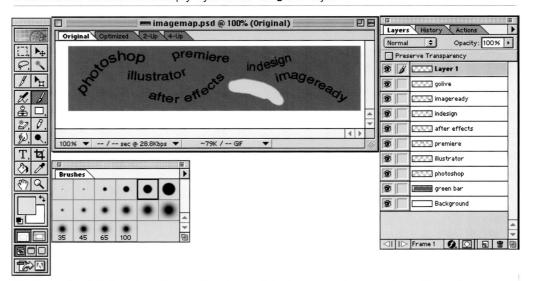

5. Using the **Paintbrush** tool, paint the shape of the letters on the empty layer. The color you pick will never show, so it doesn't matter what it looks like.

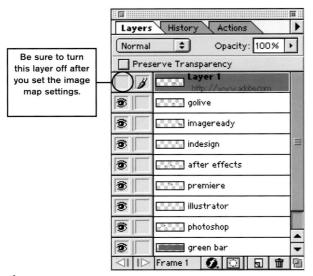

Be sure to turn this layer off after you set the image map settings.

6. Double-click the new layer that includes your paint stroke. In the **Layer Options** dialog box, check **Use Layer as Image Map** using a **Polygon**, enter a URL, and click **OK**. It's essential that you now turn off the visibility for the layer that includes the paint stroke. (The visibility is set by turning off the eye icon to the left of **Layer 1** in your **Layers** palette.)

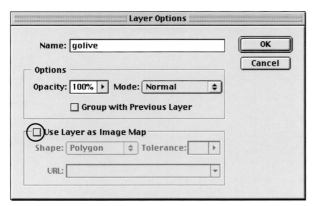

7. Double-click the **golive** layer inside the **Layers** palette to see its **Layer Options**. Uncheck **Use Layer as Image Map** and click **OK**. This will deactivate the image map settings for the **golive** layer.

Note: It's important to deactivate the settings, or else you will generate unnecessary code for the wrong layer.

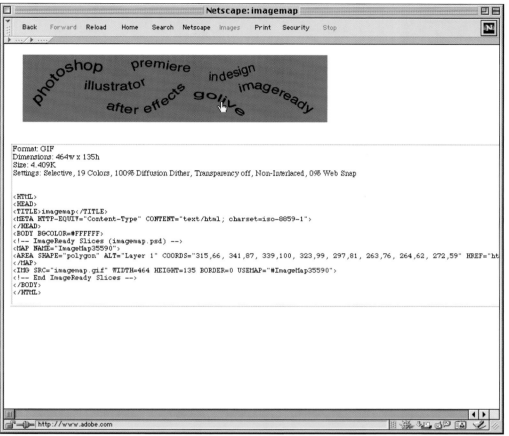

8. Choose **File > Preview in** and choose a browser. This time notice that there is only one line for **COORDS**. That means that ImageReady took the coordinates from the painted layer instead of the layer that is showing. You could use this technique for every layer in this document, and ImageReady would allow you to basically paint your regions.

9. Choose **File > Save** and leave this document open for the next exercise.

Voila! You just made a layer that was there for the purpose of the image map coordinates but wasn't visible because you turned it off. It's a handy trick that's useful when you want to "paint" the shape of your image map.

3. —————————Jumping to Photoshop with an Image Map

In the introduction to this chapter, I mentioned that Photoshop honors image map information from ImageReady even though it cannot display it. This exercise will put that promise to practice.

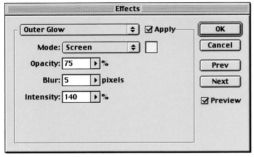

1. With **imagemap.psd** open from the last exercise, click the **Jump To** button at the bottom of the ImageReady toolbar. This will open Photoshop. Select the **golive** layer and choose **Layer > Effects > Outer Glow....** In the **Effects** dialog box that will appear, change the **Intensity:** settings to **140** as shown above and click **OK**.

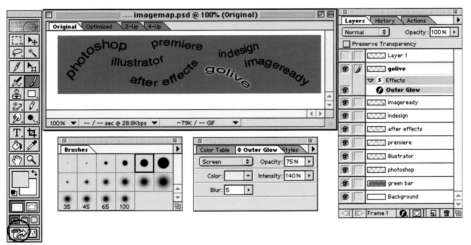

*The glow should appear on the **golive** layer and an f-shaped **Layer Effect** icon should appear in the **Layers** palette.*

2. Click the **Jump To** button at the bottom of the Photoshop toolbar. Save when you are prompted.

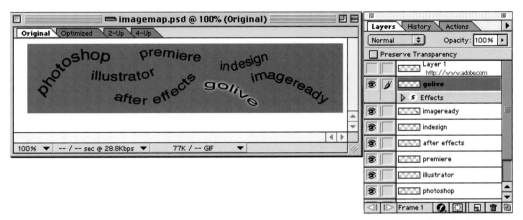

You should now be back in ImageReady and the change should appear. Notice that the image map information that was not visible in Photoshop is still intact inside ImageReady. Told you so! You can edit freely between these two programs and even though image maps are not directly supported inside Photoshop, they will still be honored.

You can **Preview**, **Save Optimized** and/or **Save** now by practicing what you've learned in the other exercises in this chapter. Close the file when you're finished and remain in ImageReady for Chapter 10, "Slicing."

10.
Slicing

What are Slices	Slice Icons	Slicing and Selecting
Slice Preferences	Previewing and Saving Slices
What is Spacer.gif	Slice Palette	No Image Slices

chap_10

Photoshop 5.5 / ImageReady 2.0
H•O•T CD-ROM

Being able to slice a document into as many pieces as you want is new to ImageReady 2.0. This feature offers the ability to cut apart a single image into multiple images in order to reassemble them inside an HTML table. You might wonder why anyone would want to do such a thing. For starters, you can optimize different parts of an image with different compression settings and file formats in order to reduce file size. You'll learn to do this in this chapter. Later chapters will show other uses for slices, such as producing rollovers and animations.

Slicing is simple and complex at the same time. It's easy to cut apart the image, but managing all the resulting files takes practice and going under the hood to set HTML preferences. This chapter will walk you through a complex slicing example so you can learn the nuances of making slices and generating table code from ImageReady.

It is not possible to slice images in Photoshop 5.5, which is why all the exercises in this chapter are conducted in ImageReady. If you open in Photoshop a sliced document that was created in ImageReady and saved as a .psd file, Photoshop will not display the slices, but it will also not destroy them. If you make a change in Photoshop, save the change, and re-open the .psd file in ImageReady. All the slices you created will still be there.

What Are Slices?

Slices are the result of cutting up an image into multiple pieces. A single document is cut into smaller pieces and those pieces (slices) are reassembled to look like a single image again using an HTML table.

When you create slices in ImageReady, the program generates multiple images and HTML table code. The table allows the browser to assemble all the separate images seamlessly so it looks like one document again.

The source code that ImageReady generated once an image was cut apart into slices and viewed in Netscape.

In the example with which you will work in the following exercises, ImageReady will cut a document into 21 pieces and reassemble them inside an HTML table. The program's settings will affect how the code is written and how the 21 slices are named and saved.

Slice Icons

Once you start to make slices, ImageReady will display icons that show what type of slice is being used.

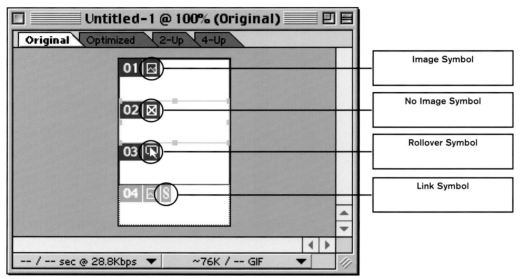

*This example shows the different types of icons that identify differ-ent **slices: Image, No Image, Rollover,** and **Link**.*

GoLive or ImageReady Code?

When writing the HTML for slices, you will have to choose whether to save it as GoLive code or ImageReady code. If you plan to use GoLive, have ImageReady write the code that way and if not have it write the code as ImageReady code. Either way, the code will work just fine in any browser, it's just that GoLive will recognize the code as its own if you change your **Preferences** to this setting. This has advantages if you are planning to build your site in GoLive because it will recognize the code as one of its own **Actions**, making it possible to copy and paste the code easily between pages. To learn how to incorporate ImageReady code inside GoLive or another HTML editor, check out Chapter 14, *"Importing/Exporting."*

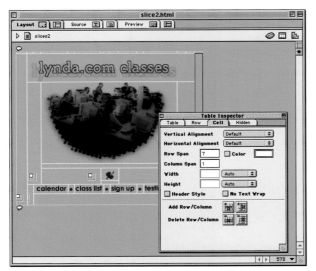

The sliced file that ImageReady generated shown opened in GoLive.

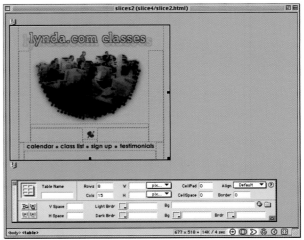

The sliced file that ImageReady generated shown opened in Dreamweaver.

The nice thing is that any HTML editor or browser will recognize and honor the table that ImageReady writes regardless of whether you choose **ImageReady** or **GoLive** HTML preferences. Best of all, you don't have to figure out how to write the complex table that holds all the images in place. ImageReady does this for you automatically.

[IR]

I. ————Slicing and Selecting

When slicing artwork in ImageReady, you will use two new tools — **Slice** and **Slice Selection**. This first exercise will demonstrate how to slice up an image using these two tools.

I. Open **slices.psd** from the **chap_10** folder you transferred to your hard drive from the **H·O·T CD-ROM**.

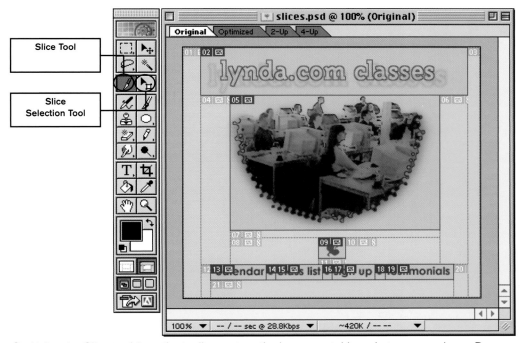

Slice Tool

Slice Selection Tool

2. Using the **Slice** tool from the toolbar, cut up the image, matching what you see above. Drag the **Slice** tool around the "**classes logo**" (including the blurry shadow), the "**photo**," the "**leaf**," each "**dot**," and each word in the **navigation bar**. **Important Note:** Your numbers might not perfectly match the ones shown above if you do not slice your document identically. If that's the case, you should still be able to do the exercise, but realize that your numbered slices might be different than those I describe.

*If you need to adjust any of these slice shapes, choose the **Slice Selection** tool and you'll be able to drag the shape's handle into a new position. You can also delete any slice by selecting it first and then pressing your **Delete** key. The standard **Move** tool will not work. You can only use the **Slice Selection** tool to select a slice or multiple slices (by holding down the **Shift** key) when working in ImageReady.*

*Notice that some of these slices have been marked with a bright blue color, while other slices appeared without you even defining them. ImageReady creates slices for all the areas the user doesn't define with the **Slice** tool so that all the areas are divided into slices. The bright blue slices are called **User-slices** and the rest are called **Auto-slices**.*

Note: *The advantage to cutting all the type into separate pieces is that each piece can contain a separate URL this way. Wouldn't it be easier to make one giant slice that covered all the type and purple dots? Yes, it would be, but you couldn't give each slice a separate URL.*

Tip | **Zooming In and Out**

When slicing the image to match the slices that I show in this chapter, it might be easier if you zoom into the document. You can use the **Zoom** tool to click on the document to zoom in and **Option+Click** (Mac) or **Alt+Click** (Windows) with the same tool to zoom out.

3. The slices have also discolored the image, leaving a screened-back appearance to the document. You might be wondering if there's a way to turn slices off so you can see the image without discoloration or the numbers of the slices. To toggle the preview of slices on and off, click between the **Hide Slices** and **Show Slices** buttons or press the shortcut key, **Q**. When you're finished trying this tool, leave the **Show Slices** button turned on so the slices are visible again.

4. Save and leave this file open for the next exercise.

Note | **Slice Preferences**

If you want to preview **Slices** without seeing the numbers for each cell, you can change ImageReady's **Preferences** to display **Slices** without numbers. Alternately, you can make the numbers bigger if they're too small to read. To change the **Preferences** for **Slices**, choose **File > Preferences > Slices....**

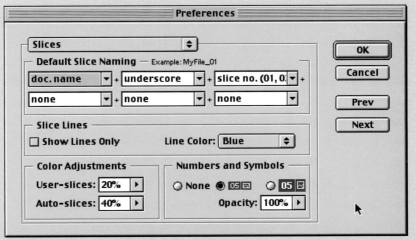

*At the bottom of the **Preferences Slices** dialog box, notice that you can change the **Slice Lines**, **Color Adjustments**, and **Numbers and Symbols**.*

[IR]

2. _____Optimizing Slices

One reason to cut apart the document is to optimize the different sections appropriately. This image is a mixture of areas with solid color that would better be compressed as GIF and areas of continuous tone photographic content that would be better compressed as JPEG. This is where slicing comes in really handy.

Link Symbol

1. Notice that all the gray **Slices** (**Auto-slices**) contain a link symbol? That means that they are linked to each other and that any optimization setting that is applied to one will apply to all. You can link the **User-slices** together, too. For example, the words in the bottom navigation bar contain the same color artwork in the same style. Use your **Slice Selection** tool, hold down the **Shift** key, and click on each of the four of the words in the navigation bar to select them, as shown above. Choose **Slices > Link Slices** and the color of all the selected slices will change and the link symbol will appear on them.

2. Next, use the **Slice Selection** tool and hold down the **Shift** key to select the **leaf** and all the "**purple dots**" (these are similar in color and appearance as well, and will therefore be best optimized with the same settings). After you've selected them, choose **Slices > Link Slices** to create a group of these slices as well. The slices are too small to show the link symbol, but the color change indicates that these are linked as a group. Every time you link slices together, the color will change to indicate they are linked.

*Why are all those slices numbered, you ask? When ImageReady creates the **User-slices** and the **Auto-slices**, it keeps track of them by assigning numbers to them.*

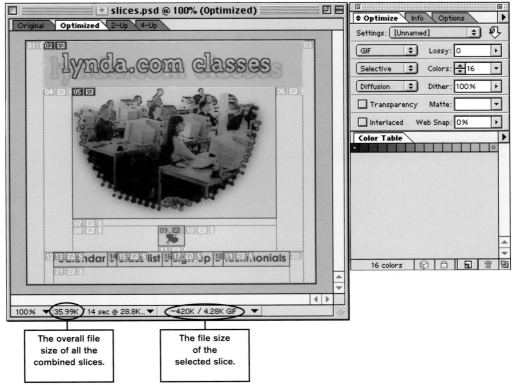

The overall file size of all the combined slices.

The file size of the selected slice.

3. Click the **Optimized** tab in the document window. Using the **Slice Selection** tool, select the slice that contains the **lynda.com classes** type (**slice #02** in the figure above). If your **Optimize** palette isn't visible, select **Window > Show Optimize**, and change the settings to those shown above. Notice the readout at the bottom of the document window? It's showing that this particular slice is under 4.2K but the overall document is 35K. That will change soon. There is still more optimizing left to do.

Note: Your optimization results might differ from mine in the above figure since your slices might be different sizes.

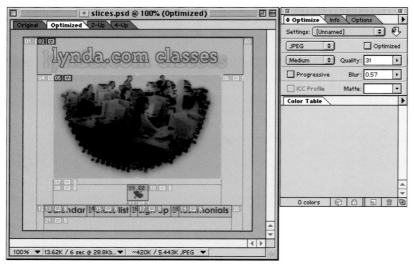

4. Next, select the slice for the "**photo of the class**"(**slice #05** as shown in the figure above). Set the settings for this slice in the **Optimize** tab. This slice is best optimized as a **JPEG**, as shown above. Notice that the overall image size is coming way down.

5. Click on the "**leaf**" slice (**slice #09** as shown above) to select it. Change the settings to what you see above. Once you've set this slice, click on the other green slices with the **Slice Selection** tool. You'll see that they have also changed to the exact same optimization settings. That's because they're linked, which you already knew, right?

6. Click on **slice #13** which slices the word "**calendar**," shown above. Change its optimization settings inside the **Optimize** tab to **GIF**, **Selective**, **Colors: 4**. Try clicking on the other red slices; you'll see they share the same settings that you just set for **slice #13**. Reselect **slice #02** and **slice #05**. You'll see that each slice has memorized the settings that you made in earlier steps.

7. Click on any of the gray slices, which are the **Auto-slices** that ImageReady generated. These are grouped automatically (note the **Link** icon on each gray slice), but these slices need optimization settings as well. In the **Optimization** palette, enter **Colors: 2**. Any change that you make will be applied to all the **Auto-slices** in the gray group because they too are linked.

*Next you're going to set the **Auto-Slices** so they contain a **Matte** color. If you set a **Matte** color to these slices, it will set the* BODY BGCOLOR *tag in the resulting HTML. This means that the background color of the Web page will match the green color of the slices.*

8. Toggle off the **Show Slices** button so the slices disappear for a moment. I toggle this button frequently so I can double check the optimization settings, because the **Show Slices** mode slightly discolors the document's appearance. Choose the **Eyedropper** tool from the toolbar, and click on the green color of the background so it appears inside the **Foreground Color** swatch.

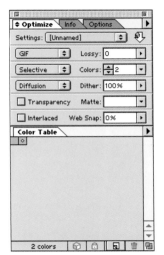

9. In the **Optimize** palette, hold down the arrow next to the **Matte:** field and select **Foreground Color** from the pop-up menu. This will put the shade of green into the **Matte** field.

The overall file size is now around 12K. Optimization makes a huge difference in file size and appearance. Again, my readout of 12K might differ from yours since you might have sliced your document differently.

10. Leave this file open for the next exercise, as you will learn all of the nuances of saving there.

Note | **Smaller Files Versus Smaller HTML**

In our classes I am always asked, which is better — to make the slices tight around the images and make more slices or to make fewer but larger slices, but have them looser around the images? Fewer slices equal less HTML and fewer images, thus faster pages. Sometimes you will still opt to draw your slices tightly around images because unless you use an image map, the shape of the slice dictates the bounding area of a linked graphic or rollover. Therefore, there is no one right way to handle this. If your objective is small file size and faster downloading, make fewer slices that are looser around the image area they encompass. If you want to assign links to buttons that are based on slices, it might be a good idea to synch in tightly.

3.⎯⎯⎯⎯**Previewing and Saving Slices**

It's not enough to slice and optimize, you've also got to save the slices and the resulting HTML. This next exercise will cover previewing and saving.

I. With **slices2.psd** still open from the last exercise, preview what you've done so far. Choose **File > Preview in** and select the browser of your choice.

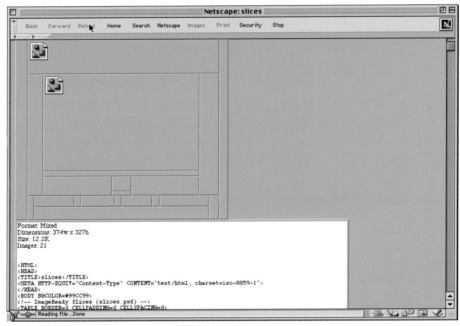

If it takes a while to preview, don't worry. ImageReady is doing a lot of things – writing an HTML table, cutting apart 21 images, and optimizing each one according to your specifications. You couldn't do it any faster yourself if you tried! As the preview loads into the browser, you'll be able to briefly see the slices loading into the HTML table. Once the file is finished loading, the regions of the table should be totally invisible.

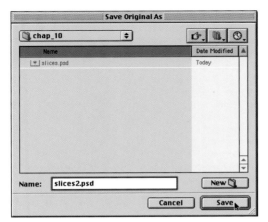

2. Previewing is a great way to test the slices, but it doesn't save a permanent record of any of the hard work you've done. It's time to do some real saving now. Return to ImageReady and choose **File > Save As...** and name this **slices2.psd**.

*When you choose **Save As...** you have the opportunity to make a copy of the .psd document. Now you'll have two versions of the file – the unsliced version and the sliced version. You don't always want to keep two versions of your .psd documents, but I often do when I make a significant change in case I want to revert quickly back to the original. It's important to note that ImageReady saves all the slice information when you save a file in the .psd format.*

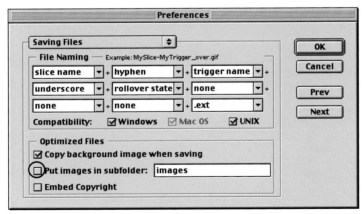

3. Choose **File > Preferences > Saving Files**, and uncheck **Put images in subfolder: images**, as circled above. This will change the **Preferences** so that the HTML file you save will be stored with your images in one folder. I'm suggesting you make this change because you'll be looking closely at how the files get saved in this exercise, and it's easier to see how everything works together if all the files (images and HTML) are in one single folder.

4. Next, it's time to save the actual slices and HTML. Choose **File > Save Optimized As...** and make sure **Save HTML** and **Save Images** are checked. This new folder will automatically be selected as the destination for your HTML and images. It's important to save the results into a separate folder because otherwise it's really messy – files scattered about your hard drive!

• (Mac) Click on the **New Folder** button. Name the new folder **slices**, and click on the **Create** button and then the **Save** button.

• (Windows) Click on the **yellow Folder** icon to make a new folder. Name the folder **slices** and double-click so that it opens. Click on the **Save** button, and all the files will populate the new folder you just created.

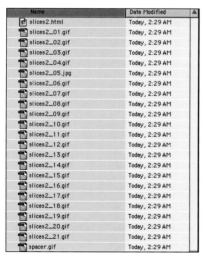

5. Navigate to your hard drive to locate the **slices** folder you just made. If you look inside the **images** folder that was automatically created, you'll see the fruit of ImageReady's labor – a folder filled with 21 image files and one HTML file. Not bad for a few minutes' work! Notice that one of the documents is a JPEG? If you'll recall, you gave **slice #05** a JPEG setting in the **Optimize** palette. You might also notice that there is a file called **spacer.gif** that you did not make. When you're done admiring your handiwork, return to ImageReady for the next exercise.

Note | **What Is the spacer.gif?**

The **spacer.gif** is a single-pixel transparent GIF that ensures that a table will open to the width that was specified inside ImageReady. If you go to choose **File > Preferences > HTML...** you will see a setting for **Spacer Cells**. The default setting is for ImageReady to automatically create a **spacer.gif** whenever slicing is invoked. This is written into the HTML because tables can change their shape if they aren't forced to open to a certain size with images.

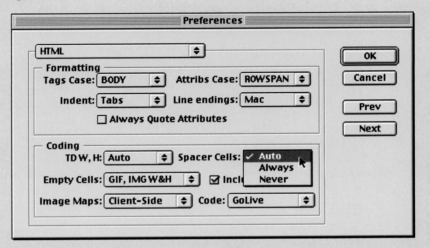

Some HTML programmers prefer not to have the **spacer.gif** written into the table. You can customize the way the HTML table is generated from slicing. I usually leave it at the defaults, shown above, but I am not a programmer so I don't really mind that ImageReady puts this GIF into the code. You can experiment with the code by choosing **File > Preferences > HTML...** and choosing to **Save Optimize As...** again if you'd like to see how the table is generated with different settings.

[IR]

4. —————**Using the Slice Palette**

New to ImageReady 2.0, the **Slice** palette offers a means to manage the way slices are named when they are saved. In this exercise, you will learn to name and set **ALT** text for the critical image files inside a document that contains slices. **ALT** text is what the end-users will see if their images are turned off.

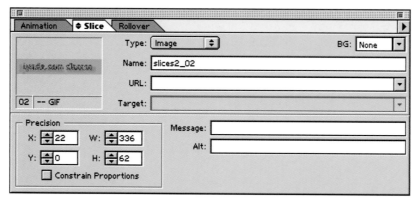

I. Make sure the **Slice** palette is open by choosing **Window > Show Slice**. Expand this palette all the way by going to the upper-right arrow and choosing **Show Options**. **Note:** Your **X**, **Y**, **W**, and **H** settings will probably differ from what this figure shows since you sliced your own file, and mine was sliced by *moi*.

2. With the **Slice Selection** tool, select **slice #02**. Inside the **Slice** palette, change the **Name:** to **classes_headline**. **Tip:** It's important not to use any spaces in the name for the file, or you might have problems with broken images once you upload this file to a live Web server. However, text in the **Alt:** field can contain spaces.

3. Set the ALT text inside the **Slice** palette to **lynda.com classes**.

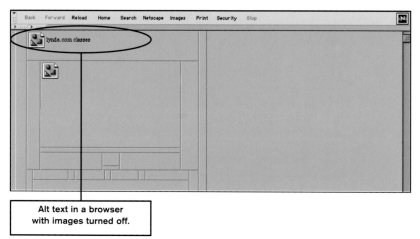

Alt text in a browser
with images turned off.

ALT *text shows on a browser if you turn off your images or if you are accessing a Web page with a text-only browser. Some people turn their images off when they surf the Web, to speed up downloading. Sight-impaired visitors to your site might have an automatic reader machine "read" the Web pages to them since they can't see them.* **ALT** *text should not be added for every single slice, just the critical information that would be needed if someone were viewing this page without images.*

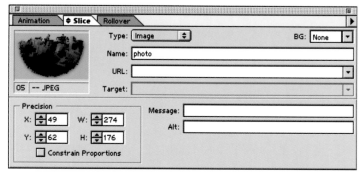

4. Using the **Slice Selection** tool, click on **slice #05**. Enter **photo** into the **Name:** field. Click on **slice #9** and enter **Name: leaf**. In the same way, name **slice #13**, **calendar**; **slice #14**, **dot1**; **slice #15, class_list**; **slice #16**, **dot2**; **slice #17**, **sign_up**; **slice #18**, **dot3**; and, finally, name **slice #19, testimonials**.

If your slice numbers are different than what I show here, just enter the correct names into the ***Name:*** *field, and your document will be just fine. You might also want to add appropriate* **Alt** *messages for each name, too. Man, you are the slicing machine!*

5. Choose **File > Save Optimized As...** and make sure **Save HTML** and **Save Images** are checked. Once again, this prevents the files from being scattered about your hard drive.

• (Mac) Click on the **New Folder** button. Name the new folder **slices2**, and click on the **Create button** and then the **Save** button.

• (Windows) Click on the **yellow Folder** icon to make a new folder. Name the folder **slices 2**, and double-click so that it opens. Click on the **Save** button, and all the files will populate the new folder you just created.

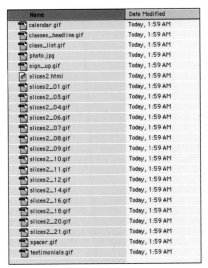

6. Return to your hard drive to look at the contents of the **slices2** folder. This time, the important (user-defined) images are named in a way that you can tell what they contain, rather than having to memorize which numbered cell relates to which image. However, there are still a lot of images in here that don't have names. Those were made from the **Auto-slices**. The next exercise will show you how to get rid of them, if you want to.

7. Return to ImageReady and leave the file open for the next exercise.

Setting Auto-Slices to No Image

The table that ImageReady is writing contains two types of slices — **User-slices** and **Auto-slices**. It creates **User-slices** automatically whenever you draw a slice using the **Slice** tool. Sometimes, it also generates slices that you didn't define, and those are called **Auto-slices**. Behind the scenes, ImageReady is always making an HTML table, so it can't have any regions that are not sliced. What if you don't want the **Auto-slices** to be generated as separate images? It's laborious, but you can turn each one off so it won't be written as a separate file. This exercise shows how to do this, plus how to change your **Preferences** so that the **spacer.gif** won't be used.

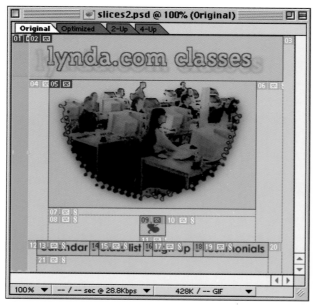

I. Using the **Slice Selection** tool, select **slice #1** (as shown in the figure above).

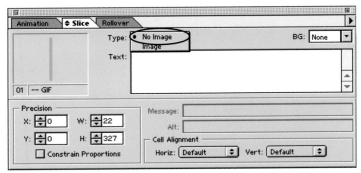

2. Inside the **Slice** palette, change the **Type:** to **No Image**. Notice that **slice #1** is now blue? This indicates that it has been changed from an **Auto-slice** to a **User-slice**. If you select every **Auto-slice** (indicated here by all the light gray slice areas) and change it to **No Image**, you will be able to get rid of all the cryptically named files when you save the optimized files again. It's unfortunate that there is no quick way to do this operation. You must go through and select each **Auto-slice** and change it to **Type: No Image**.

*The **No Image** setting creates a table cell without an image in it. ImageReady can't preview this setting, you must view it in a browser to see the result. **Warning:** Once you change the **Auto-slices** to contain **No Image**, they will no longer be linked.*

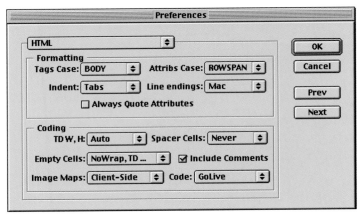

3. Choose **File > Preferences > HTML...** Change the **Empty Cells:** to NoWrap, TD... and **Spacer Cells:** to **Never**. Click **OK**.

*NoWrap means that text will not wrap if it is added later to this cell. Choosing **Never** for **Spacer Cells** means that ImageReady will not put any image into the **No Image** slices.*

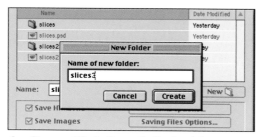

4. Choose **File > Save Optimized As...** and make sure **Save HTML** and **Save Images** are checked. This new folder will automatically be selected as the destination for your HTML and images. It's important to save the results into a separate folder, this prevents the files from being scattered about your hard drive.

• (Mac) Click on the **New Folder** button. Name the new folder **slices3**, and click on the **Create** button and then the **Save** button.

• (Windows) Click on the **yellow Folder** icon to make a new folder. Name the folder **slices3** and double-click so that it opens. Click on the **Save** button, and all the files will populate the new folder you just created.

5. If you look on your hard drive at the contents of the **slices3** folder, you will only see files that you named because it didn't write an image or a **spacer.gif** for the **Auto-slices** based on your changes to the HTML **Preferences**. While this list of files looks better and you might feel more in control of what ImageReady has named and written, there is a problem with this file that you might not be aware of. The problem will be revealed when you preview this sucker in the upcoming step.

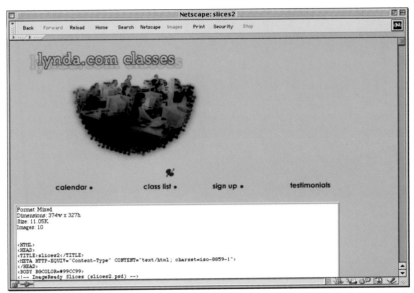

6. If you choose **File > Preview in** and select a browser of your choice, you will see that the table got messed up. That **spacer.gif** is actually a pretty useful component because it holds the empty table cells in position so nothing will slip.

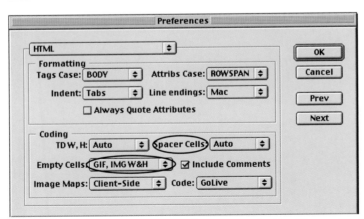

7. Return to your ImageReady **Preferences** to fix this. Choose **File > Preferences > HTML...** and change the settings to **Empty Cells: GIF, IMG W&H** and **Spacer Cells: Auto**. Click **OK**.

*GIF, IMG W&H means that ImageReady will insert transparent GIF files that include **Width** and **Height** attributes to the* IMG *tag.*

8. Choose **File > Save Optimized As...** and make sure **Save HTML** and **Save Images** are checked. This new folder will automatically be selected as the destination for your HTML and images. I cannot stress the importance of a separate folder enough, it prevents the files from being scattered about your hard drive.

- (Mac) Click the **New Folder** button. Name the new folder **slices4**, and click on the **Create** button and then the **Save** button.

- (Windows) Click on the **yellow folder** icon to make a new folder. Name the folder **slices4**, and double-click so that it opens. Click on the **Save** button, and all the files will populate the new folder you just created.

9. When you view the results in a browser this time, all the empty table cells will hold their shape, and your document will look great.

10. Return to ImageReady. You're finished with this exercise and can close **slices2.psd**.

Saving Slices Recap

Confused? If you are, don't beat up on yourself. Making and saving slices in ImageReady is new to everyone, and it can easily become confusing. It will probably help if I recap the differences between what you did in each of the slice folders that you've made over the past several exercises.

• The **slices** folder that you created in Exercise 3 contained 21 images that were all named by ImageReady. This resulted in a folder with a lot of files that are not named by content but instead by numbers. This saving method is not ideal since it's better to be in control of the way you name your files. When and if you bring ImageReady slices into an HTML editor, it's important that you know what the file's name is so you can troubleshoot any problems.

• The **slices2** folder that you created in Exercise 4 contained all the **Auto-slices** and **User-slices** in one folder. This worked fine but had a lot of extra images that weren't doing much except holding the table cells in place in the resulting HTML file. The **Auto-slice** images were also named with automatically created names, instead of the **User-slices** which contained the names you assigned in the **Slices** palette. If you like to be in control of the names of your files, as I do, this saving method isn't ideal.

• The **slices3** folder that you created in Exercise 5 contained images and an HTML file but removed the **spacer.gif** file that ImageReady automatically generated. You had also changed an **HTML Preference** to turn off the setting to hold the table cells open with an image (**NoWrap**). This resulted in far fewer files that all possessed the names you assigned. The only trouble was that it fell apart in Netscape and didn't look good. Not ideal either.

• The **slices4** folder that you also created in Exercise 5 contained images, an HTML file, and the automatically generated **spacer.gif**. It didn't have any automatically generated **Auto-slices** because they had all been changed to **No Image**. You changed the **HTML Preference** to contain **Spacer Cells: Auto** and **Empty Cells: GIF, IMG W&H**. This is the way I like to set up slices in ImageReady because it leaves me only with images that I've named, as well as the spacer GIF which ensures that my table will display in the browser exactly as I intended.

*This chapter is a wrap. This last exercise showed that it's best to name your slices and leave your **Preferences** set to use spacers so that your slices will hold together in the browser. Slices were used in this chapter for optimization purposes, but in future chapters you'll get to use them again for rollovers and animation.*

11.

Rollovers

Single Button Rollovers	Saving Rollovers	Preferences for Saving Rollovers
Layer-Based Rollovers	Saving Remote Rollovers	Complicated Rollovers
Navigation Bar Rollovers	Alignment with Link Symbols

chap_11

Photoshop 5.5 / ImageReady 2.0
H•O•T CD-ROM

A rollover is a type of element on an HTML page that changes when the end-user's mouse moves over it. Normally, you would need to know how to program JavaScript or how to use an HTML editor such as GoLive, Dreamweaver, or FrontPage, to create rollovers. What's great is that Image-Ready 2.0 not only lets you create the graphics for rollovers, but it then creates the code for them, so you don't have to learn a line of code if you don't want to.

While you can work with .psd files that originated from Photoshop, you can't program rollovers in Photoshop. ImageReady is the tool of choice for the job of creating rollovers. For this reason, all the exercises in this chapter take place in ImageReady, not Photoshop.

In the last chapter you learned how to slice up an image. This chapter will put those skills to practice again by having you cut up artwork in preparation for multiple rollover images. You will also have another chance to work with **Styles** and **Layer Effects**. This is where all the skills you've learned so far culminate in some pretty exciting results. Dig in, and prepare to be challenged (in a good way, of course!).

[IR] **I.** Single-Button Rollover with Styles

This first exercise will introduce you to the basic principles of making rollovers. Rollovers are often defined with "states," meaning that the **Normal** state is the image before the mouse moves over it, and the **Over** state is the image while the mouse moves over it. Starting simple, with a single button, you'll learn how to add two rollover states by using **Styles**.

I. Make sure you are in ImageReady. Remember, it's not possible to program rollovers in Photoshop. Open **rollover.psd** from the **chap_11** folder you transferred to your hard drive from the **H•O•T CD-ROM**.

As a tangential aside for Macintosh users only, notice that the readout on the bottom of the image states that it is 97K? This is the size of the uncompressed graphic. Chances are this readout is different on your screen. That's because on a Macintosh (only) the uncompressed file size is affected by the size of your hard drive. It has to do with partitions and rounding off of numbers. Have you ever noticed that the exact same image will be a different size if it's transferred to another disk, like a zip or a floppy? That's because the partitions of the different media are different than the partition of your hard drive. The uncompressed size really doesn't matter much for Web graphics anyway; the important part is how small you make the graphic when it is compressed.

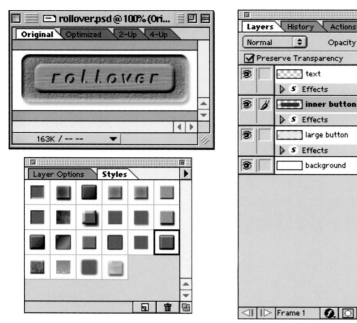

2. Add a **Style** to each layer. If the **Styles** and **Layers** palettes aren't open, you will find them under the **Window** menu. Then, either select a layer and double-click on a **Style**, or drag a **Style** onto a layer in either the **Layers** palette or the actual document. It doesn't matter which **Styles** you choose or whether or not you customize them. Settle on a look and feel for your rollover's first state and then move on to the next step. **Tip:** For a more in-depth refresher on adding **Styles**, revisit Exercise 10, in Chapter 6, *"Type."*

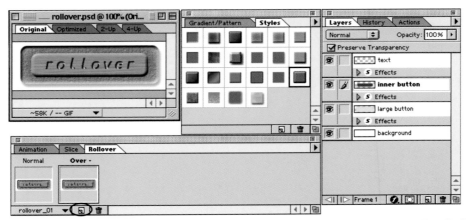

3. Choose **Window > Show Rollover** to get the **Rollover** palette. Click on the **New Rollover State** icon at the bottom of the palette to create an **Over** state.

*When you make a new state in ImageReady, it duplicates the previous state. The **Normal** state and the **Over** state thumbnails should look identical in the **Rollover** palette at this point.*

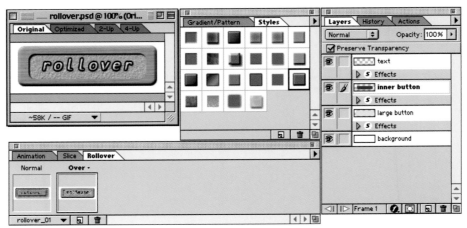

4. Notice that the **Over** state is selected (the black border around it indicates this). Modify the **Styles** that you've applied to the **Normal** state to create a different look for the **Over** state (how the button will look when the user's mouse moves over it).

*As you do this, you are creating the graphic for the **Over** state. If you click between the **Normal** and the **Over** states you'll see that ImageReady memorizes which **Styles** you put on each state.*

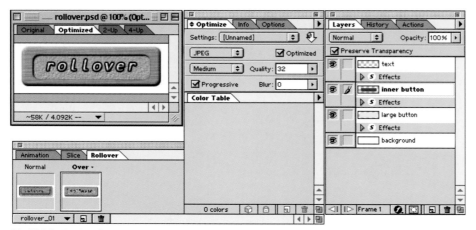

5. While in the **Over** state, click on the **Optimized** tab of the document. Open the **Optimize** palette (**Window > Show Optimize**) and change the settings to whichever type of compression is appropriate for the graphics you just made.

*See if you can figure out which is better, GIF or JPEG. See if lowering the number of colors helps the file size, or if it's best as a JPEG if lowering the quality or adding some blur might help. The object is to make the smallest possible graphic, and because I don't know what **Styles** you used, I have no way to instruct you on exactly how to do this. Hey, it's good practice for the real world once you've finished this book! If you need to refresh your memory on how to optimize graphics in ImageReady, revisit Chapter 4, "Optimization."*

6. Click back and forth between the **Normal** and **Over** states in the **Rollover** palette.

See how the compression settings you chose are applied to both states? Sadly, you cannot choose different settings for each state. Sometimes one state would be better compressed as a GIF than a JPEG or vice-versa, but ImageReady can only set compression to a slice, not to an individual state.

7. When you're ready to see the rollover work choose **File > Preview in** and select a browser of your choice. Move your mouse over the graphic and you'll see your rollover in action. Scroll down the browser window and check out all the code ImageReady wrote in order to achieve this effect. Impressive, whether or not you know how to write JavaScript!

Notice when you move your mouse over the graphic that it changed outside its border? That's because the rollover was based on the size of the ImageReady document, not on the artwork itself. This happens automatically, unless you know how to change it. In the next exercise, you'll learn how to base the rollover on an image map to avoid the problem of having images like this that roll over when the mouse isn't directly over the graphic.

8. Return to ImageReady and leave **rollover.psd** open for the next exercise. Don't save just yet.

2. —————**Image Map-Based Rollovers**

The last exercise yielded impressive results with little effort. The only criticism might be that the button changed when the mouse moved outside the graphic image. There's an easy fix for that and it involves image maps, about which you already learned in Chapter 9, *"Image Maps"* although not in the context of rollovers.

1. With **rollover.psd** still open from the last exercise, switch the view to **Original** instead of **Optimized**.

*It's always best to edit images in the **Original** view because ImageReady doesn't try to optimize every change you make.*

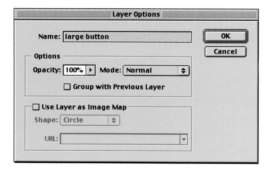

2. In the **Layers** palette, double-click the **large button** layer since it is the biggest shape of the graphic and the box around it encompasses everything else. The **Layer Options** dialog box will appear.

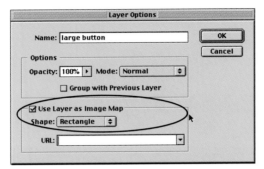

3. In the **Layer Options** dialog box, click on **Use Layer as Image Map** and select the **Rectangle** shape. If you are online and want to test a URL, enter a link inside the URL field. Click **OK**.

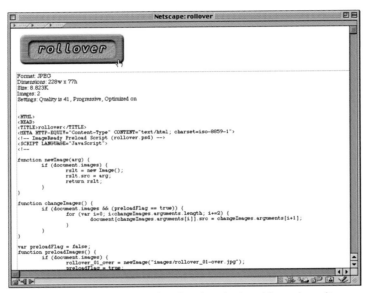

4. Preview in a browser and notice that the hand icon doesn't appear until your cursor is directly over the area that was defined as the large button layer. Told ya an image map would do the trick.

I often combine image maps with rollover graphics so that the rollover region more tightly matches the shape of my button. This is especially true on irregularly shaped buttons, because ImageReady always bases the shape of the rollover on a rectangular slice or the document itself.

5. Return to ImageReady and leave the same file open for the next exercise. Don't save it yet. That's what the next exercise is all about.

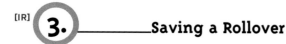

[IR] **3.**————————**Saving a Rollover**

Saving a rollover is similar to saving a transparent GIF or an image map, and you already know how to do those things, right? The one big difference is that a rollover is nothing more than two static images unless it retains the HTML code that contains the JavaScript. Therefore, you must not only save the images but the HTML code, too. When this happens, ImageReady automatically creates a subfolder for you, which you may or may not want it to do. This exercise will explain this and more.

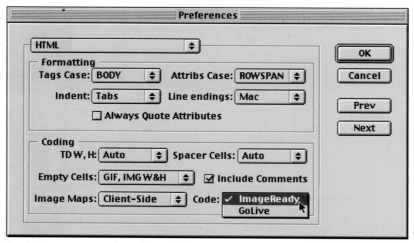

I. Before you save the rollover, find out whether the **Preferences** are set to generate **ImageReady** or **GoLive** code. Check your settings by going to **File > Preferences > HTML....** The only reason to change this code to **GoLive** code is if you are a GoLive user. Otherwise, leave it set to **ImageReady**. If you've made a change, click **OK**. Otherwise, click **Cancel**.

You might want to read the introduction to Chapter 10, "Slicing," to refresh your memory about this choice between ImageReady and GoLive. There's also great information about getting rollovers into an HTML editor in Chapter 14, "Importing/Exporting." Don't skip ahead just yet though, there are important and challenging tasks to complete first ;-).

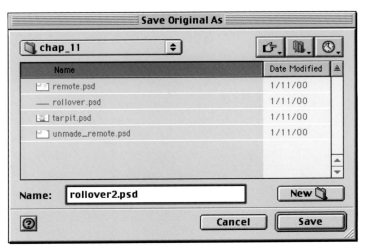

2. Choose **File > Save As...** and name the file **rollover2.psd**. Navigate to the **chap_11** folder that you transferred to your hard drive from the **H•O•T CD-ROM** and click **Save** to place this file in there.

*Saving the modified file as a **.psd** ensures that you can access the **Layers** and **Styles** settings. You haven't saved this file for the Web yet, but you've saved it as a .psd file in the event a client asks you to change something or you ever want to edit parts of it again. The only format that stores the rollover states, layer information, Styles information, etc., is the.psd format. It's important to save a master .psd file and the necessary GIFs and JPEGs, in addition to HTML, when you're working on projects, so all your bases are covered.*

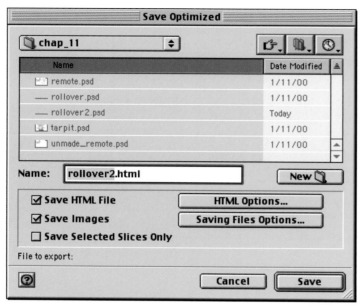

3. Choose **File > Save Optimized As...** and save it as **rollover2.html**. ImageReady will probably offer to name it for you that way anyway because by default the application bases the name
of the rollover HTML document on the name of the .psd file. The images will also get saved as
rollover2.gif or **rollover2.jpg**, depending on what optimization setting you specified in Exercise
1. By default, the images will go into another, newly created folder called **images**. Look to the
following section to understand how to change this, if you want to.

4. You're done with this example and you can close **rollover2.psd** now.

*The files are saved both as a master, editable Photoshop file (**rollover2.psd**) and as a working
HTML document (**rollover2.html**) with associated images (**rollover2_01-over**, **rollover2_01**)
that could be brought into any HTML editor or opened directly from within a browser.*

Preferences for Saving Rollovers

There might be times when you'll want to change the way ImageReady writes the files for a rollover. If so, you will want to visit the **Preference** settings for **Saving Files**. To do this, choose **File > Preferences > Saving Files**....

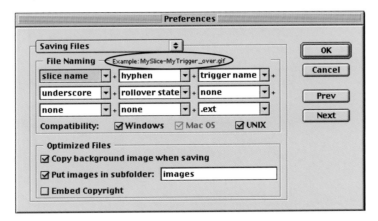

Of all the settings in the **Saving Files Preferences, File Naming** is the most overwhelming. Its settings have to do with how ImageReady names the rollover files. It's important to realize that naming rollover graphics is a lot more tricky than naming a single image. So far, you have learned to make a simple rollover. What you might not realize is that, by default, every ImageReady document contains one default slice. When you build a simple rollover, it uses the single slice even though you never had to define it. Later in this chater you will learn to make much more complex rollovers that contain many slices.

Consider that when a rollover is made, two graphics, at minimum, have to be generated — the **Normal** and **Over** state. There are all kinds of factors that contribute to defining which image is being saved, including the name of the slice, the name of the rollover state, and the number of the cell that is triggering the rollover event.

Notice that each one of the settings, such as what's currently set to **slice name, hyphen, trigger name, underscore**, etc., is a pop-up menu? Some of the pop-up menus are set to none. If I had named a slice and created an **Over** state for a rollover, the **Preference** is currently set up to create a name that is shown in the **Example:** area (circled above) — **MySlice-MyTrigger_over.gif**. If you wanted to change the format for ImageReady's automatic file naming, you would change the pop-up menus to select a different formatting option. These options are explained on the following pages.

slice name
rollover state rollover abbr.
trigger name trigger no.
doc. name
slice no. (1, 2, 3 ...) slice no. (01, 02, 03 ...) slice no. (a, b, c ...) slice no. (A, B, C ...)
mmddyy (date) mmdd (date) yyyymmdd (date) yymmdd (date) yyddmm (date) ddmmyy (date) ddmm (date)
underscore hyphen space
none

You can actually click on each item on the pop-up menu to change its setting. This chart should help you understand what these settings mean.

File Naming Options	
Setting	**Description**
slice name	If you have given the slice a name in the **Slices** palette, then that name will appear in the saved file name.
rollover state	The graphics will be saved with the name of the state, such as **Rollover-Over.gif**.
rollover abbr.	The graphics will be saved with the name of the state, but in abbreviated form, such as **Rollover-O.gif**.

Continued...

trigger name	Remote rollovers are triggered by a slice that is different than the slice in which the rollover appears. This choice lists the name that was assigned in the **Slices** palette of that trigger slice.
trigger no.	Same as above, only the slice number would be used instead of the slice name.
slice no. (I, 2, 3...)	The graphics will be saved with the name of the slice plus a number – such as **Rollover-1.gif**.
slice no. (01, 02, 03...)	The graphics will be saved with the name of the slice, plus a number starting with 0, such as **Rollover-01.gif**.
slice no. (A, B, C...)	The graphics will be saved with the name of the slice, such as **Rollover-A.gif**.
mmddyy (date)	The graphics will be saved with the date, starting with the month, day and then the year, such as **Rollover-110100.gif**.
mmdd (date)	The graphics will be saved starting with the month and then the day, such as **Rollover-1101.gif**.
yyyymmdd (date)	The graphics will be saved starting with the year, month, then day, such as **Rollover-20001101.gif**.
yymmdd (date)	The graphics will be saved starting with the year, then month and day, such as **Rollover-001101.gif**.
yyddmm (date)	The graphics will be saved starting with the year, then day and month, such as **Rollover-000111.gif**.
ddmmyy (date)	The graphics will be saved starting with the day, then month and year, such as **Rollover-011100.gif**.
underscore	An underscore will be placed between items, such as **Rollover_01.gif**.
hyphen	A hyphen will be placed between items, such as **Rollover-01.gif**.
space	A space will be placed between items such as **Rollover 01.gif**. I don't recommend this because it might cause broken links on some Web servers.
none	If you don't want any of the selections available, choose **none**.

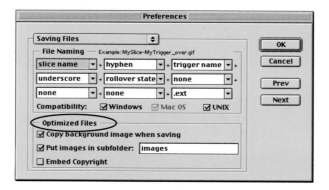

The different optimization settings in the **Saving Files Preferences** and their definitions are listed in the chart below. It should help you understand what these settings mean.

File Optimization Options	
Setting	**Description**
Copy background image when saving	If this box is checked and you've specified an external file as a background, that file will be copied to the folder of final images for your rollover graphics.
Put images in subfolder	Because rollovers can often produce numerous image files, it is a good idea to put the images in a subfolder just to keep things organized. You can change the default name "images" by typing in a name of your choice. If you uncheck this setting, the images and HTML will not be separated.
Embed copyright	This setting will embed a copyright into a comment tag in the HTML.

Movie | **savingprefs.mov**

To learn more about the ImageReady Preferences for saving rollovers, watch **savingprefs.mov** located in the **movies** folder on the **H•O•T CD-ROM**.

Single-Button Rollover with Layers

You made the first rollover by using **Styles** to change the appearance of each state. This next exercise will show you how to create a rollover by showing or hiding layers instead of using **Styles**.

1. Open **tarpit.psd**.

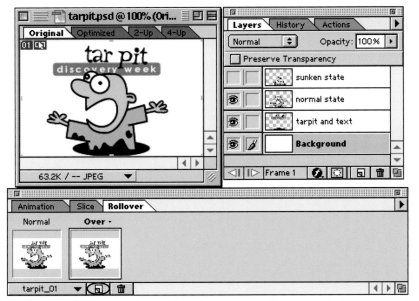

2. Click on the **New Rollover State** icon in the **Rollover** palette to duplicate the previous state.

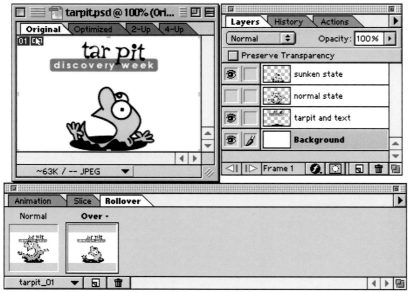

3. With the **Over** state selected in the **Rollover** palette, turn off the visibility eye icon for the **normal state** layer and turn on the eye icon for the **sunken state** layer. Leave the **tarpit and text** layer icon turned on.

*Notice how ImageReady has memorized which eye icons were turned on and off for both the **Normal** and the **Over** state? Go back and forth between the two in the **Rollover** palette and you'll see what I mean.*

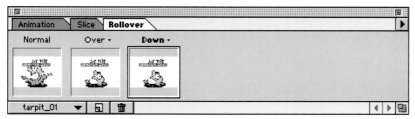

4. Again, click on the **New Rollover State** icon, this time to make a third state that is automatically called **Down**.

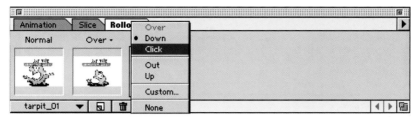

5. Put your mouse over the word **Down** and click to access a pop-up menu. Choose **Click**.

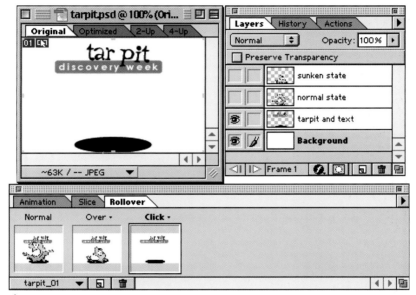

6. Turn off the eye icon for the **sunken state** layer. Only the two bottom layers should be visible.

7. Preview your work in a browser, roll your mouse over the image, and click your mouse on it.

*Way to go! You just made a multiple rollover that included a **Normal**, **Over**, and **Click** state. This exercise demonstrated an alternate way to make rollovers – set up the different states on different Photoshop layers and use the **Rollover** palette to memorize which layers were on or off.*

8. Close this file. You can save it if you want. Just follow the steps in Exercise 3.

What JavaScript States Are Allowed?

When you are specifying a rollover state in ImageReady, you are invoking a JavaScript call. Now that you see there are more than just a **Normal** and **Over** state with rollovers, here's a handy chart to describe what they are.

JavaScript Rollover States	
State	**Definition**
Over	When the mouse enters the slice.
Down	When the mouse is depressed inside the slice.
Click	Older versions of Netscape don't support the **Down** state, so some developers prefer to use **Click**, which is supported.
Out	When the mouse leaves the slice. If there is no defined **Out** state, the document will automatically return to the **Normal** state.
Up	When the mouse is released inside the slice. If there is no defined **Up** state, the slice will return to the **Over** state when the mouse is released.
Custom	Available to hand coders who want to write their own JavaScript event.
None	Not supported by browsers — this is a placeholder for when you want to experiment with different states but don't want to assign a real one yet.

5. _____**Remote Rollovers**

The ways you just made rollovers resulted in one type of rollover, in which an image swaps itself for another image. The next type you'll learn to make is a remote rollover in which multiple pieces of artwork change when the mouse enters a specified region. This exercise is going to combine what you learned in Chapter 10, _"Slicing,"_ and use **Layer**-based rollovers and **Style**-based rollovers.

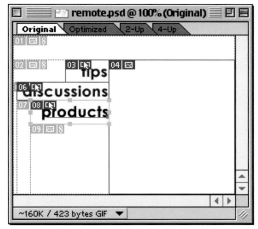

1. Before you get going, it might be nice to visualize what you are about to build. Open **remote.psd**, which I've sliced up for you and filled with pre-programmed rollovers.

2. Preview this file in a browser of your choice. Roll your mouse over the words "**tips**," "**discussions**," and "**products**."

See how each word changes color to red and that additional information appears to the right? This is what I meant when I said that in a remote rollover multiple pieces of artwork change at once. A rollover, in this case, is triggering a change in other slices. This is very impressive!

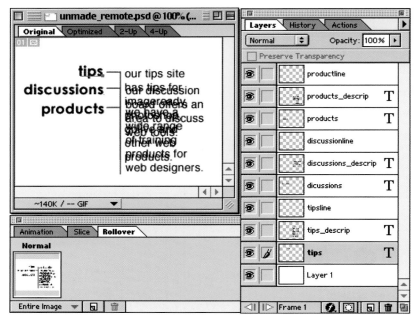

3. Close this file and open **unmade_remote.psd**. Turn all the layers on in the entire document so you can see what's on all of them at one time. I usually do this so I can see how to slice the artwork properly. **Tip:** You can click one eye icon on, leave your mouse depressed and drag over the rest to turn them all on in a more easy fashion than clicking them individually.

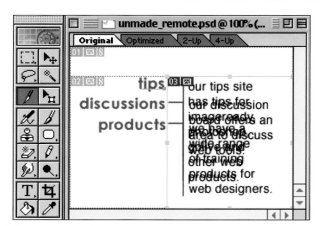

4. Using the **Slice** tool (the shortcut is the letter **Y** on your keyboard), drag a slice around an area that encompasses all the line and description images. **Tip:** If you make a mistake or want to adjust the boundaries of the slice, use the **Slice Selection** tool (the shortcut is the letter **A**).

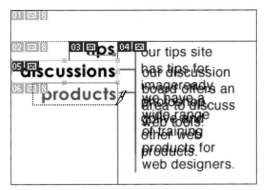

5. Next, drag slices around the words "**tips**," "**discussions**," and "**products**." **Tip:** When working with multiple slices and rollovers, it's very important that you specify your slices before you begin creating the rollovers. That's because it's much harder to change your mind to add a slice later after you've set up rollovers.

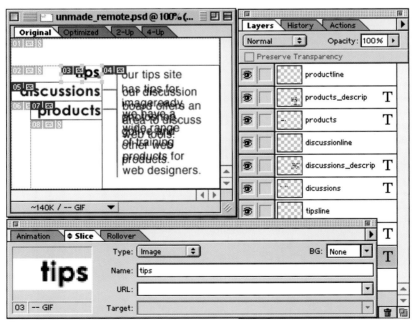

6. Click on the **Slice** tab of the **Rollover** palette. With the **Slice Selection** tool, select each of the slices you just created and name them respectively: **descriptions**, **tips**, **discussions**, and **products**. (You need to select each one first with the **Slice Selection** tool before you can rename them in the palette.) As you learned in the Chapter 10, *"Slicing,"* naming each region is important so that the resulting files will be named in a recognizable way.

Movie | **naming_slices.mov**

To learn more about naming slices, shown in Steps 3 through 6, check out **naming_slices.mov** from the **movies** folder on the **H·O·T CD-ROM**.

Now that you've named the slices, you are ready to set up the rollovers. The first thing to do is to imagine how this series of images should look in the **Normal** state, before anyone has moved his or her mouse over the words. The object of this exercise is to make these three words — **tips**, **discussions**, and **products** — visible first.

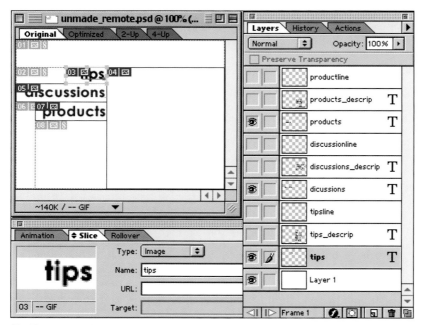

7. Turn off the layers named **productline**, **products_descrip**, **discussionline**, **discussions_ descrip**, **tipsline**, and **tips_descrip**, so that only the words **tips**, **discussions**, **products**, and **Layer 1** are visible.

> Note | **Slices and Layers**
>
> You might wonder which layer should be selected while you are slicing. It actually does not matter. **Slices** "drill" through each layer that's turned on in the document. The only time it matters which layer is selected is when you're adding a **Layer Effect** or editing a specific layer. You do not need to select a layer to turn its visibility on or to slice through it.

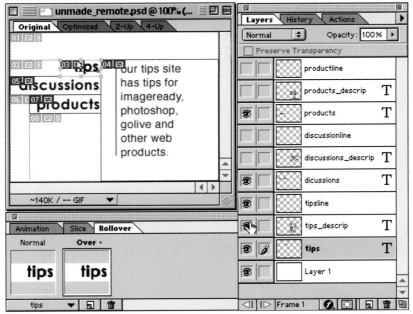

8. With the **Slice Selection** tool, select the **tips** slice. Click on the **Rollover** tab and click on the **New Rollover State** icon.

9. Turn on the eyes for **tipsline** and **tips_descrip**.

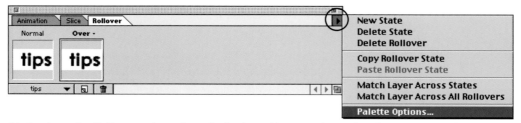

*Notice how the **Rollover** palette doesn't display a big enough preview for you to see the changes that you just made on the **Over** state? You can change this so you can view the whole document with the pop-up menu (circled above).*

IO. Click on the **Rollover** palette's upper-right arrow to select **Palette Options....**

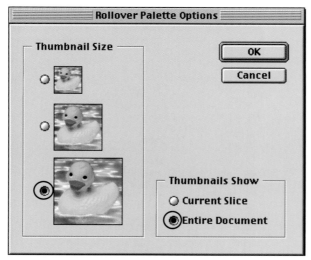

II. In the **Rollover Palette Options** window that will open, click on the large thumbnail icon and **Entire Document**, then click **OK.**

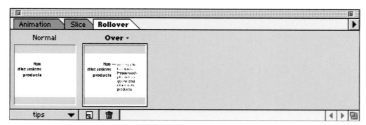

*With the **Rollover Palette Options** set to show the largest icon and the entire document, the **Over** state offers much better feedback.*

*Next, you need to change the word "**tips**" so it lights up in red. You'll use the **Color Fill Layer Effect** for this task, because the only type of color change that can be memorized between states is one made with a **Layer Effect**.*

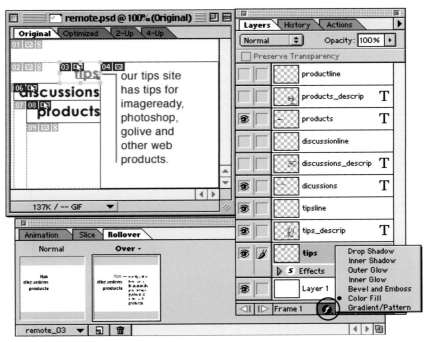

12. Select the **tips** layer in the **Layers** palette. Click on the *f*-shaped **Layer Effect** icon at the bottom of the palette and select **Color Fill**. The type will turn red in the **Over** state but remain black in the **Normal** state.

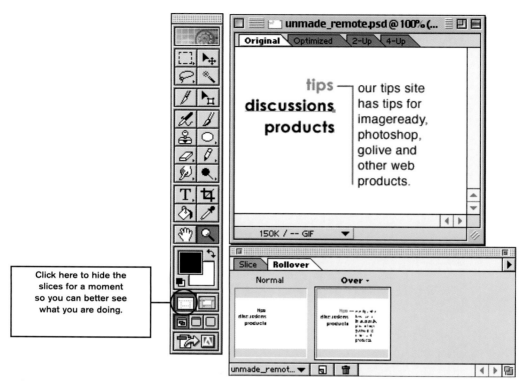

Click here to hide the slices for a moment so you can better see what you are doing.

13. If you want to see how things look without the slices showing (which can be very distracting at times) click on the **Hide Slices** button at the bottom of the toolbar. You can toggle this on and off whenever you want (the quickest way is to press your keyboard's letter **Q**, which lets you toggle between hiding or showing slices). Try clicking on the **Normal** and **Over** state with it off so you can more easily see the results of your labor so far.

14. Be sure to turn the **Show Slices** button on before the next step so you can select a new slice and continue programming this remote rollover.

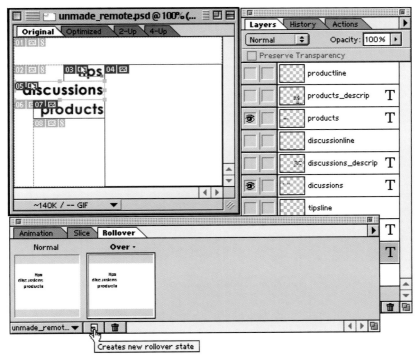

15. Select the slice that contains the word **discussions**. Notice that there is no **Over** state set yet. Click back onto the slice that contains the word **tips** and you'll see that the work you just did wasn't lost. It was associated with the **tips** slice and that's because every slice in a document can possess its own distinct set of rollover states. Click back on the **discussions** slice and click on the **New Rollover State** icon to create an **Over** state for that slice.

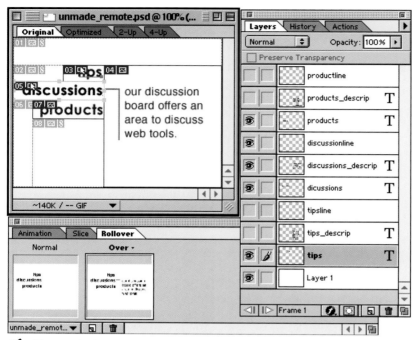

16. Turn on the layer visibility for the layers **discussionline** and **discussions_descrip**.

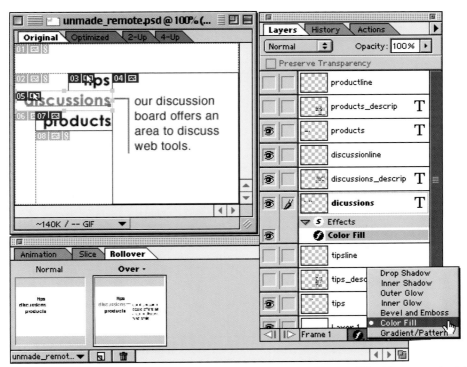

17. Select the **discussions** layer and click on the *f*-shaped **Layer Effect** icon to select **Color Fill** from the pop-up menu. The word "**discussions**" should turn red.

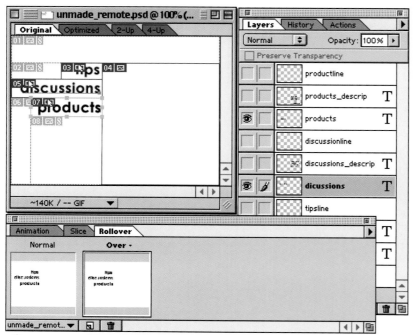

18. Select the **products** slice. Click on the **New Rollover State** icon at the bottom of the **Rollover** palette to create an **Over** state.

19. Turn on the visibility for the layers **productline** and **products_descrip**.

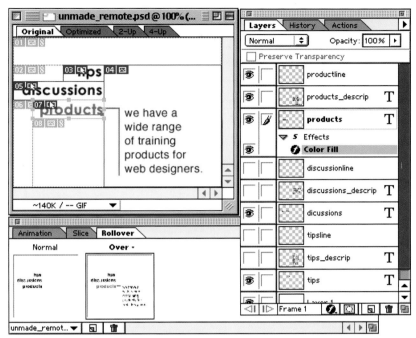

20. Now, select the **products** layer and click on the **Layer Effect** icon at the bottom of the **Layers** palette to select **Color Fill** from the pop-up menu.

21. Preview all this work in a browser. Your **remote rollover** file should function identically to what you previewed at the beginning of this exercise.

*Not only did you program a remote rollover, but you combined techniques from other chapters and exercises as well, including layer visibility and **Layer Effects**. The slices were key to creating multiple rollovers inside a single document.*

22. Return to ImageReady and leave this document open. Don't save just yet. You'll learn the nuances of saving this file in the next exercise.

6. ⎯⎯⎯⎯**Saving Complicated Rollovers**

[IR]

You've already learned to save rollovers and sliced documents. The last exercise you completed contained both rollover graphics and slices. This next exercise is mostly a review, but it never hurts to review the steps, especially when saving rollovers is such a new practice to most Photoshop and ImageReady users.

I. With **unmade_remote.psd** still open from the previous exercise, choose **File > Save As...** and name this file **remote2.psd**. Navigate to save it in your **chap_11** folder. Saving a .psd master document will allow you to make a change in the future since only a .psd file can store all the slicing and layer information.

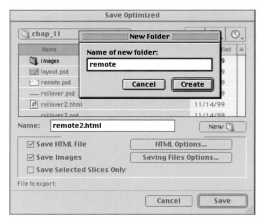

2. Choose **File > Save Optimized As...** and create a new folder called **remote**. To save all the HTML and image files inside this new folder, do one of the following.

• (Mac) Click on the **New** button, which will bring up the **New Folder** icon before you save the contents. Make sure that **Save HTML File** and **Save Images** are both checked and click **Save**.

• (Windows) Click on the yellow **New Folder** icon and name the new folder **remote**. Double-click to open the **remote** folder and then click **Save** in the **Save Optimized** dialog box.

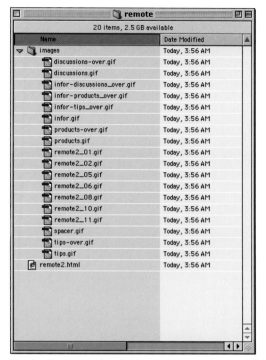

3. Look on your hard drive to ensure that you did, indeed, create a folder called **remote** and that it contains the HTML and a folder called **images**.

4. Return to ImageReady and close the file.

*Are you curious why ImageReady wrote all those separate images and HTML? A rollover, by nature, has to generate an image for every single state and slice. If there is a **Normal**, **Over** and **Click** state in one slice, ImageReady needs to generate three separate images. The HTML contains the JavaScript that makes the rollover work.*

*You might wonder why I asked you to make a folder called **remote**. If you don't make a separate folder, all the pieces of the rollover will still work but if you save it to a folder that already contains files, then the HTML and images will mix in with your other files, making it difficult to keep your files organized.*

7. Creating Navigation Bar Layers

Navigation bars are one of the most common uses for rollovers. Because a rollover graphic gives the visitor to your Web site great feedback about which images contain links, its popularity for this purpose is understandable. However, of all the types of rollovers you'll learn to make in ImageReady, this will be the most challenging. This exercise will teach a number of new skills, including automatic slicing and alignment using linked layers.

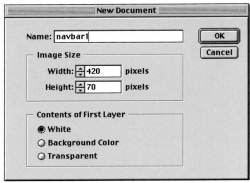

I. Choose **File > New** and create a new document with the same settings and name as you see above. Click **OK**.

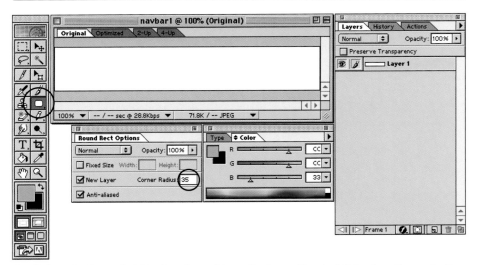

2. Select the **Rounded Rectangle** tool from the ImageReady 2.0 toolbar. If you don't see this tool, hold your mouse down on the **Rectangle** or **Ellipse** tool and select it.

3. Double-click the **Rounded Rectangle** tool to make the **Round Rect Options** palette appear. **Tip:** Sometimes the **Options** palette will be behind another palette and this technique won't work. In that event choose **Window > Show Options**. In the **Round Rect Option**s palette, type in **Corner Radius: 35**. This is going to make a more rounded rectangle shape than the default radius provides.

*These new shape tools are a great addition to ImageReady 2.0. The **Rectangle**, **Rounded Rectangle**, and **Ellipse** tools are perfect for making Web buttons of all shapes and sizes.*

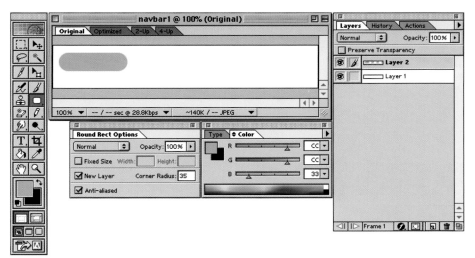

4. Select a color of your liking before you draw the shape. As you can see above, the color will be dictated by whatever color is in the **Foreground Color** swatch on the toolbar. If you don't like the color you chose, you can always practice the coloring skills that you built in Chapter 5, *"Web Color."* Drag a rounded rectangle shape on to the document window. Make the size similar to what you see on the screen above. **Note:** Don't worry about aligning this shape yet.

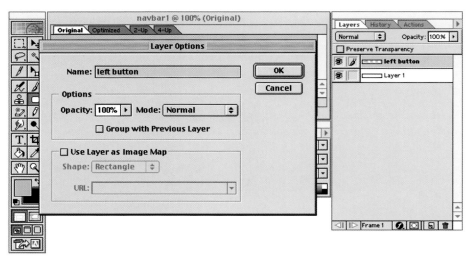

5. Double-click **Layer 2** to name it **left button** and click **OK**. **Tip:** When you work with multiple layers you will find that naming your layers makes it much easier to navigate around the document.

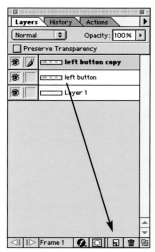

6. Drag the **left button** layer onto the **New Layer** icon at the bottom of the **Layers** palette. This will make a copy. **Note:** The copy will only show in the **Layers** palette, but it will not be visible in the document because it is in the exact same location as the original layer from which it was copied. You will move it to a new location in the next step.

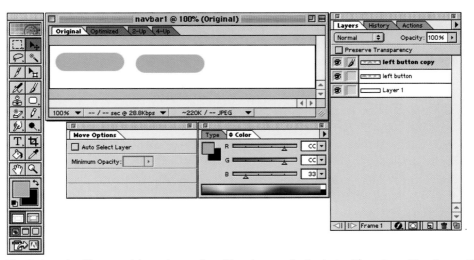

7. Select the **Move** tool from the toolbar (the shortcut is the letter **V**) and position it over the **button** shape. Click and drag to the right, and you'll see the copy move away from the original. **Note:** You still don't have to worry about alignment. You'll get to that in a future exercise.

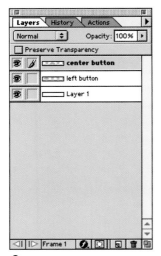

8. Double-click the **left button copy** layer to rename it **center button**.

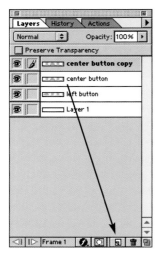

9. Drag the **center button** layer on to the **New Layer** icon at the bottom of the **Layers** palette. This will make a copy, which, again, won't be visible in the document window because it is hidden behind the original from which it was copied – in this case, the **center button** layer.

10. The **Move** tool should still be selected, so just click and drag the **second button** over to the right with your mouse depressed. You'll see the **center button copy** appear to the right of the **center button** original.

Tip | **Using the Shift Key with the Move Tool**

You can constrain the artwork to be moved in a straight line on a parallel path if you use the **Shift** key when you click and drag with the **Move** tool.

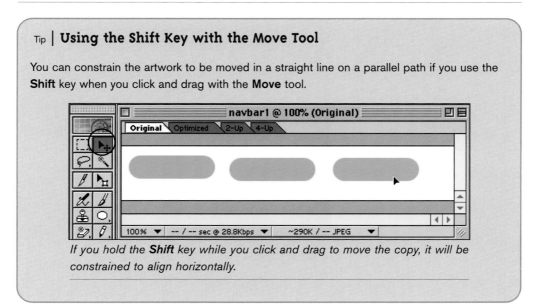

*If you hold the **Shift** key while you click and drag to move the copy, it will be constrained to align horizontally.*

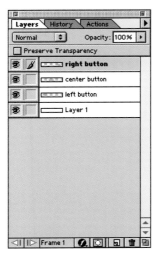

II. Double-click the **center button** copy layer and rename it **right button**.

I2. Choose **File > Save**. Leave this document open for the next exercise.

Note | **Why Duplicate Layers?**

When you are making navigation bars, there are a few important goals. You will most likely want all your buttons to be the same size. You could have dragged the rounded rectangle shape out three times on your screen to make three distinct layers. Instead, this last exercise walked you through the steps of duplicating the layers. You might wonder why.

By duplicating the layers, you ensure that they are the same size. There are other methods to ensure this, such as setting the **Rounded Rectangle** tool options to be a fixed size. I prefer the method you learned here, which was to duplicate each layer.

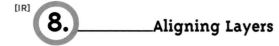

Aligning Layers

Learning to align layers is actually a pretty tricky thing. I predict that you might find this exercise frustrating. There's a movie to guide you on this one, (align_layers.mov), and you might want to watch it before you start the exercise. It's easier to understand some things if you see them performed than if they're explained with mere words. But before you watch the movie, take note that aligning layers involves learning to use the **Link** function of the **Layers** palette.

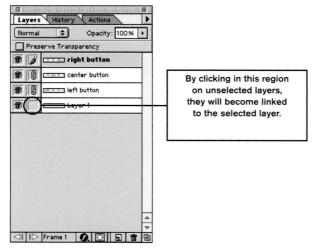

By clicking in this region on unselected layers, they will become linked to the selected layer.

I. With the **right button** layer of **navbar1.psd** still selected from the end of the last exercise, click inside the **Link** region of the **Layers** palette on the **center button** and **left button** layers. This caused the unselected layers (**center button** and **left button**) to be linked to the **right button** layer. **Tip:** To get 100 percent clear on what I mean, try moving any of these layers with the **Move** tool on your screen. You'll see that they move together because they are linked.

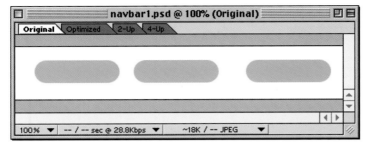

2. Choose **Layer > Align Linked > Vertical Center**. You'll see that all the layers align so they are at one horizontal level. One of the benefits to using the **Layers** palette's **Link** function is this powerful alignment function.

Now that you've aligned all of the button shapes horizontally, it would be nice to align them so they have equal distance between them, wouldn't it? Here's how.

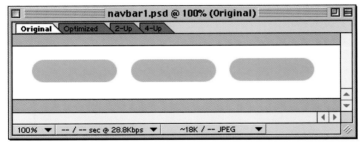

3. Choose **Layer > Distribute Linked > Left**. This will perfectly distribute all the buttons. **Tip:** You can use the **Move** tool to move the block of three buttons around the screen to put them wherever you want because they are linked.

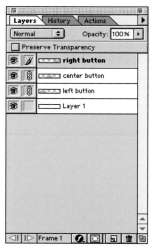

4. Now it's time to add some words for the buttons. Make sure you select the top layer in the **Layers** palette (**right button**) before adding the type. This will ensure that the type you add for the button will be above the other layers, which will become important later for alignment reasons.

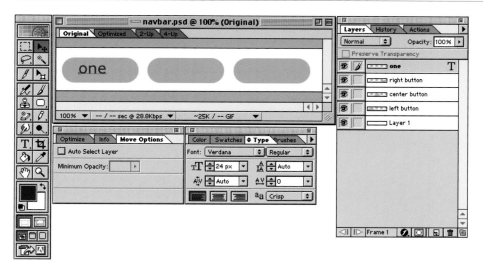

5. Pick a different color than what you chose for the **Rounded Rectangle** shape. **Hint:** You can use the **Color Picker**, the **Swatch** palette, or the **Color** palette from which to choose a new color. Using the **Type** tool (the shortcut is the letter **T** on your keyboard), click in the middle of the first button and type the word "**one**." The layer **one** should appear at the top of the **Layers** palette. Switch to the **Move** tool, and the type will appear with ImageReady's blue editable text underline. Now it's selected so that it can be changed in the next step.

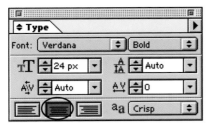

6. Drag the **Type** palette out (**Window > Show Type**). Change the alignment to center, as circled above. This will likely cause the type on your screen to look offset to the button, but that's OK because you'll learn to fix that in a minute. Pick a different font if you want.

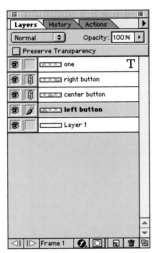

7. Click on the **left button** layer to select it. Notice that it is still linked to the **center button** as well as the **right button**.

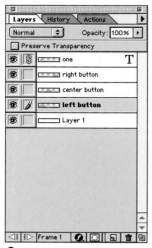

8. Turn off the link icons on the **center** button and **right** buttons. Click in the **Link** region on the editable type layer named **one**. This links the **left button** layer to the editable type **one** layer.

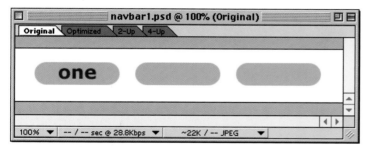

9. Choose **Layer > Align Linked > Horizontal Center** and then choose **Layer > Align Linked > Vertical Center**. This should perfectly align that **left button** and type layer **one** to each other without disturbing the alignment that was achieved in earlier steps.

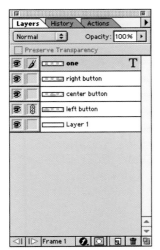

10. Make sure you select the top layer in the **Layers** palette (**one**) before adding the other type. This will ensure that the type you add for the other two buttons will be placed at the top of the layer stack.

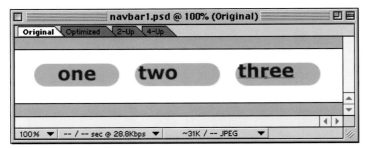

11. With the **Type** tool, click on the **middle** button and type the word **two**. Click on the right button twice, once to deselect the type you just created and again to type the word **three**. Click on the **Move** tool, and you'll see that the last type layer you created will become selected, as evidenced by the blue underline.

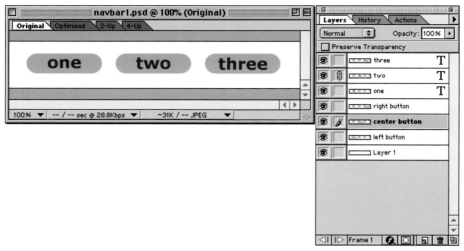

12. Select the **center button** layer and then click on the **Link** region for type layer **two**. Choose **Layer > Align Linked > Horizontal Center** and then choose **Layer > Align Linked > Vertical Center**. Repeat this procedure for the **right button** layer and **three** layer.

13. With your document created and aligned, you're ready to move to the next step, which is to slice and create the rollovers. Save the document and leave it open.

Movie | **align_layers.mov**

To learn more about using alignment features, check out **align_layers.mov** from the **movies** folder on the **H•O•T CD-ROM**.

Adding Slices to a Navigation Bar

The next step toward completing the navigation bar is to slice it using the **Divide Slice** feature and, after that, to add the rollovers to it. You've learned to do these things in other exercises and chapters, but it never hurts to get extra practice in a different context.

I. With **navbar1.psd** open from the previous exercise, use the **Slice** tool (the shortcut is the letter **Y** on your keyboard) to drag a slice around all three buttons.

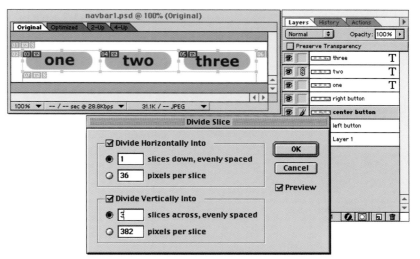

2. Choose **Slices > Divide Slice....** In the **Divide Slice** dialog box, enter the value of **3 slices across, evenly spaced**, and click **OK**. **Note:** The pixels per slice might differ on your screen than on this one, because your buttons might be slightly smaller or bigger than what the buttons show here. The important thing is to divide it by **3 slices across, evenly spaced**.

This method works because your artwork was aligned perfectly, so you could choose a mathematical way of creating three perfect slices.

3. Choose **File > Save As...** and name this **navbar2.psd**. Leave the file open for the next exercise, in which you will set the rollovers for this navigation bar, which now has slices for exactly that purpose.

[IR] **IO.** _____Adding Rollovers to a Navigation Bar

You've already learned how to make rollovers, but you might not grasp all the steps involved when there are multiple slices. This exercise will give you more practice in building your rollover skills.

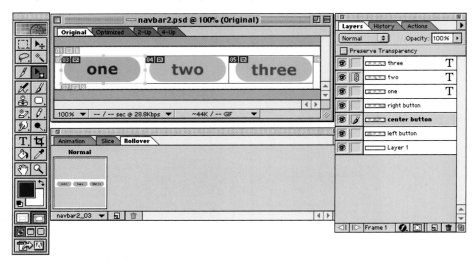

I. In **navbar1.psd**, which you should still have open from the previous exercise, select the left slice using the **Slice Selection** tool. Make sure the **Rollover** palette is visible (**Window > Show Rollover**). Notice that all three rollover images are showing in the thumbnail view of the **Normal** state of the **Rollover** palette? This is because you changed the settings for the **Rollover** palette in Exercise 5. For the purposes of this exercise it will be better if you change it back to how it was originally. The next steps will show you how.

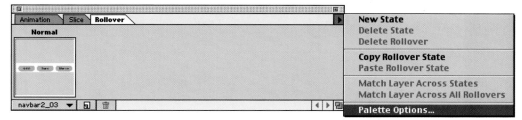

2. Click on the upper-right arrow of the **Rollover** palette to select **Palette Options...** from the pop-up menu.

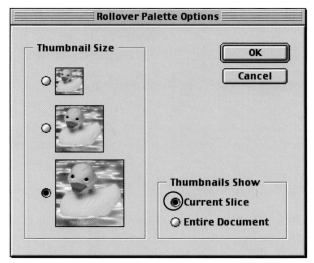

3. Click on **Current Slice** and click **OK**.

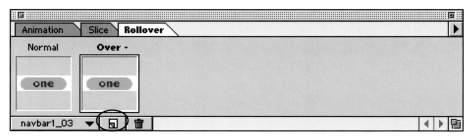

4. Your **Rollover** palette will now only display the slice that is selected. Click on the **New Rollover State** icon at the bottom of the **Rollover** palette.

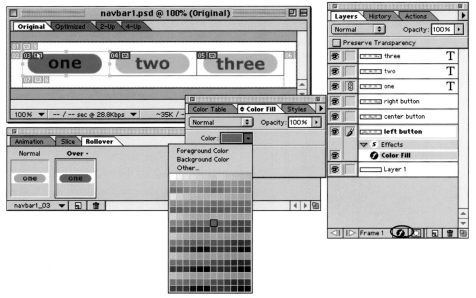

5. Select the **left button** layer in the **Layers** palette. Click on the **Layer Effect** icon at the bottom of that palette and select **Color Fill** from the pop-up menu. **Tip:** If you want to change the red default color, click on the arrow next to the color field in the **Color Fill Options** palette (**Window > Show Layer Options/Effects**).

6. Choose **Layer > Effects > Copy Effects** to put a copy of the **Color Fill** setting you just created into the clipboard of your computer so you can copy it on other layers to maintain a consistent appearance.

7. You should still be in the **Slice Selection** tool. Click on the middle slice to select that slice.

8. Click on the **New Rollover State** icon at the bottom of the **Rollover** palette.

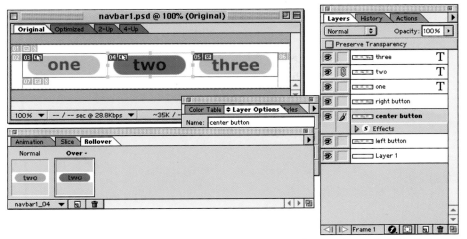

9. Select the **center button** layer in the **Layers** palette. Choose **Layer > Effects > Paste Effects**. Beautiful! The rollover state of the middle slice now matches that of the left slice.

10. See if you can figure out how to do the same to the **right button** layer. I bet you can!

11. Preview this in a browser and you should see each button change as you roll over it. If you don't like the way it looks, experiment with the compression settings.

12. Save and close this file. You should be proud; this was a challenging chapter and you made it through alive ;-).

Movie | **multiple_roll.mov**

To learn more about making a navigation bar rollover, shown in this last exercise, check out **multiple_roll.mov** from the **movies** folder on the **H•O•T CD-ROM**.

12.
Animated GIFs

Frame-by-Frame	Setting Speed and Looping	Optimizing and Saving
Transparent Animated GIFs	Tweening	Reversing and Looping Frames
Animated GIF Rollovers	Designing Entire Interfaces

chap_12

Photoshop 5.5 / ImageReady 2.0
H·O·T CD-ROM

One of the coolest things about authoring for the Web is that you can include animation on pages, which is something that print publishing obviously can't offer. It's likely that this is the first design medium you've ever worked in that supports animation, and that learning animation is new to you. If that's the case, you're very lucky that you get to learn on such great tools as Photoshop 5.5 and Image-Ready 2.0. If you've done animation before, you'll still be grateful for these tools, but you likely had to learn on systems that were much more difficult.

While animation appears to move when seen on a computer screen, that movement is actually created from a series of still images. The GIF format is the most popular file format for Web animation because it can contain a series of static images and display them one after the other in sequence, much like a slide show. It's also popular because it is backwards compatible with older browsers.

While you can prepare images for animation in Photoshop, the only place that you can write animated GIFs is inside ImageReady. For this reason, all the exercises in this chapter take place in ImageReady.

Animation Terms

If you are new to creating animation in ImageReady, here is a handy list to help familiarize you with several new terms and interface elements.

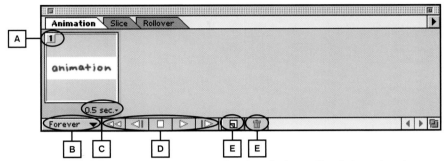

Animation palette: You'll create animations in ImageReady by using the *Animation* palette. *A:* This displays the frame number. *B:* Here is where you set how many times the animation plays. *C:* Here is where you set the delay of each frame. *D:* These are the playback controls. *E:* The **New Frame** icon creates a new frame by duplicating the selected frame. *F:* Use the **Delete Frame** icon to delete a frame.

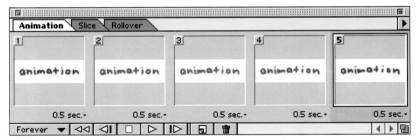

Frames: ImageReady's *Animation* palette numbers frames sequentially. A single frame indicates that the image is static, while two or more different frames displayed in sequence will create the illusion of movement.

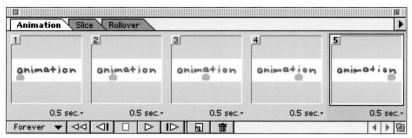

Frame-by-Frame Animation: *You can create this by turning on and off different layers over a series of frames.*

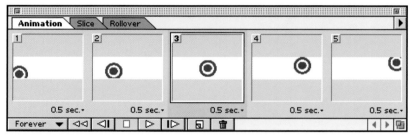

Position Tween: *When this is applied, one layer of artwork changes position over a number of frames. You can create a **Tween** in ImageReady by taking two different frames (called keyframes) and applying the **Tween** command, which will create the additional frames automatically.*

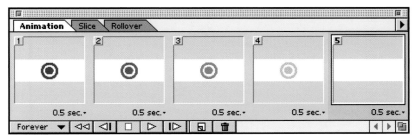

Opacity Tween: *This is something you apply so that one layer of artwork changes opacity over a number of frames.*

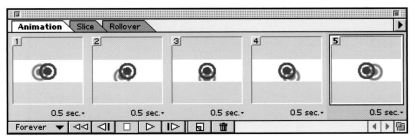

Layer Effect Tween: *You can also apply to one layer of artwork a **Layer Effect** which changes over a number of frames.*

Animated GIF Format

The GIF file format supports animation, while the JPEG format does not. A Web browser treats an animated GIF file no different than a static GIF file, except that it displays multiple images in a sequence instead of a single image, much like a slide show. Because different frames can contain different timings, one frame can hold for a few seconds while other frames can display in much less time.

Animated GIF files do not require Plug-Ins, which means they are accessible to all Web browsers (with the exception of text-only or 1.0 browsers). The HTML code to include an animated GIF is no different from that of a static GIF, so working with these animation files requires no extra programming expertise. Animated GIF files can be instructed to loop (or repeat endlessly), to only play once, or to play a specific number of times. The number of repeats is stored in the file itself, not in the HTML code.

Compression Challenges

The animated GIF format uses the same principles of compression that apply to static GIF images. Large areas of solid color compress better than areas with a lot of noise or detail. If you do use photographic-style images, be sure to add **Lossy** compression – it will make a substantial difference in file savings.

Animated GIFs will always be larger than static GIFs. By default, ImageReady turns on two features – **Bounding Box** and **Redundant Pixel Removal**. What this means is that ImageReady will only add file size to the areas that have changed in your animation. If you have a photographic background and the only thing that changes is some lettering that fades up over it, the photographic area will only be written once to the file, causing it to decrease in file size. If you change every pixel of an animation, such as this chapter's animated slide show example, the **Bounding Box** and **Redundant Pixel Removal** features won't be able to help.

When you compress animated GIFs, keep in mind that the file will stream in, meaning that frames will appear before the entire file has finished loading. For this reason, I usually divide the file size by the number of frames, and that makes me feel a lot better about big file sizes. For example, if I have a 100K animated GIF file that is 10 frames long, in reality each frame is only 10K, which makes me feel more at ease about publishing such a big file to the Web.

Controlling the Timing of Animated GIFs

Animation is time based, meaning that it depends on time passing as well as its artwork changing. If you alter artwork very slowly in an animation, it doesn't appear to move but to sit for a long time and then change. If you change artwork very quickly, it appears to have more fluid movement.

Sometimes slide-show-style animation is what you'll want and other times you'll want to make movement happen more quickly. The GIF format supports delays between frames, which allows for the timing to change within a single animation file.

Video and film animation are also time-based mediums, with one key difference from animated GIFs. They play back at specific frame rates (30 frames per second for video, 24 frames per second for film). Unfortunately, animated GIF files may play back at different speeds depending on the computer upon which they are viewed. A slow Mac or PC (386, 486, 030, 040, or Power PC) will play an animation much more slowly than a new G3, G4, Pentium II, or III. There's no controlling that the animation you author will play back at different speeds on different processors. The only suggestion I can make is that you view your work on an older machine, if you can, before you publish it to the Web. This isn't always possible or practical, and the truth is that most people don't have a lot of old computers lying around to test with. It doesn't stop anyone from publishing animation, but it does mean that you might be surprised when you view your work on older machines.

Animation Aesthetics

Animation is going to draw your end-user's eye much more than a static image. Make sure that the subject matter you pick for animation is worthy of more attention than other images on your screen. I've seen Web pages contain so much animation that it distracts from the important content rather than enhance it. Good uses for animation might include ad banners, making certain words move so they stand out, diagrams brought to life, slide shows of photographs, or cartoon characters. You'll learn how to do all these different kinds of animation in this chapter.

[PS] **I.** _____Frame-by-Frame Animation with Layers

ImageReady can work with existing Photoshop files, or you can work with artwork you create in ImageReady. It is important to note, however, that Photoshop 5.5 cannot write animated GIF files, which is why this entire chapter takes place in ImageReady. This exercise walks you through the process of establishing frame-by-frame animation by turning on and off layers.

I. In ImageReady, open **animation_finished.psd** from the **chap_12** folder that you transferred to your hard drive from the **H•O•T CD-ROM**.

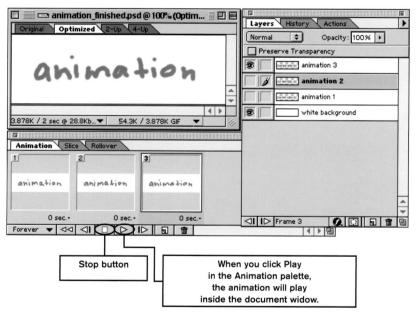

2. Make sure the **Animation** and **Layers** palettes are open (**Window > Show Anima-tion** and **Window > Show Layers**). Click **Play** to watch the animation play inside the document window. You should see the letters in the word "**animation**" dance on the screen. Click **Stop** once you've watched the animation.

 Movie | **framebyframe.mov**

To learn more about Exercise 1, "Frame-By-Frame Animation with Layers," check out **frame-byframe.mov** from the **movies** folder on the **H•O•T CD-ROM**.

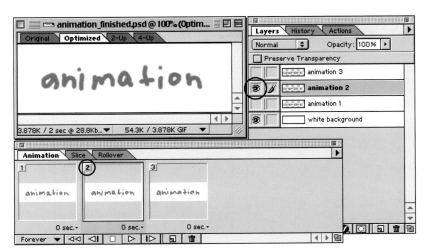

3. Select each frame in the **Animation** palette, and notice that different layers in the **Layers** palette turn on and off.

*This animation was created by writing the word "**animation**" three times on three different layers. The layers were then selectively turned on and off. You will learn how to build this file in the following steps.*

4. Close the file and do not save if prompted. Open **animation.psd**, which contains only a single frame in the **Animation** palette. That's because the **Animation** palette must contain at least two frames with different content in each one. One way to achieve this is to turn the visibility of different artwork on and off between frames, as you just witnessed. You will learn to create new frames and turn layers on and off in the following steps.

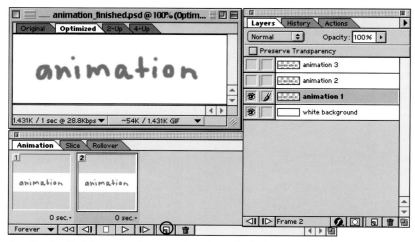

5. On the first frame, make sure that the visibility is turned on for **animation 1** and **white background**. Click the **New Frame** icon at the bottom of the **Animation** palette to create a duplicate of the first frame before it.

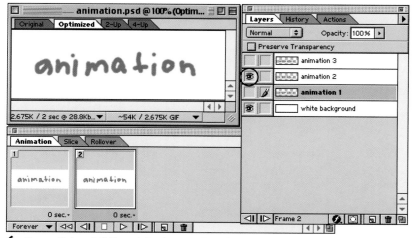

6. Turn off the visibility of the layer **animation 1**, and turn on the visibility of the layer **animation 2** by clicking on and off the eye icons. Leave the layer **white background** turned on.

*It does not matter which layer is selected in the **Layers** palette when you are turning on or off with the eye icons. That's because ImageReady and Photoshop allow you to turn layers on and off without selecting a specific layer.*

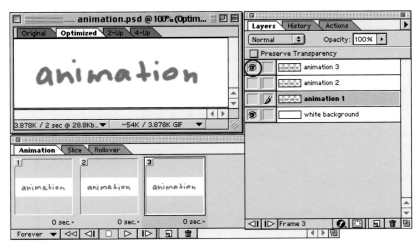

7. Click the **New Frame** icon again to create a third frame. This duplicates the second frame until you make a change, such as turning on or off a different layer. For **frame 3**, turn off **animation 2** and turn on **animation 3** in the **Layers** palette. Leave the layer **white background** turned on.

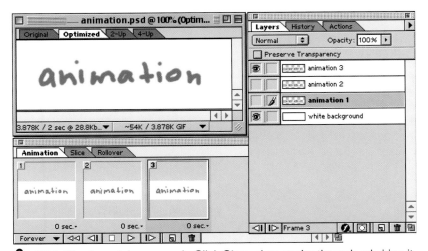

8. Click **Play** to watch your work. Click **Stop** when you're through admiring it.

9. Choose **File > Save** and leave the file open for the next exercise.

You might be surprised at how easy it was to set up your first animation in ImageReady. Animated GIFs have never been easier to make as far as I'm concerned!

2. ——————Setting the Speed and Looping

This exercise focuses on how to slow down the speed and change the looping from a **Forever** setting, like the one you just played and stopped, to a specific number of repeats.

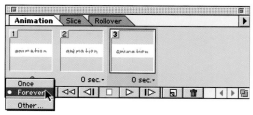

1. With **animation.psd** open from the last exercise, play the animation again by clicking **Play** on the **Animation** palette. Notice that it loops indefinitely? Click and hold down on the **Forever** pop-up menu at the bottom left of the **Animation** palette. Change it to **Once** and press **Play** again. The animation should only play once. Return the setting to **Forever** once you've explored this setting.

*Tip: If you want the duration of the animation to play more than once or less than forever, choose the **Other...** setting and enter the number of repeats you prefer. This particular animation will look best if it loops forever, but now you know how to change the looping if you want to for future animation projects.*

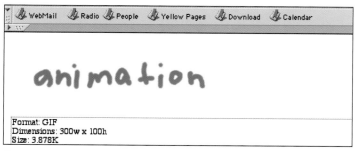

2. Preview this in a browser (**File > Preview in**). Notice that the animation plays much faster than it did when you previewed it by pressing **Play**. That's because ImageReady builds the animation as it plays back, while the browser plays the animated GIF that is already built. You'll notice that the animation plays too fast now. Return to ImageReady to slow down the pacing.

It's impossible to tell the true speed of the animation unless you preview it in a browser. In most cases, this one included, the animation plays much faster in the browser than it does in ImageReady. For this reason, it's always important to view the animation in a browser before you finalize your speed settings.

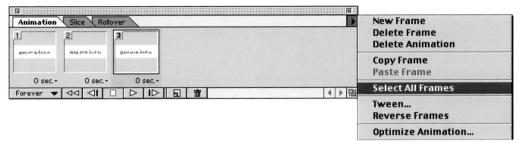

3. Click the upper-right arrow of the **Animation** palette and choose **Select All Frames**.

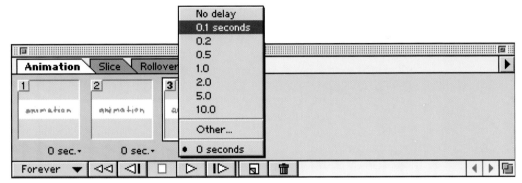

4. Hold down on any of the frame settings that currently read **0 sec**. From the pop-up menu select **0.1 seconds**. All the frames should change at once.

5. All of the frames should now appear with the **0.1 sec**. timing in the pop-up menu. Preview in the browser (**File > Preview in**) to see how the timing of the animation slowed down a little. **Tip:** You can change the rate of individual frames if you want, or change all of them at once by selecting all the frames first, as you did here.

6. Choose **File > Save** and leave the document open for the next exercise.

3.————————**Optimizing and Saving an Animated GIF**

Has all of this seemed too simple so far? It's easy to create and edit animation in ImageReady. Perhaps you are thinking that there must be something more to it? Nope. The only thing left to do is to optimize this animation and save it as a GIF. You'll see that there is little difference between saving an animated GIF or just a plain old static GIF.

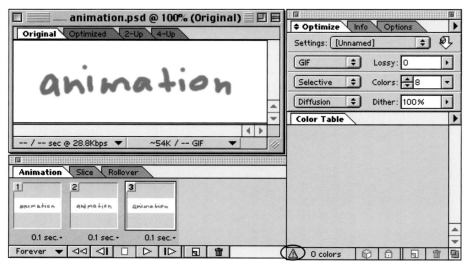

I. Make sure that the **Optimize** and **Color Table** palettes are open (**Window > Show Optimize**). Note that there is nothing in the **Color Table**, and the warning symbol appears at the bottom left of the **Color Table** palette. If you get a warning symbol, (circled), it is there to alert you to the fact that this document has never been optimized. Switch to the **Optimized** tab of the document and the warning symbol will disappear.

Note | **Animation Must Be Saved as GIF**

When creating animation, it's essential that you use the GIF setting instead of JPEG. There is no such thing as an animated JPEG. The good thing is, if you ever accidentally try to save animation as a JPEG or PNG, ImageReady will let you know that those formats cannot support animation.

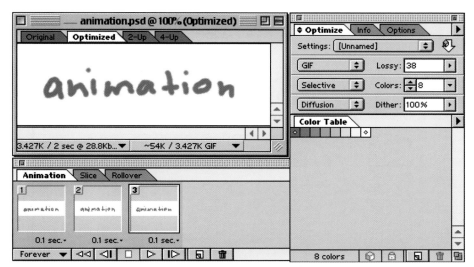

2. Now it is your turn. Go ahead and experiment with changing the settings.

*Notice that I have set **Lossy: 38**? Lossy compression will often help animated GIFs (as well as static GIFs) get much smaller than was ever possible before ImageReady 2.0 introduced this new compression feature.*

3. Choose **File > Save Optimized As...**, and you'll be prompted to save this as **animation.gif**. You do not need to save HTML in this instance, just make sure **Save Images** is checked. Click **OK**. That's all there is to it.

*You might wonder why I suggested that you save the images but not HTML in this instance. An animated GIF file knows to function properly with or without the accompanying HTML. You can insert this animated GIF into an HTML editor just as you would insert any static GIF. The GIF file format can display multiple frames with or without the accompanying HTML. You can even load an animated GIF directly into a browser without having any HTML. Try it, if you'd like. Go to the browser of your choice, and choose **File > Open** to open **animation.gif**, or simply drag and drop it into an open browser window. How does it know? ImageReady recognizes that a GIF is an animated GIF any time there are multiple frames in the **Animation** palette. The browser recognizes an animated GIF if more than one frame has been saved in the file.*

4. Save and keep the file open for the next exercise.

4.————————Making a Transparent Animated GIF

What if you want to make a transparent animated GIF? The process is almost identical to making a transparent static GIF, with a few other issues thrown into the mix, like how to affect a change throughout an entire animation by using the **Match Layers Across Frames** setting. This exercise lets you practice in this technique.

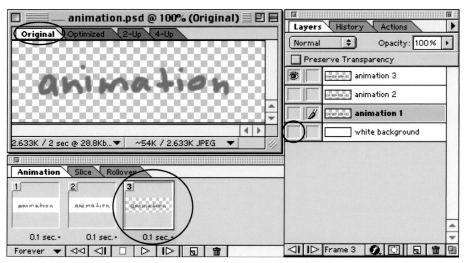

I. With **animation.psd** still open from the last exercise, turn off the eye icon for **white background** in the **Layers** palette. Click on the **Original** tab, and you should see inside the document window a checkerboard background; this indicates a transparent GIF.

*If you look carefully at the **Animation** palette, you will see that this change was only made for the frame that was selected, which means that ImageReady doesn't yet know that you want this change to occur throughout the entire animation. You'll get to remedy that next.*

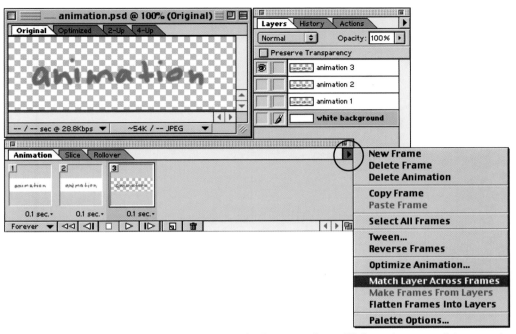

2. Select the **white background** layer inside the **Layers** palette. Click on the upper-right arrow in the **Animation** palette to select **Match Layer Across Frames**. After making this change, you'll see that all the frames will change at once.

*When using the **Match Layer Across Frames** feature, it's essential that the layer you are matching is selected inside the **Layers** palette.*

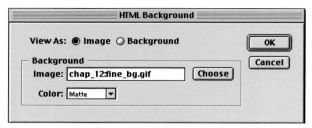

3. Choose **File > HTML Background...** and click on **Choose** to select **fine_bg.gif** from the **chap_12** folder. Click **Open** and then **OK**.

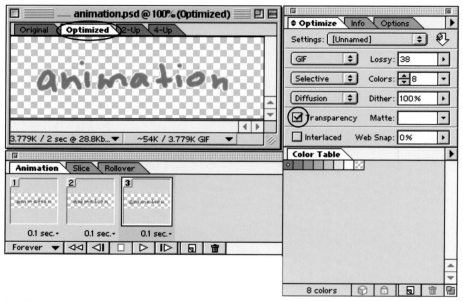

4. Click on the **Optimized** tab to check the settings. Make sure the **Optimize** and **Color Table** palettes are open. Make sure that **Transparency** is checked. If you cannot see the **Transparency** checkbox, click on the upper-right arrow of the **Optimize** palette to select **Show Options**.

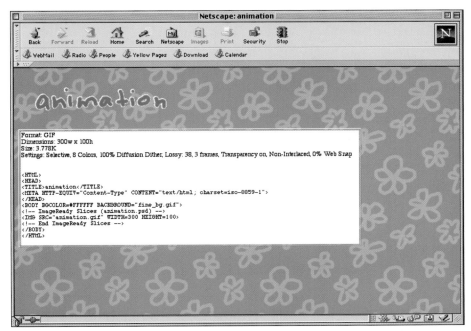

```
Format: GIF
Dimensions: 300w x 100h
Size: 3.778K
Settings: Selective, 8 Colors, 100% Diffusion Dither, Lossy: 38, 3 frames, Transparency on, Non-Interlaced, 0% Web Snap

<HTML>
<HEAD>
<TITLE>animation</TITLE>
<META HTTP-EQUIV="Content-Type" CONTENT="text/html; charset=iso-8859-1">
</HEAD>
<BODY BGCOLOR=#FFFFFF BACKGROUND="fine_bg.gif">
<!-- ImageReady Slices (animation.psd) -->
<IMG SRC="animation.gif" WIDTH=300 HEIGHT=100>
<!-- End ImageReady Slices -->
</BODY>
</HTML>
```

5. Preview this in the browser. The file should appear over the background image.

There's that unattractive white edge again you might remember from making transparent GIFs in Chapter 8, "Transparent GIFs." The next step will show you how to fix the problem.

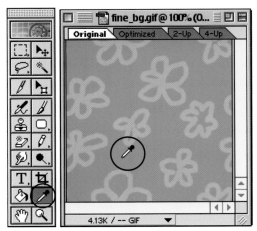

6. Return to ImageReady and open **fine_bg.gif**. Use the **Eyedropper** to capture the color. Go back to **animation.psd** (you can either click on it to make it active, or choose **Window > animation.psd**).

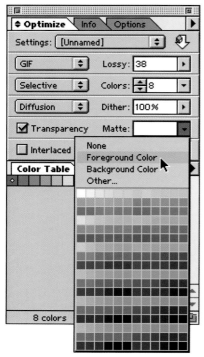

7. In the **Optimize** palette, click on the arrow to the right of the **Matte** field and select **Foreground Color** from the pop-up menu. Changes in the **Optimize** palette apply to all the frames in the animation. Preview in the browser again and you should see a perfect transparent animated GIF.

If you need help running through this process, revisit Chapter 8, "Transparent GIFs," to jog your memory. Making an animated transparent GIF has the same challenges as a static animated GIF. It's my hope that you can now transfer the skills you built in Chapter 8 to this new application of the same principles.

8. Save **animation.psd** and close it, as well as **fine_bg.gif**.

[IR] **5.**————————**Tweening with Opacity**

So far, you've been making animation by turning on and off layer visibility. This is one way to do it, but ImageReady has a few other tricks up its sleeve. This next exercise will introduce you to the **Tween** feature.

I. Open **flower.psd**.

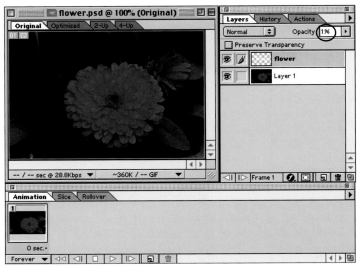

2. Make sure that the **flower** layer is selected in the **Layers** palette, then enter **Opacity: 1%**. The word "**flower**" should disappear.

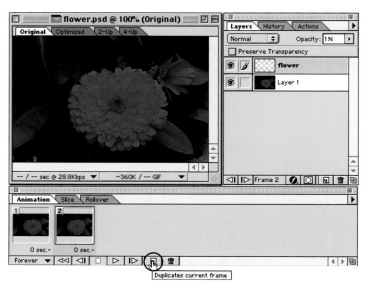

3. Click the **New Frame** icon at the bottom of the **Animation** palette.

*This will duplicate the exact settings that were in frame 1. To create another **Opacity** setting, which you need for the **Tween**, you'll change the second frame in the next step.*

4. The new frame you selected will be highlighted, so any changes you make will apply to it. Select the **flower** layer in the **Layers** palette and enter **Opacity: 100%**. This should make the word "**flower**" visible in that frame.

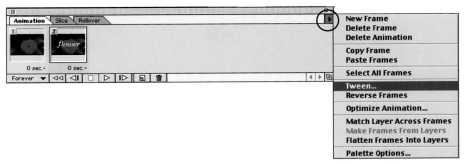

5. Click the upper-right arrow of the **Animation** palette to select **Tween...** from the pop-up menu.

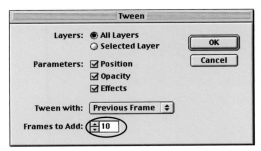

6. When the **Tween** dialog box appears, enter **Frames to Add: 10**. Click **OK**.

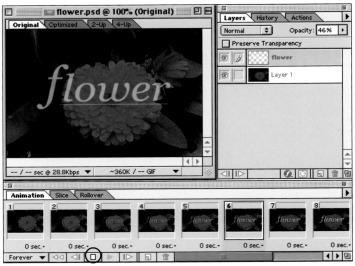

7. Click **Play** to test the animation. You should see the word "**flower**" fade up over the photographic background. Click **Stop**.

*This particular animation might look best if it only plays once. Do you remember how to change the **Forever** setting? If not, revisit Exercise 2 in this chapter. While this looks one way when you preview it in ImageReady, don't forget to test this file in the browser. That's because you'll always get the best indication of speed in the browser, not in ImageReady. When you preview this animation, you'll see that you haven't set any optimization settings yet, and that ImageReady is using the optimization settings from the last image that you worked on. Don't get too worried about optimizing this image just yet. This exercise was created to familiarize you with **Tweening**, and a later exercise will cover optimization techniques for animated GIF files.*

8. Save and leave the file open for the next exercise.

Movie | **tweening_opacity.mov**

To learn more about Exercise 5, "Tweening with Opacity," check out **tweening_opacity.mov** from the **movies** folder on the **H•O•T CD-ROM**.

[IR]

6. _____Selecting, Duplicating, and Reversing Frames

What if you wanted to make the words fade up, then hold, then fade out? This type of change is not only possible to do in ImageReady, but it's easy once you know the steps.

I. With **flower.psd** still open from the previous exercise, click on **frame 1** in the **Animation** palette. Hold your **Shift** key down and click the last frame. All the frames should be selected.

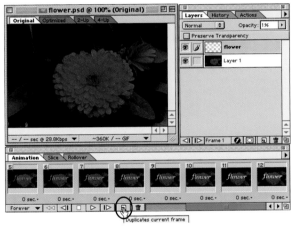

2. With all the frames selected, click on the **New Frame** icon at the bottom of the **Animation** palette. This duplicates all the selected frames and appends them to the end of the frames that were already there.

*Tip: This technique doesn't just offer a fast way to copy and paste, it's also the only way to get the animation to copy and paste without generating new layers in the **Layers** palette. See the note "Different Ways to Duplicate Frames" later in this chapter.*

3. Use the scroll bar at the bottom of the **Animation** palette, and you'll see that the 12 frames you copied were just pasted at the end of the animation sequence. They should already be selected. **Note:** If you accidentally click off of them, you can use the **Shift+Click** method to reselect them. Click **frame 13**, hold your **Shift** key down, and click **frame 23**. This selects all the frames that you just duplicated.

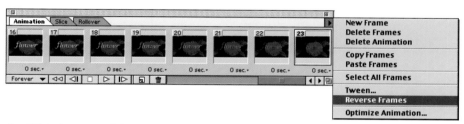

4. Click the upper-right arrow again and select **Reverse Frames**. This puts all the selected frames in the reverse order.

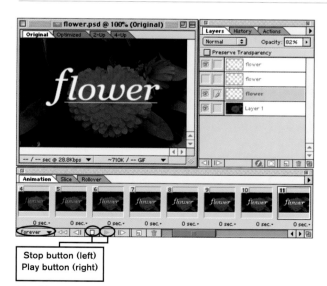

Stop button (left)
Play button (right)

5. Change the **Once** setting to **Forever** and click **Play**. You should see the animation fade up and down. Click **Stop** when you're through admiring your handiwork.

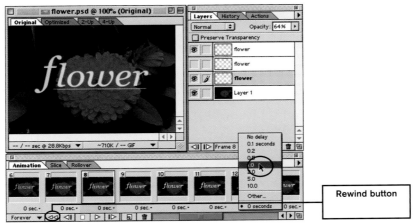

Rewind button

6. Click on **frame 12** and change the timing to **1.0** second, as shown above. Rewind the animation by clicking on the **Rewind** button at the bottom of the **Animation** palette. Click **Play** to watch the result of this change. The animation should now stop and hold in the middle and then continue to play. When you're finished watching, click the **Stop** button.

You can change the timing of all the frames, like you did in Exercise 2, or you can change the timing of individual frames.

This exercise taught you how to set the number of repeats with which an animation will play. You learned to create a loop by selecting, duplicating, and reversing frames, and how to set delays on individual frames.

7. Now that you've seen the power and ease with which ImageReady lets you select, duplicate, and reverse frames, save and leave the file open for the next exercise.

 Movie | **reversing.mov**

To learn more about Exercise 6, "Selecting, Duplicating, and Reversing Frames," check out **reversing.mov** from the **movies** folder on the **H•O•T CD-ROM**.

7. ——————————Tweening a Tweened Sequence

You can also **Tween** the animation in the **Animation** palette more than once. This is useful in the event that you change your mind about a **Tween** setting. In the type of animation that you've built so far, this would produce a shimmery effect instead of a smooth fade up and down.

1. In **flower.psd**, be sure that the **flower** layer is selected in the **Layers** palette. Next, click on **frame 3** in the **Animation** palette to select it. In the **Layers** palette on the **flower** layer enter **Opacity: 100%**.

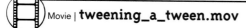

Movie | **tweening_a_tween.mov**

To learn more about Exercise 7, "Tweening a Tweened Sequence," check out **tweening_a _tween.mov** from the **movies** folder on the **H•O•T CD-ROM**.

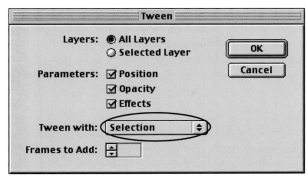

2. Select **frames 1-3** by using your **Shift** key. Click the upper-right arrow of the **Animation** palette to select **Tween...**. Click **OK**.

Notice that you are not given the option to choose the number of frames but that the **Tween with:** *setting is on* **Selection**. *That's because you selected multiple frames before you selected the* **Tween...** *option.*

3. Play the animation or preview it in a browser. You'll see a short fade up at the beginning and an abrupt change in **Opacity** as a result of the changes you made.

ImageReady allows you to **Tween** *either by defining a selection or defining a number of frames to insert between two keyframes.*

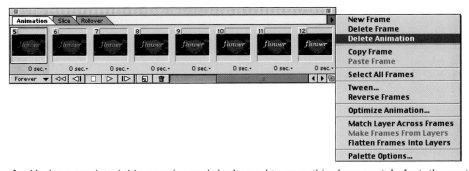

4. You've completed this exercise and don't need to save this document. In fact, the next exercise will require this same file without any animation. Delete the animation in **flower.psd** by clicking the upper-right arrow of the **Animation** palette and selecting **Delete Animation**. When prompted, click **Delete**. This will leave intact the layers in the **Layers** palette but delete all the frames in the **Animation** palette.

5. Leave this file open for the next exercise.

Different Ways to Duplicate Frames

In the last exercise, you learned to duplicate a series of frames that were selected by clicking on the **New Frame** icon. Before you duplicate frames, you must first select them. You can select frames by holding down the **Shift** key or you can use the upper-right arrow to choose **Select All Frames** from the pop-up menu. There are a few different ways to duplicate frames, and this chart outlines them.

Methods for Duplicating Frames	
Method	**Results**
From the **Animation** palette, select frames and click on the **New Frame** icon.	Duplicates the frames and appends them to the end of your animation.
Click on the **upper-right** arrow of the **Animation** palette to access the **Copy Frames** and **Paste Frames** features.	Copies all the frames, but when you paste them, it not only pastes the frames, it also pastes whatever layers the animation used in the **Layers** palette. For this reason, I only use this method when I'm copying animation from one document to another. In that event, it's great that ImageReady copies all the appropriate artwork to the target document. Other considerations when pasting: If you don't select a frame to paste into on the target document, the pasted animation will append to the end of the existing animation. If you select a frame within the animation, the pasted frames will overlay the existing frames. Overlaying might be good if you had, let's say, an animation of a logo in one .psd file that you wanted to transfer to an ad banner that was being built inside a different .psd file.

8. _____Tweening with Position

So far, you've learned to create animations two different ways. Exercise 1 showed you how to create animation by turning on and off layers on different frames. Exercise 5 introduced you to creating animation by using the **Tween** setting and adjusting opacity between frames. There are two other types of **Tween** parameters you can work with — **Position** and **Effects**. This exercise will show you how to **Tween** with **Position**. ImageReady will memorize the position of a layer between two frames, and those two stored positions can be **Tweened**. You'll see how in this exercise.

I. With **flower.psd** still open from the last exercise, make sure the **flower** layer is selected in the **Layers** palette and that **Opacity** is **100%**.

2. Using the **Move** tool from the toolbar, click and drag inside the document window to move the lettering to the top.

3. Click on the **New Frame** icon at the bottom of the **Animation** palette. With the second frame selected, move the lettering to the bottom of the document window using the **Move** tool. It's even **OK** to position the artwork so that it goes off the edge. **Tip:** You can use arrow keys to move the artwork instead of clicking and dragging. To do this, you must have the **Move** tool selected.

Movie | **tweening_position.mov**

To learn more about Exercise 8, "Tweening with Position," check out **tweening_position.mov** from the **movies** folder on the **H·O·T CD-ROM**.

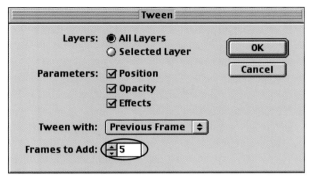

4. Click on the upper-right arrow of the **Animation** palette and select **Tween...**. Enter **Frames to Add: 5**. Click **OK**.

5. Preview the results.

*If you aren't pleased by what you see, you should know how to make any adjustments that you want, but the main point is that you have now learned how to **Tween** with position changes.*

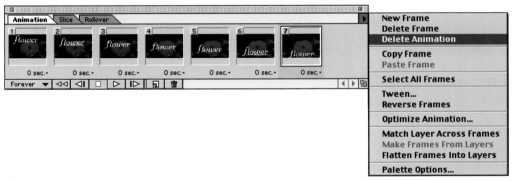

6. You've just learned to create an animation by letting ImageReady **Tween** between two different positions on the screen. You won't need this animation for the next exercise, so go ahead and delete it. Delete the animation in **flower.psd** by clicking the upper-right arrow of the **Animation** palette and selecting **Delete Animation**. When prompted, click **Delete**. Leave the document open for the next exercise.

[IR] 9. ————————Tweening with Effects

ImageReady can also **Tween** effects using **Styles** or **Layer Effects**. This next exercise will walk you through the process.

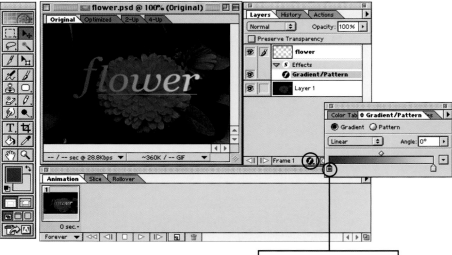

You can change colors by double-clicking on these tabs.

I. In **flower.psd**, which should still be open from the last exercise, select the flower layer in the **Layers** palette. Use the **Move** tool to move the word "**flower**" back into the center of the document window. In the **Layers** palette, click on the *f*-shaped **Add Layer Effect** icon at the bottom of that palette, and select **Gradient/Pattern** from the pop-up menu.

*Notice how the **Gradient/Pattern Layer Effect** pulls colors from the foreground and background colors in the ImageReady toolbar? If you want to change the colors, you can double-click on the tabs at the bottom of the **Gradient/Pattern Options** palette.*

 Movie | **tweening_effects.mov**

To learn more about Exercise 9, "Tweening with Effects" check out **tweening_effects.mov** from the **movies** folder on the **H·O·T CD-ROM**.

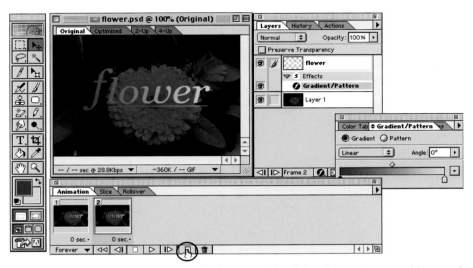

2. Click on the **New Frame** icon at the bottom of the **Animation** palette to add a new frame.

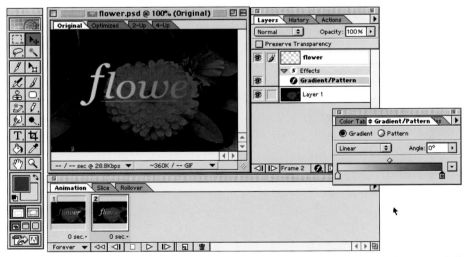

3. Change the gradient settings in the **Gradient/Pattern Options** palette. If you can't find the options, choose **Window > Show Gradient/Pattern Options**. **Tip:** I simply reversed the gradient by moving the tabs to opposite sides of the gradient slider.

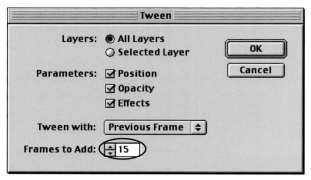

4. In the **Animation** palette, click on the upper-right arrow to select **Tween...**, **Tween with: Previous Frame**. Enter **Frames to Add: 15**. Click **OK**.

5. Preview the results in a browser. You could also press the **Play** button of the **Animation** palette, but you would get less accurate feedback of the timing.

*You should know how to make any adjustments that you want if you aren't pleased, but the main point is that you have now learned how to **Tween** with effects. What you might not realize is that you can combine animating **Opacity**, **Position**, and **Effects** in a single **Tween**. Try your own experiments with this and you'll see.*

6. Save and, finally, close the file.

Note | **How Many Frames?**

You might be wondering why I chose different numbers of frames to add in the **Tween** dialog box in different exercises. Some types of animations look better if they happen over a longer or shorter amount of time. How did I know how many frames to instruct that you add, or, more importantly, how will you know how many frames to add when you make your own animated GIFs? Experience has led me to have a good instinct about timing. I can imagine how something will look if it happens quickly versus if it happens slowly. You will be able to build this same skill if you make a lot of animated GIFs yourself. In the interim, don't be afraid to experiment! You can always delete the animation and try again, right?

10.—————**Animated Slide Show**

Let's say that you have a number of photographs from which you want to create a slide show. There are two types of **slide shows** that you can make. You can simply turn each image on and off and set a delay to last for a few seconds, which would be no different from what you did in Exercise 1. You can also create a slide show that fades up on one image and fades down on another (called a cross-fade in filmmaking). This is something that ImageReady does naturally without requiring that you set the **Opacity**. You'll see how simple it is — just try it!

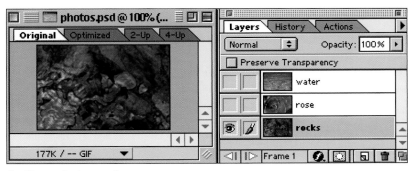

1. Open **photos.psd**.

This is a simple file that you could easily make. It contains three layers, each with a different image. The images could be photographic or graphic.

 Movie | **slideshow.mov**

To learn more about Exercise 10, "Animated Slide Show," check out **slideshow.mov** from the **movies** folder on the **H•O•T CD-ROM**.

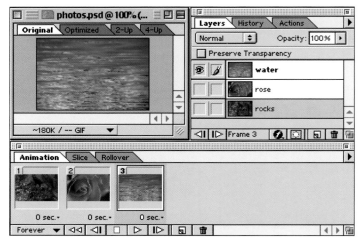

2. Make three frames and set three images so each one is on its own frame. Do this by turning the layer for **rocks** on, and the layers for **rose** and **water** off. Click on the **New Frame** icon to add a second frame, which is a duplicate of the first frame. Turn off the layer for **rocks**, turn on the layer for **rose**, and turn off the layer for **water**. Click on the **New Frame** icon to add another frame. Turn off the layers for **rocks** and **rose**, and turn on the layer for **water**. The result should look similar to what you see here.

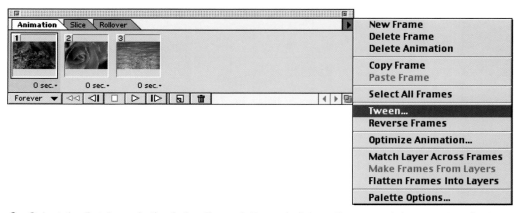

3. Select the first frame in the **Animation** palette, and click on the upper-right arrow to select **Tween...** from the pop-up menu.

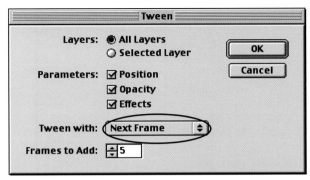

4. Notice that the **Tween** dialog box is already set to **Tween with: Next Frame**. Use the settings above (**Frames to Add: 5**) and click **OK**.

*If you click on the first frame in the **Animation** palette, ImageReady knows that you want to **Tween** with the **Next Frame**. If you click on a middle frame, ImageReady will let you set whether to **Tween with: Next Frame** or **Previous Frame**. If you click on the last frame, ImageReady will automatically be set to **Tween with:** the **Previous Frame**.*

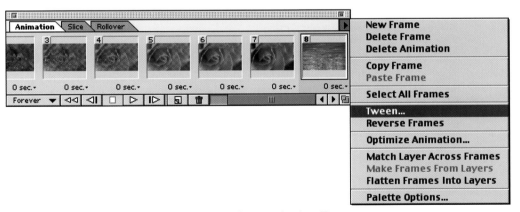

5. Select the last frame in the **Animation** palette and select **Tween....**

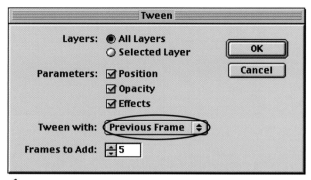

6. This time, ImageReady is set to create the **Tween with: Previous Frame** because you selected the last frame in the sequence. Click **OK**.

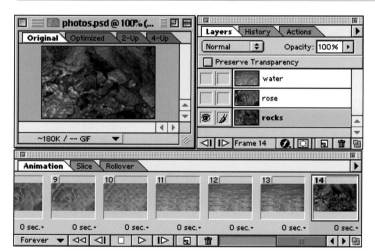

7. Click on the **Play** button or preview the animation in a browser.

It would be nice if it made a complete loop, wouldn't it?

8. Select the last frame in the **Animation** palette, and click on the **New Frame** icon to add another frame. Turn on the layer **rocks**, and turn all the other layers off.

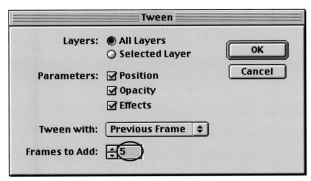

9. Select **Tween...**. Notice that the **Tween** is set to **Previous Frame**? That's exactly what you want. It's also still set to add **5** frames, which is perfect because all the other **Tweens** were set to **5** frames, and this will be consistent. Click **OK**.

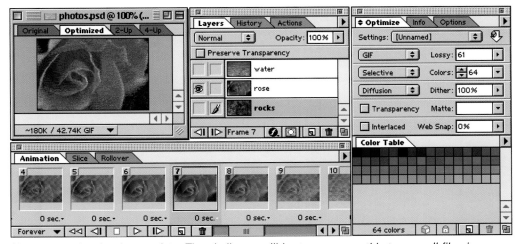

*Now your animation is complete. The challenge will be to compress this to a small file size. Remember that your content is photographic, so **Lossy** compression will really cut down on the file size. I've got my version of this animation down to **42K**. Without adding the **Lossy** compression, it would have been double the size. If you'd like a refresher about optimizing animation, revisit Exercise 3 in this chapter.*

10. To save the final animated GIF, choose **Save Optimized As**. To save the Photoshop document, chose **Save As**. Once you're finished saving your work, close the file.

Animated GIF Rollovers

It might not be obvious to you, but it is also possible to combine animation and rollover techniques in a single ImageReady document. This is the only image editor I know of on the market that can easily do this. If you've never made animated rollovers in ImageReady before, it is likely that you might find the steps in this exercise a bit strange. The steps make sense once you've gone through them and have seen the results, but I find that many students in our lab have trouble understanding this exercise until they've tried it a few times. You might like to look at the movie **animated_ roll.mov** from the movies folder on the **H•O•T CD-ROM** before you embark on these steps.

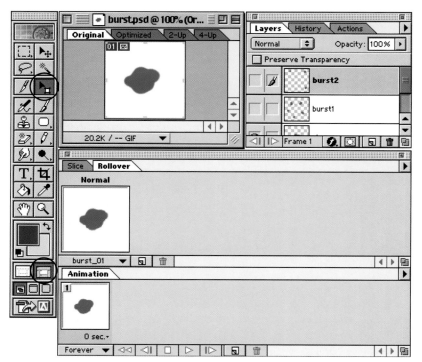

I. Open **burst.psd**. If you don't see a **Normal** state in the **Rollover** palette, it's because you haven't selected a slice. Click the **Slice Selection** tool and click on the single slice, as shown above, and the **Show Slices** button will automatically turn on.

*When I create animation and rollovers in the same document, I like to dock the **Animation** and **Rollover** palettes together, as shown here. You learned to do this same kind of docking with the **Optimize** and **Color Table** palettes in Chapter 4, "Optimization."*

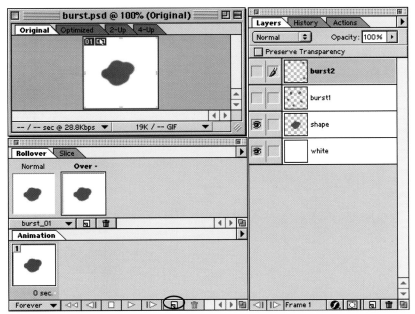

2. Click on the **New State** icon at the bottom of the **Rollover** palette. This will add a new frame to the **Rollover** palette but won't affect the **Animation** palette.

*Notice that the first frames in the **Animation** and the **Rollover** palettes are identical? This means that the **Normal** state will look just like what's on the screen.*

Note | **Preload Issues**

When designing animated rollovers, it is necessary to set the animation to play at least two cycles (the **Forever** setting that generates an endless loop is my favorite). This is because ImageReady automatically writes a script that "preloads" the images. If the animation is set to play one time only, it will play in the preloading process and will not play when you finally see the image in the browser.

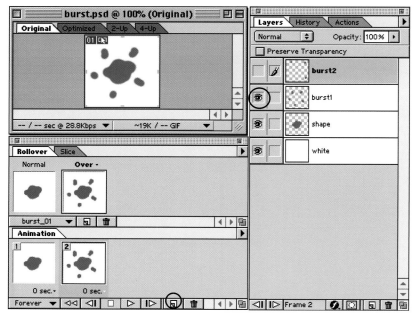

3. Click on the **New Frame** icon at the bottom of the **Animation** palette. Turn the eye on for the layer called **burst1** (leaving the eye icons on for the **white** and **shape** layers in the **Layers** palette).

This should result in two rollover states and two animation frames. If you click on the Normal state, you'll see the animation frame disappear, and if you click on the Over state, it will reappear. That's because the animation is going to be triggered by the Over state. Be sure that the Over state is selected before you go to the next step.

Warning | **Netscape Animation Bug**

Unfortunately, if you click on an animated rollover in Netscape, the animation will not resume if you move your mouse over the artwork again. This is not true in Internet Explorer. The problem is not with the code that ImageReady generates but in the way that Netscape renders animated GIF files. At this point, there is nothing I can suggest to get around this.

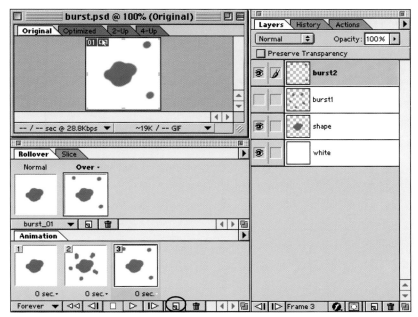

4. Click on the **New Frame** icon at the bottom of the **Animation** palette. This will create a third frame in the **Animation** palette. Turn on the layer **burst2** and turn off the layer **burst1**.

*In the last step I suggested that you click on the **Normal** and the **Over** state to watch the animation frames disappear. Now I'm going to suggest that you click on frame 2 in the Animation palette. Notice that frame 2 also appears in the Over state of the Rollover palette? This can be very confusing, but ImageReady is simply previewing whatever frame or state is selected. Be sure to select frame 3 again before progressing to the next step.*

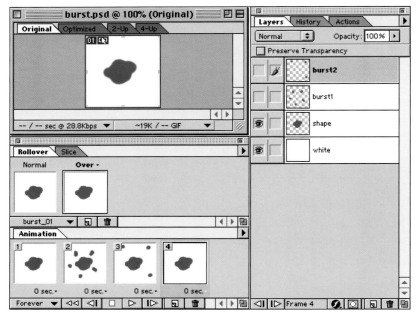

5. Click on the **New Frame** icon again at the bottom of the **Animation** palette, and turn off the **burst2** layer in the **Layers** palette.

You should see four frames of animation and two rollover states. This won't necessarily make sense until you preview the results of your work.

6. Preview in the browser (**File > Preview in**) and move your mouse over the artwork. Notice that the animation happens when the mouse is on the rollover artwork.

Assuming all went well, you just learned how to create an animated rollover. What's interesting about ImageReady is that any rollover can be made to have an animated state.

7. Return to ImageReady to save and close the file.

[IR] **12.** _____Designing Entire Interfaces

In the past three chapters you've learned about slicing, rollovers, and animation. It might not seem obvious that all these techniques can be combined to design an entire Web interface. This next exercise should bring into practice a lot of skills that you've just learned and open your eyes to further possibilities. I'll be truthful with you, however, this is a very complex exercise. Don't be surprised if you have to try it a few times or watch the movies over and over. You won't be alone; when we teach this at our training center, most of our students suffer along until the big "ah ha!" moment comes and it finally makes sense. ImageReady is a powerful and complex tool, and this exercise really shows off its strengths and challenges.

1. Open **finished_layout.psd**.

2. Preview it in a browser and notice that the camera at the bottom animates all the time. Move your mouse over the "**rose**," the "**portrait**," or the "**sunflower**" images. Notice that remote rollover words appear in the area below those images, and that when they do, the camera positions switch.

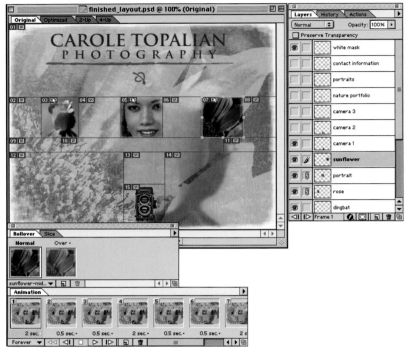

3. Return to ImageReady and make sure that the slices are visible (**Q**). Use the **Slice Selection** tool to click each of the three photographs in the middle of the image. You'll see that each has rollovers associated with it.

4. In the **Rollover** palette, click the **Over** state, and you'll see the screen change and that text appears in the area below the three photos. Notice that the **Normal** state of every single slice in this image contains the camera animation in the **Animation** palette. This means the animation will play before the end-user's mouse moves over any of the artwork. The **Normal** state is the default view of this document.

Deconstructing a finished piece can teach how to construct a complicated document like this.

 Movie | **deconstructing.mov**

To learn about deconstructing this piece, check out **deconstructing.mov** from the **movies** folder on the **H•O•T CD-ROM**.

5. Now that you have observed some of the techniques used in this exercise, close this file and open **unfinishedlayout.psd**.

*The first thing to set up is the camera animation. Why? Because this animation will take place on the **Normal** state of every single slice in this document if you do – and that's what you do want to have happen. Whenever you want animation to play at the onset of a page, you must set it up in the **Normal** state.*

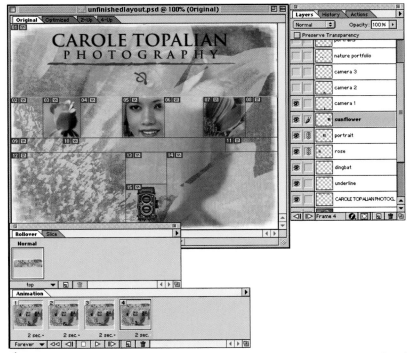

6. Do not select any slice just yet, since the goal here is to create an animation that is in the **Normal** state of the entire document. Add four frames to the **Animation** palette by clicking four times on the **New Frame** icon. On **frame 1**, turn the layer **camera 1** on. On **frame 2**, turn the layer **camera 2** on and **camera 1** off. On **frame 3**, turn **camera 3** on and **camera 2** off. On **frame 4**, turn **camera 1** on and **camera 3** off.

7. **Tween** between each frame, and add three frames each. This can be tricky because you can lose track of the original frames as you start adding **Tweens**. For this reason, I like to do this process backwards.

• Select **frame 4** and choose **Tween (Frames to Add: 4, Tween with: Previous Frame)**.

• Select **frame 3** and choose **Tween (Frames to Add: 4, Tween with: Previous Frame)**.

• Select **frame 2** and choose **Tween (Frames to Add: 4, Tween with: Previous Frame)**.

This should result in a continuous loop of the animation. If you want to preview it right now, go ahead and look at it in the browser. No rollovers will work because you haven't specified any yet. Whenever I am building a document of this complexity I preview often and after each step. I usually preview in the browser because you can't preview the rollovers in ImageReady itself.

By the way, this is no different than what you learned in the last exercise, except that this is on a more complicated sliced up document. If you want to watch me set this up, check out **complex.mov** *from the* **movies** *folder.*

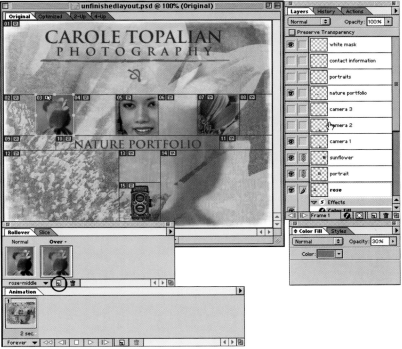

8. Using the **Slice Selection** tool, select the **rose** slice (**slice #3**) inside the document window. Add an **Over** state in the **Rollover** palette by clicking on the **New State** icon.

9. The **Over** state should now be selected in the **Animation** palette. From the **Layers** palette, select the **rose** layer and add a **Color Fill Layer Effect** to it. I chose a red color and changed the **Opacity** to **30 percent**.

10. When you're finished, turn on the text layer **nature portfolio** in the **Layers** palette. In the **Animation** palette, click the upper-right arrow to select **Delete Animation**. That's because you only want the animation to play on the **Normal** state, not on the **Over** state. Make sure that the layer **camera 1** is turned on and that the other camera layers are turned off.

You just specified that when your end-user's mouse rolls over the picture of the rose, it will change color, the words "NATURE PORTFOLIO" will appear, the animation will stop, and camera 1 will appear. Next you'll get to do the same for the rest of the pictures.

11. Using the **Slice Selection** tool, select the **portrait** slice (**slice #5**). Add an **Over** state in the **Rollover** palette.

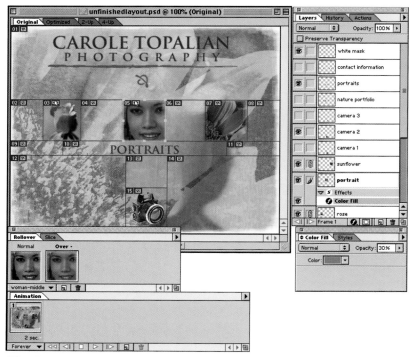

12. From the **Layers** palette, select the **portraits** layer and add a **Color Fill Layer Effect** to it. I chose a red color and changed the **Opacity** to **30 percent**.

13. When you're finished, turn on the text layer **portrait**. In the **Animation** palette, click on the upper-right arrow to select **Delete Animation**. Make sure that the layer **camera 2** is turned on and that the other camera layers are turned off.

You just specified that when your end-user's mouse rolls over the picture of the portrait, it will change color, the word "PORTRAIT" will appear, the animation will stop, and camera 2 will appear. Again, preview. If it doesn't work, retrace your to see if you can figure out what went astray. You might want to watch the movie complex.mov to see me do it.

14. Using the **Slice Selection** tool, select the **sunflower** slice (**slice #7**). Add an **Over** state in the **Rollover** palette.

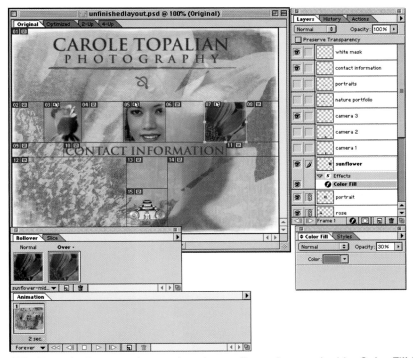

15. From the **Layers** palette, select the **sunflower** layer and add a **Color Fill Layer Effect** to it. I chose a red color and changed the **Opacity** to **30 percent**.

16. When you're finished, turn on the layer **contact information**. In the **Animation** palette, click the upper-right arrow to select **Delete Animation**. Make sure that the layer **camera 3** is turned on and that the other camera layers are turned off.

You just specified that when your end-user's mouse rolls over the picture of the sunflower, it will change color, the words "CONTACT INFORMATION" will appear, the animation will stop, and camera 3 will appear.

16. You're done. Preview in a browser to check to see if everything works. When you're finished, close and save the file. Remember that **Save Optimized** will save all the parts – the HTML, the JavaScript to make the rollovers function, and the images. **File > Save As...** will save the .psd file.

Whew! You survived this chapter. That truly is a feat. I know this is a rough one, but these skills afford wonderful bragging rights once you've mastered them!

I3.
Automation

| Web Photo Gallery | Actions in Photoshop | Batch Processive Actions |
| Actions in ImageReady | Droplets | Changing Droplets |

chap_13

Photoshop 5.5 / ImageReady 2.0
H·O·T CD-ROM

As I'm sure you've realized by this chapter, there are tons of practical and creative things that you can do with Photoshop 5.5 and ImageReady 2.0. This chapter addresses what to do when you want to do something useful and creative but to an entire folder of images at once. This can be a huge timesaver – who wants to repeat the same operation over and over when the computer can do it for you?

Photoshop and ImageReady both offer something called **Actions**, which allow you to store an operation or series of operations as a recording that can then be played back over a single image or multiple images contained inside the same folder. While it's possible to create **Actions** in both Photoshop and Image-Ready, they cannot be created in one program and played in the other.

ImageReady also has a feature called **Droplets**, which stores optimization settings that can be applied to a folder of images through drag-and-drop methods about which you'll learn. Photoshop does not support **Droplets**, so this is something distinct to ImageReady. A new Photoshop feature called the **Web Photo Gallery** is an example of the new **Automate** feature that was added for Photoshop 5.5. This chapter offers hands-on training in all features: **Actions**, **Droplets**, and the **Web Photo Gallery.** This is the sort of stuff computers were made for. Enjoy!

What is the Web Photo Gallery?

The **Web Photo Gallery** command, an exciting new feature that is new to Photoshop 5.5, automatically and quickly creates a Web site that displays a series of images. This process automatically optimizes the images and writes HTML to produce a Web site suitable for publishing online. The **Web Photo Gallery** is a great tool for artists to display their work, for architects to show renderings to clients, for photographers to show proofs, for families to share personal photos on the Web, and for many other purposes too numerous to list here.

When you make a **Web Photo Gallery**, Photoshop starts with a folder of images and does all of the following for you.

• The program copies, resizes, and optimizes the images and then creates a thumbnail and a larger JPEG of each image in the folder.

• Photoshop also writes all the HTML code and compressed images for a Web site that includes a page of thumbnails and a separate page for the larger version of each image.

• The site even includes arrow keys for next, previous, and home buttons!

You can upload that site directly to the Web, or bring it into Adobe GoLive or another HTML editor to customize it further. To do so, you simply launch another HTML or word-processing application and choose **File > Open** to open any of the .htm files that Photoshop generated. At the end of each HTML file, Photoshop puts the file extension .htm, which works just the same as .html in any Web browser. However, it should be noted that in order to put this on a live Web site, you must first obtain an account for server space, plus know how to upload and how to link to the gallery from other pages within your site.

Actions that Ship with Photoshop and ImageReady

This chapter will show you how to create your own custom **Actions**. Once you get acquainted with the **Actions** feature in both Photoshop and ImageReady, you'll notice that there are already **Actions** inside the **Actions** palette. If you'd like to try some of these, you can simply click on the **Play** button to see what happens. On playback, the **Action** can contain prompts that explain how the **Action** is supposed to work.

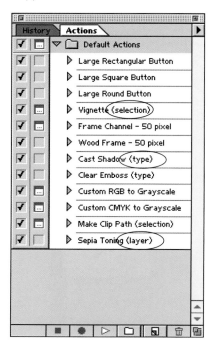

If you click on the arrow to the left of the **Default Actions** folder in the **Actions** palette, you'll see its contents. Some of the **Actions** have parentheses, such as (**selection**) on **Vignette**, (**type**) on **Cast Shadow**, and (**layer**) on **Sepia Toning**. Those are hints that some **Actions** only work under certain conditions, such as, in the above cases, when there is a selection active, editable or rendered type, or an independent layer in a document. Note that the **Actions** shown above are from Photoshop. ImageReady ships with different **Actions**.

It's very easy to try out these default **Actions**. Simply click on the **Action** you want (exactly the same as you would select a layer in the **Layers** palette) and then click on the **Play** button at the bottom of the palette. If you don't have the proper condition set up for the **Action** to play, it will either warn you or it will not work. That's the worst that can happen, so feel free to explore how they work!

I. Creating a Web Photo Gallery

This exercise walks you through the steps for creating a **Web Photo Gallery**. Once you learn how to do this to the folder of images supplied on the **H•O•T CD-ROM**, try it on a folder of your own images. I predict you'll be amazed at how simple it is to generate an entire Web site without needing any HTML coding knowledge whatsoever.

I. Select **File** > **Automate** > **Web Photo Gallery**....

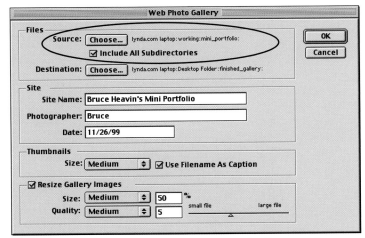

2. In the **Web Photo Gallery** window, press the **Source: Choose...** button.

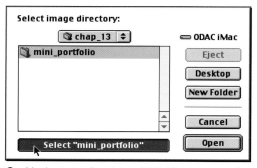

3. Navigate to the **chap_13** folder you transferred to your hard drive from the **H•O•T CD-ROM**.

• (Mac) Click on **Select "mini_portfolio"**. This will return you to the **Web Photo Gallery** dialog box. The next steps will show you how to fill out this dialog box's settings, so don't click **OK** just yet.

• (Windows) Click **OK** in the **Browse for Folder** dialog box. This will return you to the **Web Photo Gallery** dialog box. The next steps will show you how to fill out this dialog box's settings, so don't click OK just yet.

*Tip: The **Web Photo Gallery** works best with images that are of similar size to begin with. When you make a **Web Photo Gallery** with your own images, before you start putting the images into one folder, resize them to make them similar in either height or width. This can be done by choosing **Image > Image Size** and entering consistent values into the **Width** or **Height** settings. You could even make an **Action** to resize an entire folder of images to all be the same height or width. You'll learn how to create **Actions** soon enough....*

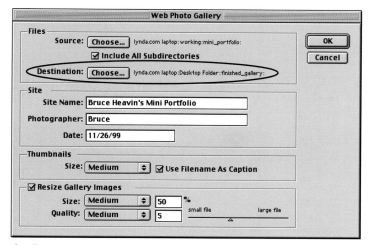

4. Press the **Destination: Choose...** button.

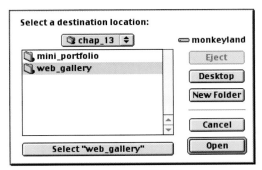

5. Navigate to the **chap_13** folder.

- (Mac) Click **Select "web_gallery"**. This will return you to the **Web Photo Gallery** dialog box. The next steps will show you how to fill out this dialog box's settings, so don't click **OK** just yet.

- (Windows) Select the **web_gallery** folder and click **OK** in the **Browse for Folder** dialog box. This will return you to the **Web Photo Gallery** dialog box. The next steps will show you how to fill out this dialog box's settings, so don't click **OK** just yet.

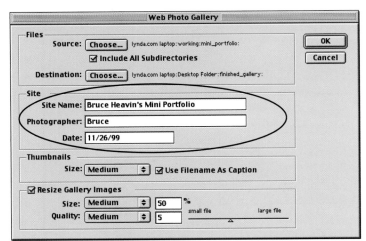

6. Enter **Site Name: Bruce Heavin's Mini Portfolio,** and **Photographer: Bruce**. (My husband Bruce created these wonderful illustrations.) Photoshop automatically fills out the **Date** field, though you can manually enter a change if you'd prefer. Leave all the other settings below at their defaults.

*The information you enter into the **Site Name**, **Photographer**, and **Date** fields will be displayed as HTML text on the first page of the site Photoshop creates for you. Notice that only JPEG (not GIF) optimization is available for the **Web Photo Gallery**. This is something I hope will change in future versions of Photoshop. For now, however, there isn't a way to change this setting.*

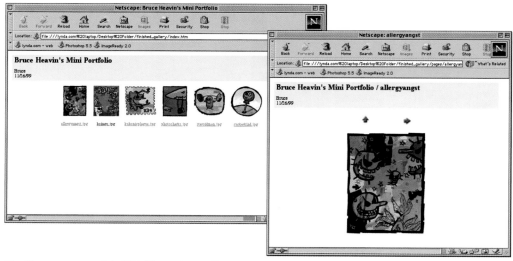

7. You can now click **OK**. Photoshop will create the site, open a browser, and show you the Web site it just built in seconds.

Warning: If you want to change the name of the Web site or the photographer, you will need to return to Photoshop and start over, or edit the HTML file in an HTML or text editor.

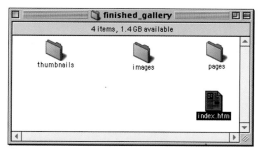

8. Go to your hard drive to look inside the **chap_13** folder, then open the **finished_gallery** folder to see that Photoshop created folders for HTML pages, images, and thumbnails for you.

What Do All the Web Photo Gallery Settings Do?

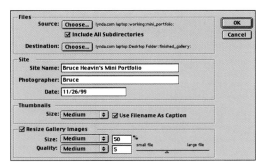

*The **Web Photo Gallery** contains many settings, most of which were left at their defaults in this exercise.*

Web Photo Gallery Settings	
Setting	**Description**
Source	This **Choose...** button lets you select the folder of images from which Photoshop will build the **Web Photo Gallery**.
Destination	This **Choose...** button lets you select the destination folder for Photoshop to write the images and HTML once it's finished creating the **Web Photo Gallery**.
Site Name	The name you put in this field dictates the name of the resulting Web site.
Photographer	Enter the name of the person who gets credit for creating the images here. Sadly, Photoshop inserts the word "**Photographer**". The **Web Photo Gallery** is used for many types of artwork — and authors are not always photographers. The good news is that once the **Web Photo Gallery** is made, the word "**Photographer**" is dropped.
Date	Photoshop automatically inserts the date that the **Web Photo Gallery** is created. You can change this manually if you want.
Thumbnails	This setting dictates the scaling factor for the thumbnail. **Large** is **75% Med** is **50% Small** is **25%** and **Custom** leaves the % field blank. This setting scales all the images in the folder to the same percent, not to the same size, so it's important to start with originals that are similar in size to begin with.
Size	This setting dictates how large the images will be that are linked from the thumbnails. You can enter a setting from **1** to **100%**. These percentages are applied to whatever size your original image is.
Quality	The **Web Photo Gallery** optimizes images only as JPEGs. You can choose a compression setting from **0** to **12** (**0** applies the maximum amount, and **12**, the minimum).

[PS] **2.**————Creating an Action

Photoshop's **Actions** feature lets you streamline your workflow by recording a series of commands and automatically applying those commands to a single file or to many files at once. **Actions** are a great way to automate repetitive tasks, like creating Web-ready thumbnails of images, which you'll get to do in this exercise. **Actions** are good for zillions of other things, but this exercise will teach you the basics of setting up your own **Actions** recording. You'll create an **Action** that resizes a copy of an image to thumbnail size and saves it as an optimized GIF. In the following exercise, you'll apply that **Action** to a whole folder of image files in just a single step with Photoshop's **Batch** command. You can also create **Actions** in ImageReady in an identical fashion, which you'll get to do later in this chapter.

I. Open **allergyangst.psd** from the **mini_portfolio** folder in the **chap_13** folder.

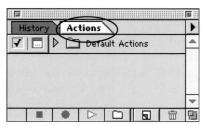

2. Choose **Window > Show Actions**. Click on the **Actions** tab to bring the **Actions** palette to the foreground. You'll notice that there is a folder called **Default Actions**. These are **Actions** that ship with Photoshop. When you get a free moment, you might try them out.

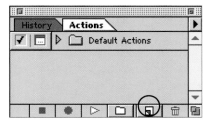

3. Click on the **New Action** icon at the bottom of the **Actions** palette.

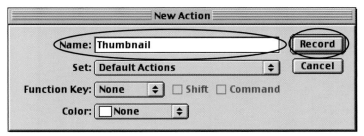

4. In the **New Action** window that will open, enter **Name: Thumbnail** to name the **Action** that you are creating.

5. Click on the **Record** button to begin recording the **Thumbnail Action**, meaning that everything you do in Photoshop from now until you stop recording will be part of the **Action**. The red dot indicates that you are now in recording mode. Notice that the word **Thumbnail** appears in a set of other **Actions**? Those are **Actions** that ship with Photoshop.

6. Select **File > Save For Web...**. This is the first step of the **Action**.

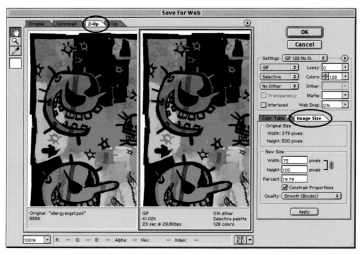

7. In the **Save For Web** dialog box that will open, click on the **Image Size** tab to bring the **Image Size** palette to the foreground.

*I set this to **2-Up** so I can see more of the image while being able to compare it to the original.*

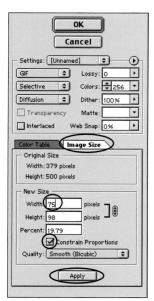

8. In the **Image Size** palette, enter **Width: 75** to set the width of the thumbnail. This is measured in pixels. Make sure there is a check in the **Constrain Proportions** checkbox so that your image does not distort when resized. Click **Apply** to resize the image.

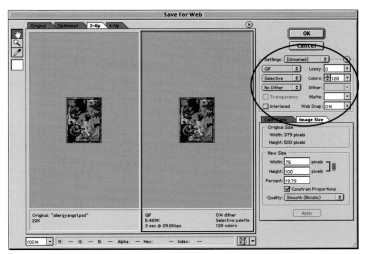

9. Choose image optimization settings. **Tip:** Try **GIF**, **Selective**, **Colors**: **128**, **No Dither**, and **Lossy: 0**. Click **OK**. I suggest these settings because they seem to create the best-looking GIF.

10. Next, you'll save the result inside a new folder that you'll create.

• (Mac) In the **Save Optimized As** window that appears, navigate to the desktop, and click on the **New Folder** button. Name the new folder **thumbnails** and click **Create**. Click **Save** to save a copy of the image as an optimized thumbnail named **allergyangst.gif**.

• (Windows) In the **Save Optimized As** window that appears, navigate to the desktop, and click on the yellow **New** folder icon. Name the new folder **thumbnails** and double-click on it so that it opens. Click **Save** to save a copy of the image as an optimized thumbnail named **allergyangst.gif** into the new folder called **thumbnails**.

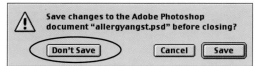

II. Back in Photoshop, close the original image without saving. This will preserve the .psd file without any changes.

*This is the last step of the **Action** and you'll program it as such in the next step.*

12. Click on the **Stop Recording** button in the **Actions** palette.

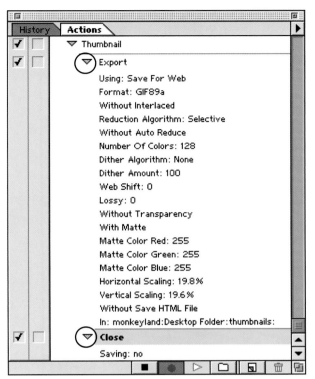

13. The arrow next to the **Thumbnail Action** in the **Actions** palette will be pointing down, revealing all of the commands included in this **Action**. Click on the arrows next to **Export** and **Close** (the **Action's** two commands) to see the settings and steps included in each command.

*You just successfully programmed an **Action**. Photoshop recorded everything you did and now you can play back the recording whenever you like. The following exercise will show you how to take this **Action** and play it over a series of images contained in a folder.*

[PS]

3. —————— Batch Processing with an Action

In this exercise, you'll use Photoshop's **Batch** feature to apply the **Thumbnail Action** you created in the last exercise to a folder full of images. You can sit back and watch Photoshop automatically create thumbnails from each of the images in the folder. It's rather wondrous when you think how long it would take to do this process manually.

I. Select **File > Automate > Batch....**

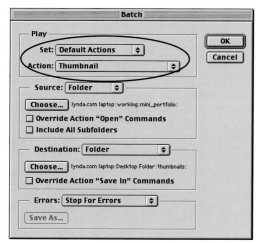

2. In the **Batch** dialog box that will open, select **Set: Default Actions**. This is the set of **Actions** in which the **Thumbnail Action** is located. Select **Action: Thumbnail**, the **Action** you created in the last exercise. **Note:** The **Default Actions** set ships with Photoshop, and because you didn't create a new set, the **Thumbnail Action** you created is stored within it.

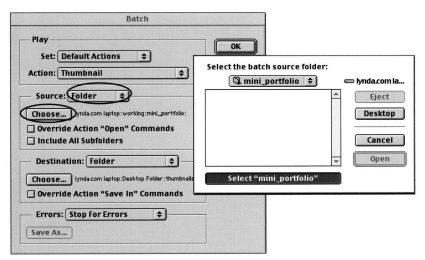

3. Select **Source: Folder** then click on the **Choose...** button directly below it to navigate to the **chap_13** folder.

• (Mac) Click on **Select "mini_portfolio"**.

• (Windows) Select the **mini_portfolio** folder and click **OK** in the **Browse for Folder** dialog box.

*If you want to try this **Action** on your own image files, first put your files into a single folder.*

Warning | **A Problem with Batch**

The **Batch** dialog box is supposed to enable you to select a **Destination** folder by clicking on the **Destination: Choose button**. Unfortunately, this doesn't work with **Save For Web**. If you record an **Action** that involves **Save For Web**, as **Thumbnail** did, the **Destination** folder you select while recording will become the **Destination** folder regardless of whether or not you select a different folder in the **Batch** dialog box.

The **Action** you just recorded and batch processed will work correctly because you selected the same destination folder in the **Action** recording and the **Batch** dialog box. If you had chosen a different destination in the **Batch** dialog box it would have still used the destination you chose when you recorded the **Action**.

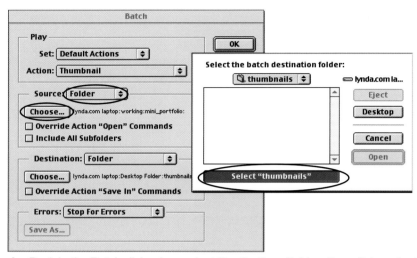

4. Back in the **Batch** dialog box, select **Destination: Folder**, then click on the **Choose...** button.

• (Mac) Click on **Select "thumbnails"**.

• (Windows) Select the **thumbnails** folder and click **OK** in the **Browse for Folder** dialog box.

*You created a **thumbnails** folder in Exercise 2 when you recorded this **Action**. If you can't find that folder, create a new **thumbnails** folder on the desktop before you begin batch processing.*

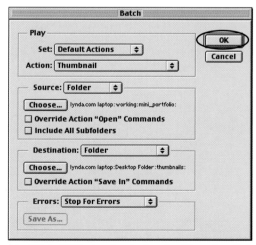

5. Click **OK** to begin playing the **Thumbnail Action** on all the images in the **mini_portfolio** folder.

Kick back and watch Photoshop automatically resize, optimize, and save a thumbnail copy of each image. This is the good life, isn't it?

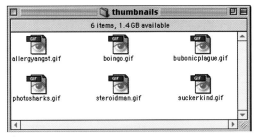

6. Open the **thumbnails** folder to see all of the thumbnails that Photoshop just created for you.

Tip | **Applying an Action to a Single File**

Batch processing is awesome, as you can already tell from Exercise 3. But what about those times when you want to work with only one file? As an alternative to batch processing, you can apply your **Thumbnail Action** to just a single file.

Here's what to do: Simply open the file on which you want to apply the **Action** and click on the **Play** button at the bottom of the **Actions** palette. The **Action** will perform its task on the one file, and will still be a great timesaver.

Note | **Actions in ImageReady**

Now that you've learned to create an **Action** in Photoshop, you might wonder if you can do the same thing in ImageReady. Yes, you can. ImageReady also contains an **Actions** palette, and recording **Actions** is done identically there. The difference is that there is no **Automate** menu item in ImageReady. If you want to apply an **Action** you make in ImageReady to a folder of images, you will need to make a **Droplet** instead. You'll learn how to make **Droplets** later in this chapter.

Adding, Changing, Deleting, or Pausing an Action

Once you've created an **Action**, you can always change it later. You can easily initiate a pause, and add or delete steps. Here's a chart to reference later if you want to do any operations with **Actions** beyond what the past exercises have taught.

Working with Actions	
Operations	**Methods**
To Add an Item Inside an Action	To add another item into an **Action**, click on the upper-right arrow of the **Actions** palette, and select **Start Recording**. Whatever you do at this point will be inserted into the existing **Action**. If you want to add another item somewhere in the middle of the recording, simply select whichever line item it should come after and then record your change.
To Delete an Item from an Action	To delete a portion of an **Action**, simply select that portion in the **Actions** palette, and click on the **Trash can** icon at the bottom or click on the upper-right arrow of the **Actions** palette and choose **Delete**. Either way, you will be asked if you want to delete that section and you should click on the **Delete** button.
To Replace an Item in an Action	To replace a part of an **Action**, select the part of the **Action** that you are replacing, click on the upper-right arrow of the **Actions** palette, and select **Start Recording** from the pop-up menu. This will insert a new section into the **Action**. When you're finished, click on the **Stop** button at the bottom of the **Actions** palette and the new section will appear inside the existing **Action**.
To Set a Pause in an Action	Setting a pause enables the **Action** to stop in the middle of playback. Let's say you want to create a new document with an **Action**. If you inserted a pause, you could enter the dimensions of the new document instead of having the new document always open at the same dimensions. To set a pause, wait until after you have completed recording the **Action**. Click in the column next to whatever command in which you want to initiate a pause.

Creating a Preview in Browser Action

I am accustomed to using the **F12** key as a quick shortcut for previewing in a browser in applications other than ImageReady. That's no problem, because you can set ImageReady up to honor the same shortcut if you program it as an **Action**. Because it's rare that you ever preview a Web graphic from Photoshop, this is a good example of when you'd want to program an **Action** in ImageReady.

1. Switch to ImageReady. Open **bg.psd** from the **chap_13** folder.

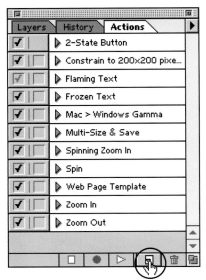

2. If the **Action** palette isn't open, choose **Window > Show Actions**. Click on the **New Action** icon at the bottom of the **Actions** palette.

3. In the **New Action** window that will open, enter **Name: preview**. Click on the pop-up menu to the right of **Function Key:** to select **F12**. Click **Record**.

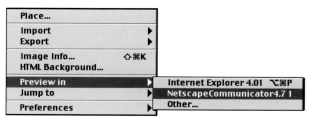

4. Choose **File > Preview in** and select a browser.

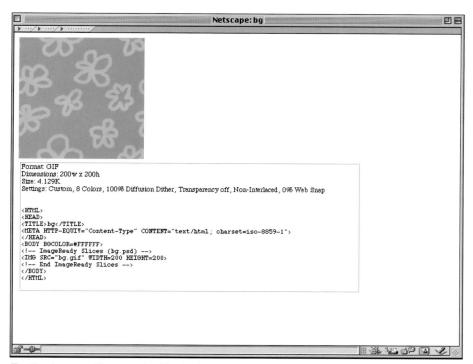

5. The image will appear inside the browser. Return to ImageReady to end this **Action**.

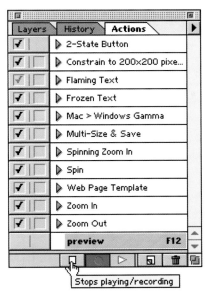

6. Make sure the **preview** layer is selected in the **Actions** palette and click on the **Stop** button.

7. Open a different image from the **chap_13** folder and press **F12**. You will grow to love how handy this shortcut will become to you.

8. Leave **bg.psd** open for the next exercise.

*From now on, any time you want to preview in the browser, simply press **F12** and your wish will be ImageReady's command! This **Action** is stored and forever there until you alter or delete it.*

5. ——————— Previewing Backgrounds with an Action

That last **Action** was great for previewing foreground images, but what about those cases when you want to preview an image as a background? This next exercise will show you how.

I. With **bg.psd** still open from the previous exercise, click on the **New Action** icon at the bottom of the **Actions** palette. In the **New Action** window that will open, enter **Name: Preview Background** and **Function Key: F12**, and put a check in the **Shift** setting. Click on **Record**.

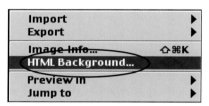

2. Select **File > HTML Background....**

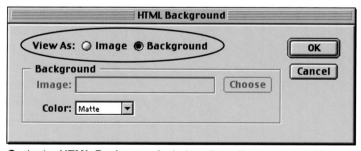

3. In the **HTML Background** window that will open, select **View As: Background** to set the optimized image as an HTML background image. Click **OK**.

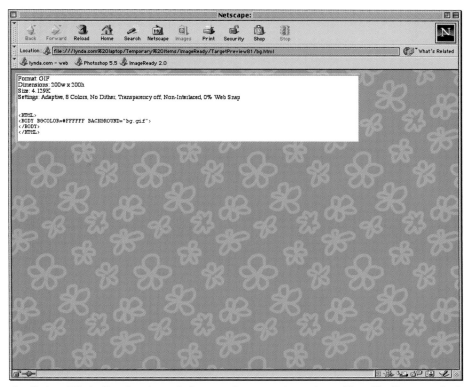

4. Select **File > Preview in** and choose a browser. A preview of **bg.gif** will appear in the browser. This is the last step in the **Preview Background Action**.

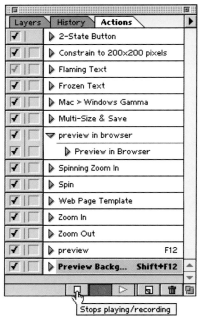

5. Return to ImageReady. Click on the **Stop** button in the **Actions** palette. Now your **Action** is recorded and good to try.

6. Close **bg.psd** and do not save. Open **bg2.psd** from the **chap_13** folder. Press **Shift+F12** and watch it preview as a repeating background.

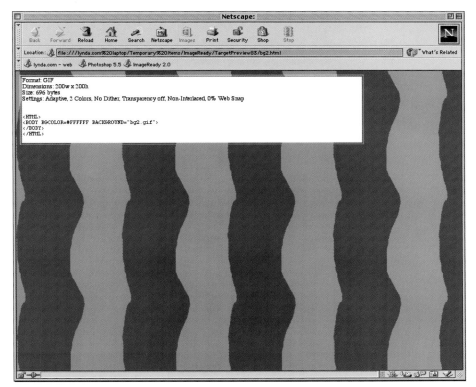

7. Close the file (you don't need to save) and you're ready for the next exercise.

Automating Optimization with a Droplet

Optimizing images can be a time-consuming, repetitive process. ImageReady 2.0's **Droplet** feature makes optimization of multiple images efficient and easy. A **Droplet** is a tiny application that runs an ImageReady **Action** on images you specify through dragging and dropping. In this exercise, you will learn to create a **Droplet** that stores the optimization settings of one image. You'll then automatically apply those settings to a folder full of images by simply dragging the folder onto the **Droplet**.

1. Open **boingo.psd** from the **mini_portfolio** folder in the **chap_13** folder.

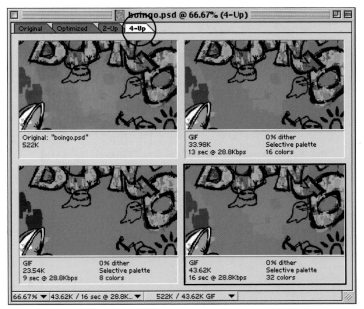

2. Click on the **4-Up** tab on the screen to open four windows in which you can view and compare the look and size of the image at various optimization settings.

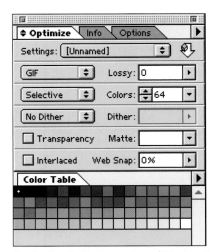

3. In the **Optimize** palette (**Window > Show Optimize**), choose compression settings that create the smallest image that is of acceptable quality. You are using this image as a trial image to determine what type of compression would work best for it, so try **GIF**, **Selective**, **Colors: 64**, **No Dither**, and **Lossy: 0**.

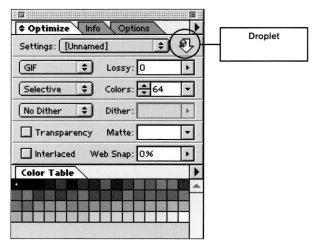

Droplet

4. Click on the **Droplet** icon on the **Optimize** palette. This will open the **Save optimized settings as droplet:** dialog box.

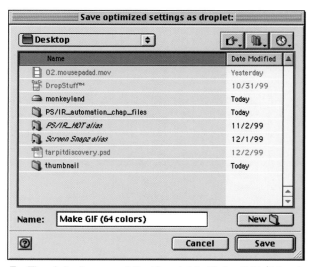

5. The default name of the **Droplet** is **Make GIF** (**64 colors**). You can change it here or type over its title on the desktop. It's a good idea to give it a descriptive name, which the default name does well. Navigate to your desktop and click **Save**. **Note:** You can save a **Droplet** to a folder or your desktop. I'm only suggesting you save to the desktop because it's easy to find it there.

6. Close the original version of **boingo.psd** without saving.

You needed the image open so you could judge the results of what kind of optimization to set. You can now use the Droplet you just created to automatically optimize a folder full of images.

Make G F (64 co ors)

mi rI_portfo io

7. Copy **mini_portfolio** from **chap_13** on the **H•O•T CD-ROM** to your desktop. Click and drag the copy of the folder directly on top of the **Droplet** icon on the desktop in order to begin the automatic batch processing.

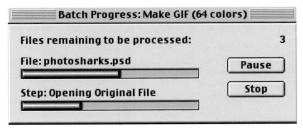

Progress bars in the Batch Progress window keep track as the Droplet optimizes each of the images in a folder, in this case mini_portfolio.

8. When the automatic optimizing is done, look in the **mini_portfolio** folder on your desktop and you will find the original .psd files and the optimized .gif files. The **Droplet** processed all the original .psd files, optimized them, and saved the optimized versions back into the same folder.

 Movie | **droplet.mov**

To learn more about creating a **Droplet**, check out **droplet.mov** from the **movies** folder on the **H•O•T CD-ROM**.

Note | **Changing the Droplet**

By default, **Droplets** save the optimized images in the same folder as the original images. If you wanted to save the optimized images in a destination folder you could use the **Batch Options** dialog box. This dialog box is only reachable by double-clicking on the **Droplet** that you saved, in this case to your desktop, and re-opening it in ImageReady.

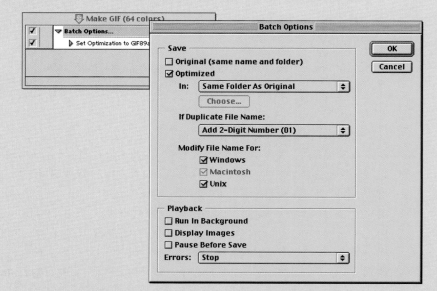

When it opens, you'll see a new window that resembles an **Action** list. Double-click on **Batch Options...** and the **Batch Options** dialog box will appear. In here, you can alter the way the **Droplet** saves the results through a number of different settings and pop-up menus.

More About Droplets

There are a few other neat things to share about **Actions**.

- A **Droplet** is similar to an **Action** in that it records and plays back over a series of images. You can only make **Droplets** in ImageReady, not Photoshop. In the last exercise you saved the **Droplet** to the desktop. That's where I like to store **Droplets** because it's easy to drag and drop files onto them when I know where to find them! However, you can put **Droplets** inside other folders on your hard drive and they will still function just fine.

- You can make **Droplets** from the **Actions** palette as well as from the **Optimization** palette (as the last exercise showed). In the **Actions** palette, select the **Action** from which you want to make a **Droplet**, and click on the upper-right arrow to select **Create Droplet...** from the pop-up menu.

- If ImageReady isn't open, you can drag a folder or image onto a **Droplet** and it will launch that application for you to execute the optimization procedures. You can't really undo a **Droplet**. If you want to change one, it's easiest if you just start over the process of creating it in the first place.

- **Droplets** are cross-platform, so you can share them among Mac and Windows users. However, for Windows machines to recognize that a **Droplet** is an application, you need to add .exe to the end of the **Droplet** name.

- ImageReady lets you drag and drop steps from the **History** palette into the **Actions** palette, which is a fast way to add steps to an **Action**.

- For the true geeks, ImageReady **Actions** are written in JavaScript, and can be edited or generated once you look at a sample **Action** to see how the instructions and settings are structured.

Another chapter down with just one mort to go. If you have any files open in ImageReady, go ahead and close them without saving.

You just successfully programmed an **Action**. Photoshop recorded everything you did and now you can play back the recording whenever you like. The next exercise will show you how to take this **Action** and play it over a series of images contained in a folder.

14.
Importing/Exporting

| Update HTML | ImageReady Rollovers Into GoLive |
| ImageReady Rollovers Into Dreamweaver |
| Illustrator 8.0 Into Photoshop 5.5 or ImageReady 2.0 |
| Earlier Illustrator Version Compatibility |
| ImageReady to QuickTime | QuickTime to Animated GIF |

chap_14

Photoshop 5.5 / ImageReady 2.0
H•O•T CD-ROM

This chapter addresses advanced issues of importing and exporting file formats other than .psd, .gif, and .jpg. I don't know whether you have some of the programs described here, such as GoLive, Dreamweaver, or Illustrator, so I can't anticipate whether or not you will know how to use those applications. It's obviously beyond the scope of this book for me to teach those applications as well as Photoshop 5.5 and ImageReady 2.0. For that reason, keep in mind that parts of this chapter are for advanced users who know how to perform tasks in those applications (GoLive, Dream- weaver, or Illustrator) without much coaching.

This chapter will be helpful to those of you who are interested in importing and exporting HTML, Illustrator, JavaScript, and QuickTime files. Most books touch upon only a single application, but because Web development almost always involves more than one program, I had an idea that this chapter might be useful to many of you readers out there ;-).

I. ————————Update HTML

Update HTML is a command that writes over existing ImageReady-generated HTML and updates only things that have changed. Suppose that you made a remote rollover in ImageReady and had saved the images and HTML in a folder on your hard drive. Your client looks at the work and likes everything but notices a spelling error. If you saved the .psd version of the file it would be easy to correct the spelling mistake, but it would require that you re-export all the optimized images and HTML. Or would it? The **Update HTML** command is useful when you make a change to an existing HTML file. It saves you the headache of managing multiple versions of a document because it updates the original HTML and images to reflect any changes you've made.

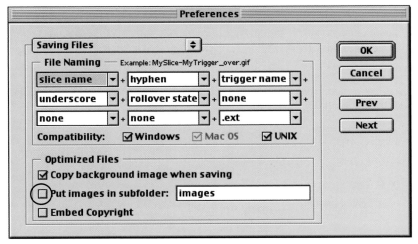

I. Before you begin this exercise, choose **File > Preferences > Saving Files...** and make sure that the **Put images in subfolder** setting is not checked. Several exercises, including this one, depend on this preference setting.

This will cause ImageReady to write HTML and images to the same folder.

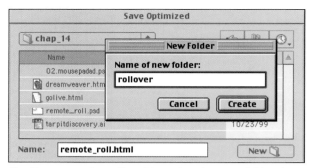

2. Open **remote_roll.psd** from the **chap_14** folder that you transferred to your hard drive from the **H·O·T CD-ROM**. Choose **File > Save Optimized As…** and navigate to the **chap_14** folder.

• (Mac) Click on the **New Folder** button. Name the new folder **rollover** and click on the **Create** button and then the **Save** button.

• (Windows) Click on the **yellow Folder** icon to make a new folder. Name the folder **rollover** and double-click on it so that it opens. Click on the **Save** button and all the files will populate the new folder you just created.

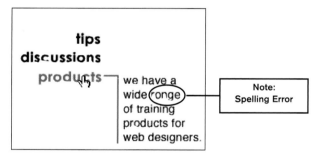

3. Navigate to the **rollover** folder you just saved, and double-click on **remote_roll.html**. This will open the HTML file in a browser. Move your mouse over the word "**products**," and notice the spelling error for "**range**." Return to ImageReady to fix this problem.

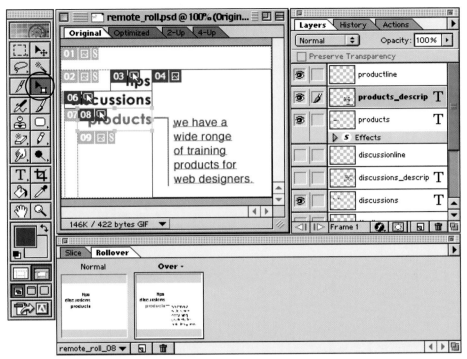

4. Back in ImageReady, use the **Slice Selection** tool to select the slice around the word "**product**" (**slice #08**). In the **Rollover** palette, click on the **Over** state. Notice the spelling error? Hey, spelling errors happen, right?

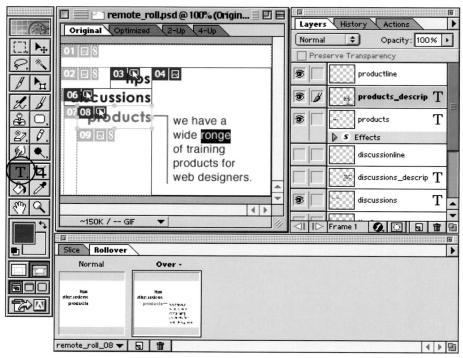

5. To fix the error, select the **Type** tool from the toolbar and select the word "**ronge**." Type the word **range** in its place.

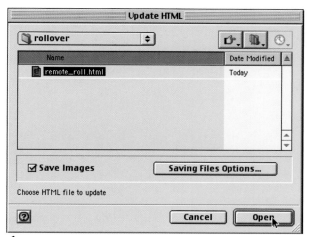

6. Once the spelling error is fixed, choose **File > Update HTML…** and navigate to open the **rollover** folder you just created inside the **chap_14** folder. Select **remote_roll.html** and click **Open**.

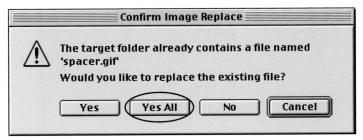

7. Click on **Yes All**. This will replace all the image files that are related to the **remote_roll.html** inside the **rollover** folder, as well as the HTML itself.

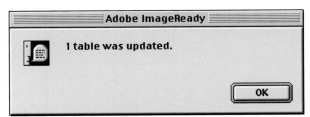

8. ImageReady will prompt you that one table was updated. It replaced all the images in the **rolllover** folder and rewrote the HTML. Click **OK**.

*ImageReady just rewrote all the files that you created in Step 2 and you avoided having to save a duplicate set just to make this one change to your file. Whenever I'm making changes to an ImageReady-generated HTML file or images, I use **Update HTML** so I don't have multiple fold-ers lying around with different versions of artwork and HTML.*

9. Close **remote_roll.psd** and click **Save** when prompted.

How Does Update HTML Work

In ImageReady, **Update HTML** uses comment tags to recognize where to replace code and images properly. Comment tags are an HTML convention that allows a programmer to write a comment inside the file without the browser showing that comment. When you use **Update HTML**, it's essential that ImageReady write its own comment tags.

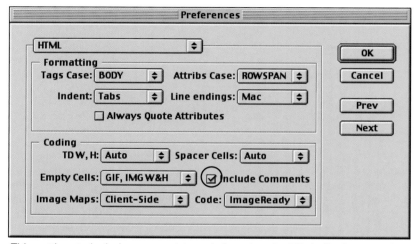

*This setting, to include comment tags, is found under **File > Preferences > HTML...** and is on by default.*

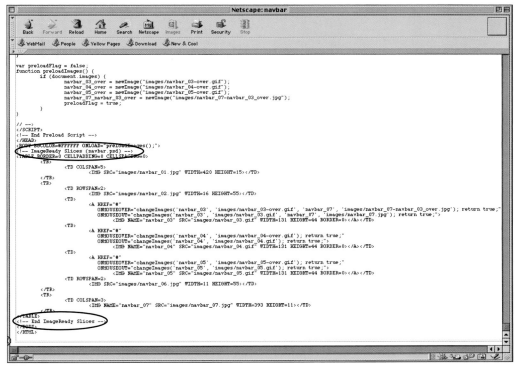

HTML comment tags always include brackets, exclamation points, and dashes. Here is an example: `<! -- comment goes here --!>`.

If you copy and paste ImageReady code into a larger HTML document, **Update HTML** *will still work if you leave the comment tags intact. For this reason, if you plan to use* **Update HTML** *and work with coders who might edit your code afterwards, be sure to tell them to leave the ImageReady comment tags alone.*

Getting ImageReady Rollovers into GoLive

Making rollovers in ImageReady was pretty fun back in Chapter 11, *"Rollovers,"* but as you followed the exercises you were probably asking yourself, "How do I get this into an HTML editor?" You can open an ImageReady HTML file inside any HTML editor and it will work properly. The harder thing to do is to integrate something you made in ImageReady (like a rollover) into an existing HTML page that you made in the HTML editor. You might want to design the rollover in ImageReady and then use it on other pages inside an existing site. This exercise will show you how to accomplish this in GoLive. The instructions are different for GoLive than for other HTML editors, probably because GoLive is an Adobe product and the engineers were able to make ImageReady files easier to use with GoLive. The main trick to getting ImageReady rollovers to work in GoLive is to be sure to set the **HTML Preferences** to write **GoLive** code.

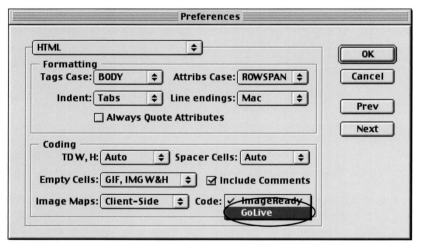

I. Access the **HTML Preferences** inside ImageReady by choosing **File > Preferences > HTML…**, choosing **Code: GoLive**, and clicking **OK**.

 Movie | **golive_rollovers.mov**

To learn more about getting your ImageReady-created rollovers to work in GoLive, check out **golive_rollovers.mov** from the **movies** folder on the **H•O•T CD-ROM**.

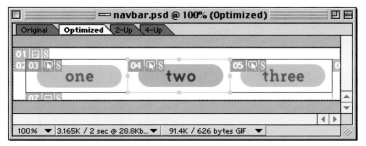

2. Open **navbar.psd**. Preview it in a browser, and you'll see that it contains a series of three simple rollovers.

*Next, you'll save this to the **chap_14** folder so it can eventually be copied into a GoLive site.*

3. In ImageReady, choose **File > Save Optimized As...** and navigate to the **chap_14** folder.

• (Mac) Click on the **New Folder** button. Name the new folder **navbar**, and click on the **Create** button and then the **Save** button.

• (Windows) Click on the **yellow Folder** icon to make a new folder. Name the folder **navbar** and double-click on it so that it opens. Click on the **Save** button and all the files will populate the new folder you just created.

*This should create a **navbar** folder inside the **chap_14** folder that contains the HTML and image files from **navbar.psd**.*

4. In ImageReady, close **navbar.psd**. You can leave ImageReady open, though you won't be using it again for another couple of exercises.

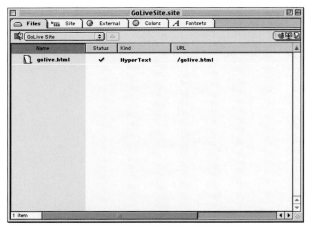

5. Open **GoLive**. To open the site that contains a single HTML file named **golive.html**, follow the directions below.

• (Mac) Choose **File > Open** and navigate to the **chapter_14** folder > **mac_golive** > **GoLive Site ƒ** > **GoLiveSite.site** and click **Open**.

• (Windows) Choose **File > Open** and navigate to **chap_14** folder > **win_golive** > **GoLiveSite Folder** > **GoLiveSite.site** and click **Open**.

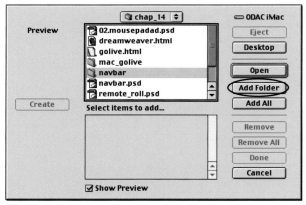

6. Choose **Site > Add Files**, then navigate back to the **chap_14** folder. Select the **navbar** folder that you made earlier, and click on the **Add Folder** button.

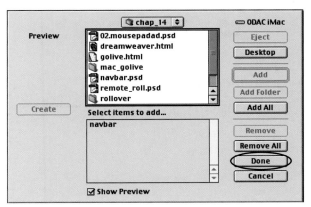

7. The folder **navbar** should now appear in the **Select items to add...** area. Click **Done**.

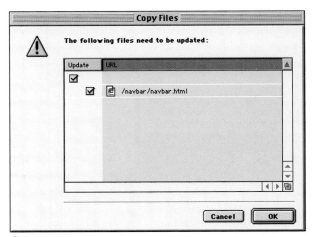

8. The **Copy Files** dialog box will appear. Click **OK**.

This is GoLive's way of updating the ImageReady HTML so that it is relative to the GoLive site. It's one of the strong points of GoLive's site-management capabilities because it ensures that all the links that were generated in ImageReady translate to GoLive properly.

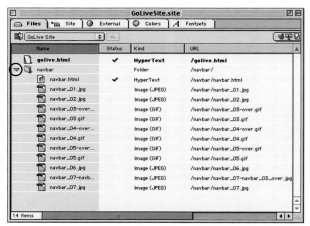

9. In the **GoLive Site** window click on the arrow to the left of the **navbar** folder (Mac) or click on the plus sign (Windows) to reveal that folder's contents. Double-click to open **navbar.html**.

Warning: If you see navbar.html outside of an images folder, you neglected to follow Step 1 in Exercise 1 and will need to start that exercise over.

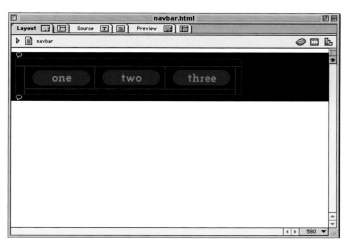

10. The file **navbar.html** should open in its own window, as shown above. Click and drag to select the contents of the file, including the comment tags. Choose **Edit > Copy**.

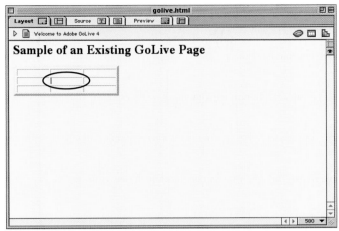

II. Return to the **Site** window by choosing **Window > GoLiveSite.site** (Mac) or **Window > GoLiveSite.site** (Windows), and open **golive.html** by double-clicking on it. The file should open in its own window. Click on the table to make it visible (it will look like a solid rectangle until you click on it), and click on the inside table cell, as shown above.

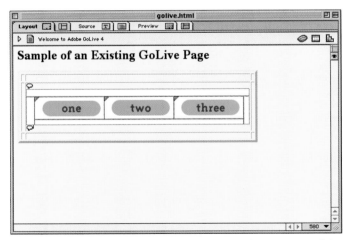

I2. Choose **Edit > Paste**. This should paste the contents of the clipboard (the rollover you copied from **navbar.html**).

I3. To preview this page in a browser, press **Cmd+T** (Mac) or **Ctrl+T** (Windows). You'll see that it works in the browser just fine.

I4. You're finished and can return to GoLive to quit. If prompted to save your changes, click **Save**.

Warning | **CyberObjects and GoLive**

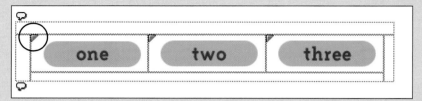

Notice the corners on each of the rollovers? That indicates that GoLive is recognizing the ImageReady rollover as a **CyberObject**. If you are not familiar with **CyberObjects** in GoLive, you can learn about them from the GoLive manual or any of the following resources.

Learning GoLive (VHS or PAL)
With Lynda Weinman
http://www.lynda.com/videos/
$49.95

Real World Adobe GoLive 4
Jeff Carlson, Glenn Fleishman
Peachpit Press
ISBN: 0201354748
$44.99

Mastering Adobe GoLive 4
Molly Holzschlag, Stephen Romaniello
Sybex
ISBN: 0782126049
$34.00

Note: If you had not changed your **Preferences** to write **GoLive** code in Exercise 2, the rollover would not appear as a **CyberObject** or work using the method described in that exercise. That is because the code gets formatted in a way that GoLive recognizes, and if it is generic ImageReady code it would be much harder to work with than what this exercise demonstrated.

[IR]

Getting ImageReady Rollovers into Dreamweaver

This next exercise shows how to put an ImageReady-generated rollover into Dreamweaver 3 or Dreamweaver 2. Again, if all you want to do is to take the ImageReady HTML in its original form, you only need open the file in Dreamweaver, and it will work just fine. This exercise shows you how to do something a little harder, which is to get the ImageReady rollover to work inside an existing HTML page that Dreamweaver generated. Unfortunately, this process is a little harder in Dreamweaver than it was in GoLive in the last exercise. It involves three different steps to copy and paste the files, which will be outlined carefully in this hands-on exercise.

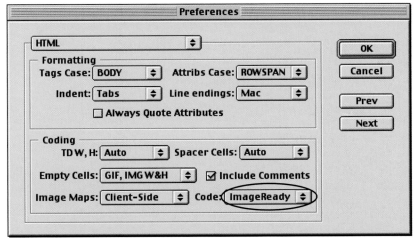

I. Go back to ImageReady and open **navbar.psd** from the **chap_14** folder again. The first thing to do is to save the HTML as **ImageReady** code instead of **GoLive** code. This is the opposite instruction from the previous exercise. To do this, access the **HTML Preferences** inside ImageReady by choosing **File > Preferences > HTML....** Choose **Code: ImageReady** and click **OK**.

2. Choose **File > Save Optimized As...** and navigate to the **chap_14** folder.

• (Mac) Click on the **New Folder** button. Name the new folder **navbar_IR**, and click on the **Create** button and then the **Save** button.

• (Windows) Click on the **yellow Folder** icon to make a new folder. Name the folder **navbar_IR**, and double-click on it so that it opens. Click on the **Save** button, and all the files will populate the new folder you just created.

The files have been saved properly. Now it's time to move the files around in your chap_14 folder before progressing any further.

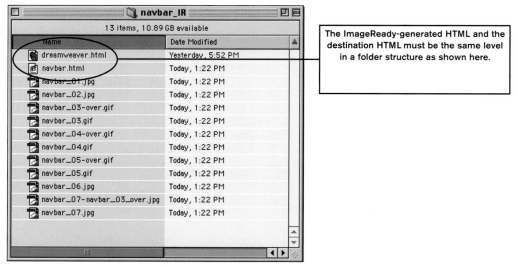

The ImageReady-generated HTML and the destination HTML must be the same level in a folder structure as shown here.

3. Look inside the **chap_14** folder on your hard drive and move the file **dreamweaver.html** into the new folder you created there called **navbar_IR**.

*When ImageReady wrote the file **navbar.html**, it contained references to all the images that appear in the rollover. If you move the HTML file away from those images, the links to them will break. That's why it's important that you make the target and destination HTML files reside in the same folder before opening Dreamweaver.*

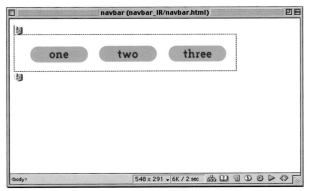

4. Open Dreamweaver and choose **File > Open**. Navigate to **navbar.html**, located inside the **navbar_IR** folder you just created, and click **Open**. Press **F12** and you'll see that the rollovers work just fine in a browser. The trick is when you want to put this rollover into an existing Dreamweaver document, which is what you'll learn to do next.

5. Return to Dreamweaver, and press **F10** to open the **HTML Source** window.

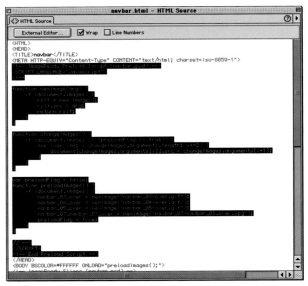

6. The first step is to copy the section of ImageReady code that is located between the first set of comment tags. Notice that these comment tags begin right after the **META** element inside the **HEAD** of the document? Select the code exactly the way you see here, from the beginning of the ImageReady **Preload Script** comment to the **End Preload Script** comment.

7. Copy the code using the command keys **Cmd+C** (Mac) or **Ctrl+C** (Windows).

Note: This technique will not work unless you use the command keys to copy, instead of the menu. It's a strange Dreamweaver 3 foible.

8. Choose **File > Open**. Navigate to **dreamweaver.html**, located inside the **navbar_IR** folder, and click **Open**.

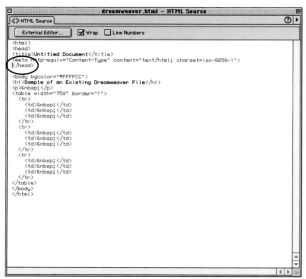

9. You should be able to see the source code of **dreamweaver.html** now. Locate the close of the HEAD tag (circled above) and click your cursor there.

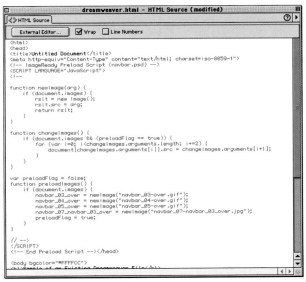

IO. Paste the code using the command keys **Cmd+V** (Mac) or **Ctrl+V** (Windows). You should see the code you copied from **navbar.html** inside the document, as shown above.

II. Return to **navbar.html** by choosing **Window > navbar.html**. Select and copy the section of code you see highlighted above using the command keys **Cmd+C** (Mac) or **Ctrl+C** (Windows).

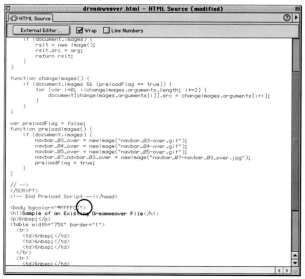

I2. Switch back to **dreamweaver.html** by choosing **Window > dreamweaver.html**. Locate the same spot inside the BODY tag and click your cursor.

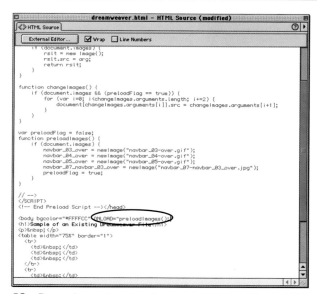

I3. Paste the code using the command keys **Cmd+V** (Mac) or **Ctrl+V** (Windows). The code should look identical to what is circled above.

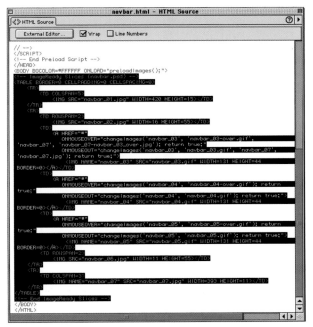

14. Return to **navbar.html** by choosing **Window > navbar.html**. Select the code that you see selected above, and copy it using the command keys **Cmd+C** (Mac) or **Ctrl+C** (Windows).

I5. Return to **dreamweaver.html** by choosing **Window > dreamweaver.html**. Click your mouse where it is circled above.

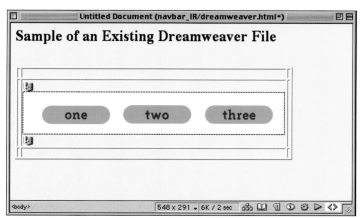

I6. Use your command keys to paste. Press **F10** again and the **Source** window will disappear, and you should see the HTML file with the ImageReady rollover inside.

17. Press **F12** to preview this in a browser. The rollover works, and you're probably blown away by how hard this was. I agree with you – it's not an easy or fun task, but it does work.

18. Quit Dreamweaver and save when prompted.

Movie | **dreamweaver_rollovers.mov**

To learn more about putting your ImageReady-created rollovers into Dreamweaver, check out **dreamweaver_rollovers.mov** from the **movies** folder on the **H•O•T CD-ROM**.

Note | **Great News for Dreamweaver Users!**

Visit the download area of lynda.com to download the free "**Insert ImageReady HTML**" Command. It will eliminate the tedious cutting and pasting that you learned to do in this exercise, by inserting the ImageReady code into any Dreamweaver document with a single instruction. This Command was written by Massimo Foti (**http://www.massimocorner.com**) for lynda.com, and can be downloaded from the following URL:

http://www.lynda.com/downloads

Warning | **Working with an Existing Dreamweaver Site**

If you are an experienced Dreamweaver user and you already have a site with which you want to try the technique covered in this exercise, the instructions are a bit different than what you just did. Instead, you would want to move the **navbar_IR** folder into the **Root Folder** of that site. It would then appear inside the **Site** window (**F5**). You would also have to move the **navbar.html** to the same level as the destination HTML file you wanted to paste it into. Be sure to move the files from within Dreamweaver's **Site** window, or you risk the possibility of all the links to the images breaking.

These are some resources I recommend for more information on learning about site management in Dreamweaver.

Dreamweaver 3 (H•O•T)
Hands-On Training
By Lynda Weinman and Garo Green
lynda.com/books and Peachpit Press
ISBN: 0201702762
$39.99

Dreamweaver 3 Bible
Joseph W. Lowery
IDG Books
ISBN: 0764534580
$39.99

Learning Dreamweaver 3 (VHS/PAL)
With Lynda Weinman and Garo Green
http://www.lynda.com/videos/

Exporting llustrator 8.0 Files

The best way to prepare documents in Illustrator for ImageReady is to first work in layers in Illustrator. This example uses an Adobe Illustrator file (**tarpitdiscovery.ai**) that contains named layers.

1. Open **Illustrator 8.0** and choose **File > Open**. Navigate to the **chap_14** folder to select **tarpitdiscovery.ai**. Notice that this file contains three layers.

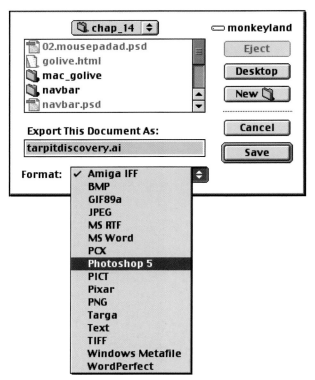

2. From Illustrator, choose **File > Export**. Select **Photoshop 5** from the **Format:** pop-up menu, navigate to the **chap_14** folder, and click **Save**. **Note:** Mac users will have to manually change the extension from **.ai** to **.psd**.

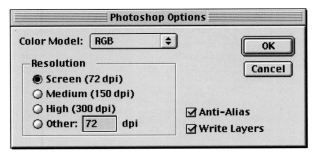

3. In the **Photoshop Options** dialog box that will appear, match your settings to those shown above and click **OK**.

4. Choose **File > Open** within ImageReady or Photoshop, and select and open the Photoshop document that you saved from Illustrator (**tarpitdiscovery.psd**). It will appear with all the layers in Photoshop layers named exactly as they were in Illustrator.

The advantage to this technique was that the Illustrator file was brought into ImageReady with layers that were pre-named and separated correctly. Now you're ready to create rollovers or animated GIF files from this layered document.

5. ———————Exporting from Earlier Illustrator Versions

If you own an earlier version of Illustrator, then you will not be able to export in the Photoshop 5.0 format. Don't worry. You can copy and paste between applications instead.

I. Open the **tarpitdiscovery.ai** file in Illustrator 8.0 or below. Select the elements that you want to paste into Photoshop or ImageReady and choose **Edit > Copy**.

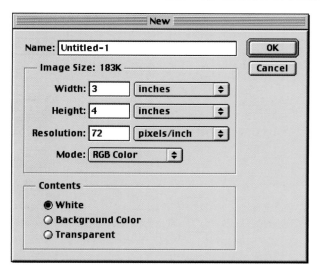

2. Open Photoshop or ImageReady and choose **File > New**. Set up the document with the same settings as you see above (ImageReady won't give you a resolution option, but don't worry about that) and click **OK**.

3. Choose **Edit > Paste**. In the **Paste** dialog box that will appear (Photoshop only), choose **Paste As Pixels** and **Anti-Alias**. **Note:** Because ImageReady doesn't support paths, it knows to paste as pixels when you choose the **Paste** command. This will change the artwork from vector (Illustrator) to bitmap (Photoshop).

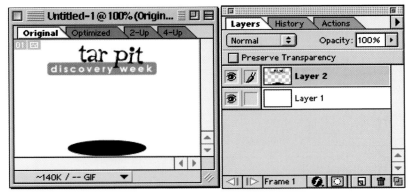

4. The artwork that you copied and pasted will appear on its own automatically named layer. If your **Layers** palette isn't open for you to see this, choose **Window > Show Layers**. If you want to name the layer differently (which I suggest you do), double-click on it and type in a better name.

You can go back and forth between Illustrator and Photoshop or ImageReady this way, copying and pasting whatever artwork you want on to new layers.

5. When you're finished with this exercise you can quit Illustrator and Photoshop, as neither is needed again.

6. _____Exporting ImageReady to QuickTime

In addition to writing animated GIF files, ImageReady will also export animation files to QuickTime. You might want to do this if you are working on a multimedia project instead of an HTML project.

I. In ImageReady, open **02.mousepadad.psd**.

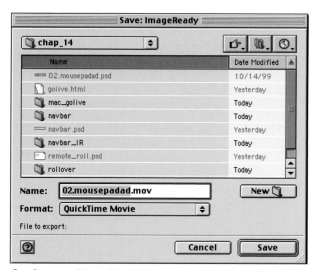

2. Choose **File > Export Original...** and then **Format: QuickTime Movie**. The .mov extension will automatically be added to the end of the file name. Navigate to the **chap_14** folder and click **Save**.

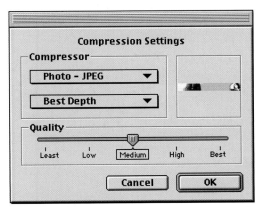

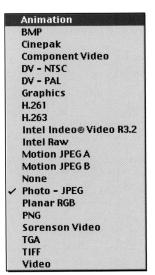

3. The **Compression Settings** dialog box will appear at its **Photo – JPEG** default. This is a good format if your animation includes continuous-tone imagery. The file you're working with is graphic in nature, so choose **Animation** from the top **Compressor** pop-up menu.

4. Click **OK** and the file will be saved. To see it, go to the **chap_14** folder where you saved it, double-click on the file **02.mousepadad.mov**, and it should open up in the Movie Player that ships with QuickTime. **Note:** A version of Movie Player is on the **H•O•T CD-ROM** in case you don't have one.

[IR] **7.**————**Converting from QuickTime to ImageReady**

You can also convert from QuickTime to an animated GIF in ImageReady. You might want to do this if someone gives you a QuickTime movie that was created for some other purpose (such as one that contained live action and was shot with a movie camera) but that you'd prefer to convert to an animated GIF.

1. In ImageReady, choose **File > Open**. Locate the **02mousepadad.mov** file that you just created and click **OK**. The **Open Movie** dialog box will appear.

You can choose to import the entire movie, a select range of frames, or skip frames to specified increments, such as every five frames or whichever setting is appropriate.

2. Click **OK** inside the **Open Movie** dialog box. These default settings will work perfectly for this example.

*The file will be converted to layers and the frames will automatically appear inside the **Animation** palette. It will take whatever timing was set as the frame rate from the QuickTime movie.*

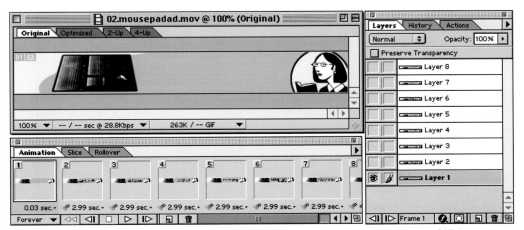

3. To save this as an animated GIF, make sure the optimization settings are in the GIF format and choose **File > Save Optimized As...**. It's that easy, really!

This exercise showed how to convert a file from QuickTime to an animated GIF. This chapter covered a lot of loose ends that weren't easily defined by the other chapter categories. I hope some or all has been relevant to your work.

You're finished with the last chapter, and now it's time to go out into the world on your own and make great Web art and movies. Rock on!

15.
Troubleshooting FAQ

| H•O•T |

| **Hands-On Training** |

Photoshop 5.5 / ImageReady 2.0

For the Web

If you've run into any problems while following the exercises in this book, this FAQ (**F**requently **A**sked **Q**uestions) is intended to help. This document will be maintained and expanded upon at this book's companion Web site:

http://www.lynda.com/books/psirhot

If you don't find what you're looking for here or there, please send an email to psirfaq@lynda.com.

If you have a question related to Photoshop 5.5 or ImageReady 2.0 that is not related to a specific exercise in this book, visit the Adobe site at:

http://www. adobe.com

or call their tech-support hotline at: (800) 49-ADOBE.

Q: I'm on Windows and all the files on the **H•O•T CD-ROM** are locked, even though I transferred them to my hard drive. What should I do?

A: There are instructions for this problem in Chapter 1, *"Introduction."* It is easy to fix as long as you follow the directions there.

Q: I'm on a Mac and I get weird refresh problems with my desktop flashing and everything running really slow. Do you have any ideas why this always happens to me?

A: You are probably running low on RAM. Close one or more applications and it should improve. You might have to quit ImageReady, Photoshop, or the browser during exercises so that you only keep one program open at a time. Consider getting more RAM if you plan to do this sort of work often.

Q: What if I use color profiles in my print work? It's kind of disconcerting to turn them off, as you suggested in Chapter 3, *"Color Management."*

A: You can always program an **Action** that will turn them off and/or back on. You learned how to make Actions in Chapter 13, *"Automation,"* but here's a brief refresher. Simply start recording an **Action** before you turn profiles on or off, and the **Action** will remember your steps. Once you've finished recording, press the **Stop** button. Bingo, you have an **Action** for that task!

Q: What should I do about CMYK images that I created for print? Can I use them on the Web?

A: You won't be able to use CMYK images on the Web. You'll have to convert those images to RGB first. Do this in Photoshop by choosing **Image > Mode > RGB Color**. There might be some color shifting during this process because CMYK and RGB are two different color spaces that cannot achieve an exact translation.

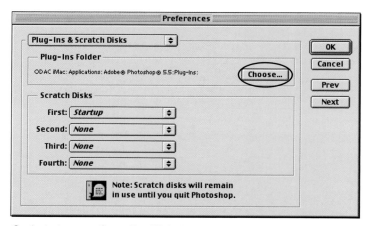

Q: I tried to use **Save For Web**, but it was grayed out in the **File** menu. How can I follow along with your book?

A: Worse than that, how can you optimize images in **Photoshop**? The problem is that the program lost track of where the **Plug-Ins** folder is located. Choose **File > Preferences > Plug-Ins & Scratch Disks...** and click on the **Choose...** button. Browse to the **Plug-Ins** folder inside the **Photoshop 5.5®** folder on your hard drive. Click **OK**. This lets Photoshop know where to find the **Save For Web** Plug-In.

Q: In Chapter 4, *"Optimization,"* you suggest that I leave the **Save For Web** dialog box open for many exercises in a row. What happens if I have to quit and come back to the exercise another time?

A: The **Save For Web** dialog box will remember the last settings you used as long as you haven't quit Photoshop. If you quit Photoshop, it will not remember any of your settings, and you will probably have to redo the exercises again from scratch.

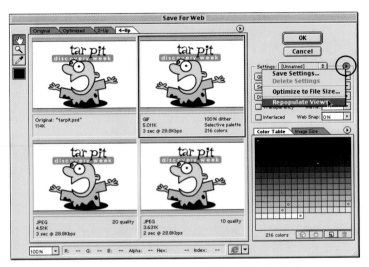

Q: What does it mean when I'm in the **Save For Web** dialog box and see an orange warning triangle?

A: Click the **Optimized** menu arrow in the **Save For Web** dialog box and choose **Repopulate Views**. This should cause all the views to refresh and the warning icon to disappear.

Q: My **Layers** palette doesn't look like yours, Lynda! What's up with that?

A: To access any palette in its entirety, not just the **Layers** palette, just drag its bottom-right corner.

Q: Anytime I go to any file in ImageReady and click the **Optimized** setting, instead of seeing the image in the background, I get a checkerboard pattern.

A: If you're having trouble seeing an image under the **Optimized** setting, go to the top-right corner of the **Optimize** palette and make sure that **Auto Regenerate** is checked in the pull-down menu. Remember, that checkerboard pattern indicates that this is a transparent GIF.

Q: Please remind me what each of the **Optimization** tabs settings means.

A: Glad to. The first is **Original** and that's self-explanatory. It's the original, non-optimized image. **Optimized** is self-explanatory, too. It shows you the optimized version of an image. I prefer to do all my work in **Original**, as **Optimized** constantly updates the image, which can really slow things down. The last two, **2-Up** and **4-Up**, offer two and four versions of the image, respectively.

Q: In Photoshop when I'm working with type I can't see the effects of what I'm doing until I bail out of the dialog box. There's gotta be a better way.

A: There is. Just make sure there's a checkmark in the **Preview** box of that very window. Doing so allows you to preview changes you make to kerning, tracking, baseline, leading, color, anti-aliasing — all sorts of type-related elements — right there on the spot. You also will want to be aware of the **Fit in Window** setting. If you work with large type, this checkbox ensures that you can see everything you need to see in the **Type Tool** dialog box. One disadvantage to using **Fit in Window** is it can be misleading when you want to see a preview of the type's actual size.

Q: Every time I save a file I get this annoying box asking me where I want to update it.

A: I know what you mean when you say it's annoying. There's a simple way to fix this and it involves changing your **Preferences**. In both applications, choose **File > Preferences > General....** In Photoshop, put a check next to **Auto-update** open documents; in ImageReady, put a check next to **Auto-Update Files**. Click **OK** and you'll never have to see that pesky box again. For more about this, revisit the third exercise in Chapter 6, *"Type."*

Q: When I type, the type shows up behind the button, not over it. Why does this happen?

A: The stacking order of layers in the **Layers** palette is from bottom to top. If your type is under another layer it might be hidden. Drag the **type** layers above all the others and you will see it. Another problem is that you might be typing in the same color as your button. Hey, it happens even to the pros, I swear it does!

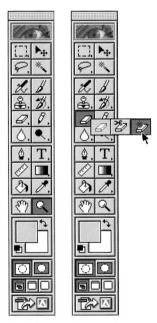

Q: I keep going to the toolbar to get to the **Magic Eraser** but it's nowhere to be found, though I do see the **Eraser**. How do I access it?

A: See the tiny arrow at the bottom right of the **Eraser** tool icon? Click there, leave your mouse depressed, and you'll see the other **Eraser** options, including the **Magic Eraser**. You can drag out to select any of the erasers in this pop-out palette. All the tools that have the same tiny arrow have more than one tool option, just like this one.

Q: Not to complain, but I get sick of zooming in and out of my files. Is there a quick way to get a big view?

A: If you double-click on the **Hand** tool inside the toolbar the image will expand to fill your screen. If you double-click on the **Zoom** tool in the toolbar it will change to **100%**. The trick is to double-click right in the toolbar, not on your image.

Q: I am working away on an image in ImageReady, and it's taking forever for the program to accept my edits. I am slowly going crazy.

A: My guess is you're working in the **Optimized** setting, which tells ImageReady to constantly optimize your graphic while you're editing it. Switch over to the **Original** tab. It will go faster, I promise.

Q: Is there a quick one-step way to hide all those palettes that are cluttering up my desktop?

A: Press the **Tab** key to toggle on and off all the palettes in either Photoshop or ImageReady. It's a beautiful thing!

Q: I keep trying to select a slice but for some reason I can't. Help!

A: Are you using the **Slice Selection** tool? It's to the right of the **Slice** tool in the ImageReady toolbar. Use the **Slice** tool to cut up an image into slices and then use the **Slice Selection** tool to adjust those slices. The **Slice Selection** tool lets you drag, reposition, delete, and select a single slice or more at one time. To select multiple slices, hold down the **Shift** key. The shortcut key for the **Slice Selection** tool is the letter **A** on your keyboard. The shortcut key for the **Slice** tool is the letter **Y**.

Q: I want to create a rollover, but nothing is showing up in the **Rollover** palette. What am I doing wrong?

A: You must first select a slice (with the **Slice Selection** tool) before the **Rollover** palette is operational. That's because you define rollovers according to a trigger slice. If you don't have a slice defined, ImageReady has no way of knowing which slice is going to trigger the rollover.

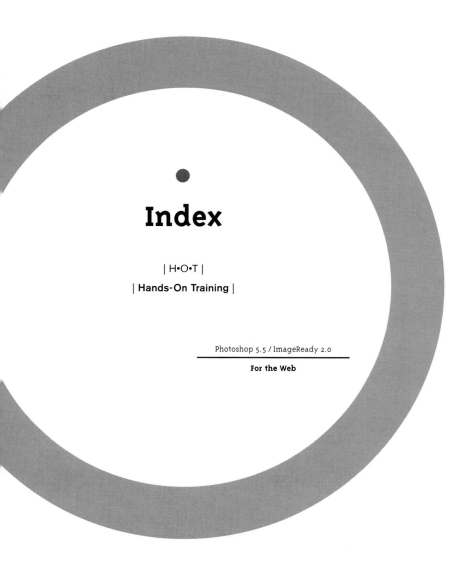

Index

| H•O•T |

| Hands-On Training |

Photoshop 5.5 / ImageReady 2.0

For the Web

H

T

Tab key, 20

tabs
    docking/undocking, 16
    dragging, 17

thumbnails
    automatic creation of, 410
    folder, 412, 418
    images linked to, 403
    scaling factor, 403
    Web-ready, 404

Tile Maker Filter, 209
    applying, 210
    Blend Edges setting, 210
    defined, 208
    dialog box, 210
    image effect, 210
    Kaleidoscope Tile setting, 210
    opening, 209

tiles. *See* background tiles

Tolerance, 193

toolbars
    Background Color swatch, 144
    Foreground Color swatch, 90, 94, 144, 172
    Hide Slices button, 270, 317
    illustrated, 14
    Jump To button, 15, 130, 132…
    152, 157, 162, 262
    showing/hiding, 20
    Show Slices button, 270, 276, 318, 384
    Switch Foreground and Background…
    Colors button, 145
    See also tools (ImageReady); tools…
    (Photoshop)

tools (ImageReady)
    Ellipse, 327
    Eraser, 66, 156, 467
    Eyedropper, 187, 233, 276
    Hand tool, 468
    hidden, viewing, 21
    Magic Eraser, 66, 192-193, 197, 467

Marquee, 140
Move, 216, 329, 373, 374, 376
Options palettes for, 21
Paintbrush, 198, 259
Rectangle, 327
Rounded Rectangle, 326-327
Shape, 144-145
Slice, 268, 269, 339, 469
Slice Selection, 268, 269, 384, 390, 393, 394, 395, 431, 469
Type, 123, 136, 334, 432
Zoom, 193, 270, 468

tools (Photoshop)
    Airbrush, 178, 179
    default settings, 21
    Eyedropper, 87
    hidden, viewing, 21
    Move, 113, 134
    Options palette, 21
    Paintbrush, 154
    Type, 123

tracking, 125

transparency
    8-bit, 225
    in Photoshop, 242-243
    preserving, 110-115
    terminology, 229
    white color substitution for, 187

transparent animated GIFs, 358-362
    challenges, 362
    creating, 358-361
    previewing, 361, 362
    saving, 362
    See also animated GIFs

transparent GIFs, 49, 73, 224-247
    1-bit limitation, 225
    alternate method creation, 247
    creating, 230-231, 247
    defined, 229
    edges, 232
    edges, fixing, 233-235

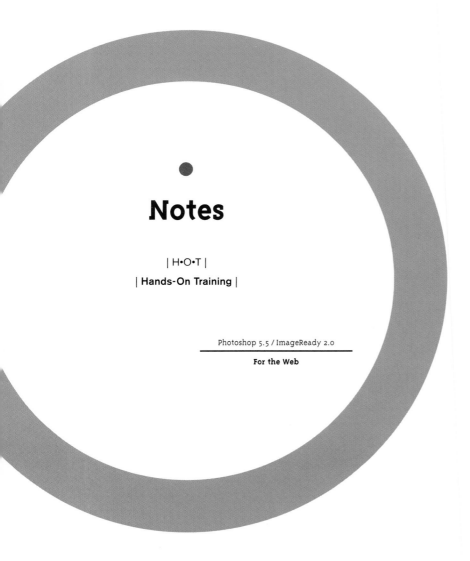

Notes

| H•O•T |

| Hands-On Training |

Photoshop 5.5 / ImageReady 2.0

For the Web

CD-ROM LICENSE AGREEMENT

THIS SOFTWARE LICENSE AGREEMENT CONSTITUTES AN AGREEMENT BETWEEN YOU AND, LYNDA.COM, LLC. . YOU SHOULD CAREFULLY READ THE FOLLOWING TERMS AND CONDITIONS BEFORE OPENING THIS ENVELOPE. COPYING THIS SOFTWARE TO YOUR MACHINE, BREAKING THE SEAL, OR OTHERWISE RE-MOVING OR USING THE SOFTWARE INDICATES YOUR ACCEPTANCE OF THESE TERMS AND CONDITIONS. IF YOU DO NOT AGREE TO BE BOUND BY THE PROVISIONS OF THIS LICENSE AGREEMENT, YOU SHOULD PROMPTLY DELETE THE SOFTWARE FROM YOUR MACHINE. TERMS AND CONDITIONS:

1. GRANT OF LICENSE. In consideration of payment of the License Fee, which was a part of the price you paid for this product, LICENSOR grants to you (the "Licensee") a non-exclusive right to use and display this copy of a Software program, along with any updates or upgrade releases of the Software for which you have paid (all parts and elements of the Software as well as the Software as a whole are hereinafter referred to as the "Software") on a single computer only (i.e., with a single CPU) at a single location, all as more particularly set forth and limited below. LICENSOR reserves all rights not expressly granted to you as Licensee in this License Agreement.

2. OWNERSHIP OF SOFTWARE. The license granted herein is not a sale of the original Software or of any copy of the Software. As Licensee, you own only the rights to use the Software as described herein and the magnetic or other physical media on which the Software is originally or subsequently recorded or fixed. LICENSOR retains title and ownership of the Software recorded on the original disk(s), as well as title and ownership of any subsequent copies of the Software irrespective of the form of media on or in which the Software is recorded or fixed. This license does not grant you any intellectual or other proprietary or other rights of any nature what-soever in the Software.

3. USE RESTRICTIONS. As Licensee, you may use the Software only as expressly authorized in this License Agreement under the terms of paragraph 4. You may phy-sically transfer the Software from one computer to another provided that the Soft-ware is used on only a single computer at any one time. You may not: (i) electroni-cally transfer the Software from one computer to another over a network; (ii) make the Software available through a time-sharing service, network of computers, or other multiple user arrangement; (iii) distribute copies of the Software or related written materials to any third party, whether for sale or otherwise; (iv) modify, adapt, translate, reverse engineer, decompile, disassemble, or prepare any derivative work based on the Software or any element thereof; (v) make or distribute, whether for sale or otherwise, any hard copy or printed version of any of the Software nor any portion thereof nor any work of yours containing the Software or any component thereof; (vi) use any of the Software nor any of its components in any other work.

8. THIS IS WHAT YOU CAN AND CANNOT DO WITH THE SOFTWARE. Even though in the preceding paragraph and elsewhere LICENSOR has restricted your use of the Software, the following is the only thing you can do with the Software and the various elements of the Software:DUCKS IN A ROW ARTWORK: THE ARTWORK CONTAINED ON THIS CD-ROM MAY NOT BE USED IN ANY MANNER WHATSOEVER OTHER THAN TO VIEW THE SAME ON YOUR COMPUTER, OR POST TO YOUR PERSONAL, NON-COMMER-CIAL WEB SITE FOR EDUCATIONAL PURPOSES ONLY. THIS MATERIAL IS SUBJECT TO ALL OF THE RESTRICTION PROVISIONS OF THIS SOFTWARE LICENSE. SPECIFI-CALLY BUT NOT IN LIMITATION OF THESE RESTRICTIONS, YOU MAY NOT DISTRIB-UTE, RESELL OR TRANSFER THIS PART OF THE SOFTWARE DESIGNATED AS "CLUTS" NOR ANY OF YOUR DESIGN OR OTHER WORK CONTAINING ANY OF THE SOFTWARE DESIGNATED AS "DUCKS IN A ROW ARTWORK" NOR ANY OF YOUR DESIGN OR OTHER WORK CONTAINING ANY SUCH "DUCKS IN A ROW ARTWORK," ALL AS MORE PARTICULARLY RESTRICTED IN THE WITHIN SOFTWARE LICENSE.

5. COPY RESTRICTIONS. The Software and accompanying written materials are protected under United States copyright laws. Unauthorized copying and/or distribution of the Software and/or the related written materials is expressly forbidden. You may be held legally responsible for any copyright infringement that is caused, directly or indirectly, by your failure to abide by the terms of this License Agreement. Subject to the terms of this License Agreement and if the software is not otherwise copy protected, you may make one copy of the Software for backup purposes only. The copyright notice and any other proprietary notices which were included in the original Software must be reproduced and included on any such backup copy.

6. TRANSFER RESTRICTIONS. The license herein granted is personal to you, the Licensee. You may not transfer the Software nor any of its components or elements to anyone else, nor may you sell, lease, loan, sublicense, assign, or otherwise dispose of the Software nor any of its components or elements without the express written consent of LICENSOR, which consent may be granted or withheld at LICENSOR's sole discretion.

7. TERMINATION. The license herein granted hereby will remain in effect until terminated. This license will terminate automatically without further notice from LICENSOR in the event of the violation of any of the provisions of this License Agreement. As Licensee, you agree that upon such termination you will promptly destroy any and all copies of the Software which remain in your possession and, upon request, will certify to such destruction in writing to LICENSOR.

8. LIMITATION AND DISCLAIMER OF WARRANTIES. a) THE SOFTWARE AND RELAT-ED WRITTEN MATERIALS, INCLUDING ANY INSTRUCTIONS FOR USE, ARE PROVID-ED ON AN "AS IS" BASIS, WITHOUT WARRANTY OF ANY KIND, EXPRESS OR IMPLIED. THIS DISCLAIMER OF WARRANTY EXPRESSLY IN-CLUDES, BUT IS NOT LIMITED TO, ANY IMPLIED WARRANTIES OF MERCHANTABILITY AND/OR OF FIT-NESS FOR A PARTICULAR PURPOSE. NO WARRANTY OF ANY KIND IS MADE AS TO WHETHER OR NOT THIS SOFT-WARE INFRINGES UPON ANY RIGHTS OF ANY OTHER THIRD PARTIES. NO ORAL OR WRITTEN INFORMATION GIVEN BY LICEN-SOR, ITS SUPPLIERS, DISTRIBUTORS, DEALERS, EMPLOYEES, OR AGENTS, SHALL CREATE OR OTHERWISE ENLARGE THE SCOPE OF ANY WARRANTY HEREUNDER. LICENSEE ASSUMES THE ENTIRE RISK AS TO THE QUALITY AND THE PERFOR-MANCE OF SUCH SOFTWARE. SHOULD THE SOFTWARE PROVE DEFECTIVE, YOU,

AS LICENSEE (AND NOT LICENSOR, ITS SUPPLIERS, DISTRIBU-TORS, DEALERS OR AGENTS), ASSUME THE ENTIRE COST OF ALL NECESSARY CORRECTION, SERVIC-ING, OR REPAIR. b) LICENSOR warrants the disk(s) on which this copy of the Software is recorded or fixed to be free from defects in materials and workmanship, under normal use and service, for a period of ninety (90) days from the date of delivery as evidenced by a copy of the applicable receipt. LICENSOR hereby limits the duration of any implied warranties with respect to the disk(s) to the duration of the express warranty. This limited warranty shall not apply if the disk(s) have been damaged by unreasonable use, accident, negligence, or by any other causes unrelated to defective materials or workmanship. c) LICENSOR does not war-rant that the functions contained in the Software will be uninterrupted or error free and Licensee is encouraged to test the Software for Licensee's intended use prior to placing any reliance thereon. All risk of the use of the Software will be on you, as Licensee. d) THE LIM-ITED WARRANTY SET FORTH ABOVE GIVES YOU SPECIFIC LEGAL RIGHTS AND YOU MAY ALSO HAVE OTHER RIGHTS WHICH VARY FROM STATE TO STATE. SOME STATES DO NOT ALLOW THE LIMITATION OR EXCLUSION OF IMPLIED WARRANTIES OR OF INCIDENTAL OR CONSEQUENTIAL DAMAGES, SO THE LIMITATIONS AND EXCLUSIONS CONCERNING THE SOFTWARE AND RELATED WRITTEN MATERIALS SET FORTH ABOVE MAY NOT APPLY TO YOU.

9. LIMITATION OF REMEDIES. LICENSOR's entire liability and Licensee's exclusive remedy shall be the replacement of any disk(s) not meeting the limited warranty set forth in Section 8 above which is returned to LICENSOR with a copy of the applic-able receipt within the warranty period. Any replacement disk(s)will be warranted for the remainder of the original warranty period or thirty (30) days, whichever is longer.

10. LIMITATION OF LIABILITY. IN NO EVENT WILL LICENSOR, OR ANYONE ELSE INVOLVED IN THE CREATION, PRODUCTION, AND/OR DELIVERY OF THIS SOFTWARE PRODUCT BE LIABLE TO LICENSEE OR ANY OTHER PER-SON OR ENTITY FOR ANY DIRECT, INDIRECT, OR OTHER DAMAGES, INCLUDING, WITHOUT LIMITATION, ANY INTERRUPTION OF SERVICES, LOST PROFITS, LOST SAVINGS, LOSS OF DATA, OR ANY OTHER CONSEQUENTIAL, INCIDEN-TAL, SPECIAL, OR PUNITIVE DAMAGES, ARISING OUT OF THE PURCHASE, USE, INABILITY TO USE, OR OPERATION OF THE SOFTWARE, EVEN IF LICENSOR OR ANY AUTHORIZED LICENSOR DEALER HAS BEEN ADVISED OF THE POSSIBILITY OF SUCH DAMAGES. BY YOUR USE OF THE SOFTWARE, YOU ACKNOWLEDGE THAT THE LIMITATION OF LIABILITY SET FORTH IN THIS LICENSE WAS THE BASIS UPON WHICH THE SOFTWARE WAS OFFERED BY LICENSOR AND YOU ACKNOWLEDGE THAT THE PRICE OF THE SOFTWARE LICENSE WOULD BE HIGHER IN THE ABSENCE OF SUCH LIMITATION. SOME STATES DO NOT ALLOW THE LIMITATION OR EXCLUSION OF LIABILITY FOR INCIDEN-TAL OR CONSEQUENTIAL DAMAGES SO THE ABOVE LIMITATIONS AND EXCLU-SIONS MAY NOT APPLY TO YOU.

11. UPDATES. LICENSOR, at its sole discretion, may periodically issue updates of the Software which you may receive upon request and payment of the applicable update fee in effect from time to time and in such event, all of the provisions of the within License Agreement shall apply to such updates.

12. EXPORT RESTRICTIONS. Licensee agrees not to export or re-export the Soft-ware and accompanying documentation (or any copies thereof) in violation of any applicable U.S. laws or regulations.

13. ENTIRE AGREEMENT. YOU, AS LICENSEE, ACKNOWLEDGE THAT: (i) YOU HAVE READ THIS ENTIRE AGREEMENT AND AGREE TO BE BOUND BY ITS TERMS AND CONDITIONS; (ii) THIS AGREEMENT IS THE COMPLETE AND EXCLUSIVE STATEMENT OF THE UNDERSTANDING BETWEEN THE PARTIES AND SUPERSEDES ANY AND ALL PRIOR ORAL OR WRITTEN COMMUNICATIONS RELATING TO THE SUBJECT MATTER HEREOF; AND (iii) THIS AGREEMENT MAY NOT BE MODIFIED, AMENDED, OR IN ANY WAY ALTERED EXCEPT BY A WRITING SIGNED BY BOTH YOURSELF AND AN OFFICER OR AUTHORIZED REPRESENTATIVE OF LICENSOR.

14. SEVERABILITY. In the event that any provision of this License Agreement is held to be illegal or otherwise unenforceable, such provision shall be deemed to have been deleted from this License Agreement while the remaining provisions of this License Agreement shall be unaffected and shall continue in full force and effect.

15. GOVERNING LAW. This License Agreement shall be governed by the laws of the State of California applicable to agreements wholly to be performed therein and of the United States of America, excluding that body of the law related to conflicts of law. This License Agreement shall not be governed by the United Nations Convention on Contracts for the International Sale of Goods, the application of which is expressly excluded. No waiver of any breach of the provisions of this License Agreement shall be deemed a waiver of any other breach of this License Agreement.

16. RESTRICTED RIGHTS LEGEND. Use, duplication, or disclosure by the Govern-ment is subject to restrictions as set forth in subparagraph (c)(1)(ii) of the Rights in Technical Data and Computer Software clause at 48 CFR § 252.227-7013 and DFARS § 252.227-7013 or subparagraphs (c) (1) and (c)(2) of the Commercial Computer Software-Restricted Rights at 48 CFR § 52.227.19, as applicable. Contractor/manufacturer: LICENSOR: LYNDA.COM, LLC, c/o PEACHPIT PRESS, 1249 Eighth Street, Berkeley, CA 94710.